RELIGION AND PSYCHOLOGY

Also by Maurice Friedman

Martin Buber: The Life of Dialogue
Problematic Rebel: Melville, Dostoievsky, Kafka, Camus
The Worlds of Existentialism: A Critical Reader
To Deny Our Nothingness: Contemporary Images of Man
The Philosophy of Martin Buber (chief Editor)
Touchstones of Reality: Existential Trust and the Community of Peace
The Hidden Human Image
*The Human Way: A Dialogical Approach to Religion
and Human Experience*
The Confirmation of Otherness: In Family, Community, and Society
Contemporary Psychology: Revealing and Obscuring the Human
Martin Buber's Life and Work: The Early Years—1878–1923
Martin Buber's Life and Work: The Middle Years—1923–1945
Martin Buber's Life and Work: The Later Years—1945–1965
The Healing Dialogue in Psychotherapy
Martin Buber and the Eternal
Abraham Joshua Heschel and Elie Wiesel: "You Are My Witnesses"
A Dialogue with Hasidic Tales: Hallowing the Everyday
Encounter on the Narrow Ridge: A Life of Martin Buber
Dialogue and the Human Image: Beyond Humanistic Psychology

RELIGION AND PSYCHOLOGY

A Dialogical Approach

MAURICE FRIEDMAN

PARAGON HOUSE PUBLISHERS
New York

First edition, 1992

Published in the United States by

Paragon House
90 Fifth Avenue
New York, N.Y. 10011

Grateful acknowledgment is made to the following for permission to reprint material:

Excerpts from *Between Man and Man*, by Martin Buber, translated by Ronald G. Smith. Copyright © 1985 by Macmillan Publishing Company. Used with permission.

Excerpts from *The Knowledge of Man*, by Martin Buber. Quoted, with permission, from *The Knowledge of Man*. Copyright © 1990 Humanities Press, Atlantic Highlands, NJ.

Excerpts from C.G. Jung, *Answer to Job* from *Collected Works of C.G. Jung*. Bollingen Series XX, vol 11. Copyright © 1958, 1969 by Princeton University Press. Used with permission.

Excerpts from *The Hero with a Thousand Faces*, by Joseph Campbell. 2nd edition. Bollingen Series XVII. Copyright © 1949 renewed 1976. Used with permission of Princeton University Press.

Excerpts from *The Myth of the Eternal Return, or Cosmos and History*, by Mircea Eliade, translated by Willard R. Trask. Bollingen Series XLVI.

Library of Congress Cataloging-in-Publication Data

Friedman, Maurice S.
    Religion and psychology : a dialogical approach / Maurice
Friedman.
        p.   cm.
    Includes index.
    ISBN 1-55778-346-2
    1. Psychology and religion.   2. Psychology, Religious.   I. Title.
BF51.F73   1992
1st ed.
291.1'75—dc20   91-30769
                                                                    CIP

Manufactured in the United States of America

CONTENTS

Part II
A CRITIQUE OF SOME PSYCHOLOGIES OF RELIGION

Part III
ISSUES IN THE MEETING BETWEEN RELIGION AND PSYCHOLOGY

Part IV
THERAPEUTIC IMPLICATIONS OF THE MEETING BETWEEN RELIGION AND PSYCHOLOGY

To Hans Trüb,

Ivan Boszormenyi-Nagy

and Barbara Krasner

in Whose Theory and Practice of Therapy

the Meeting Between Religion and Psychology

Has Become Real and Fruitful

PREFACE

ALTHOUGH THIS BOOK WILL TOUCH on subjects that have great relevance for religious psychology, psychology of religion, and pastoral psychology, it is not centrally concerned with any of these. Rather it is concerned with the *meeting* of religion and psychology and with issues that grow out of that meeting, such as attitudes toward anxiety, existential trust, the limits of the psyche as touchstone of reality, neurotic and existential guilt, and the limits of the responsibility of the helper. Even the critique of psychologies of religion in Part Two serves to illuminate these issues.

This book has two sorts of readers in mind—the mature therapist, pastor, philosopher, and interested layperson, who will find these issues important and even controversial, and the upper division college and graduate students who may be assigned this book in one or another course on psychology of religion, religion and psychology, religion and culture, and the like or will find it themselves in the bookstore or library. I hope that it may speak simultaneously and equally satisfactorily to both types of readers.

In moving from teaching this material, as I have for more than twenty years, to writing a book on it, I have found it necessary to make clear the standpoint from which I have come. Hence the subtitle *A Dialogical Approach*. The term "dialogue" as I use it is much more than two people speaking. It is real openness, presence, mutuality, and immediacy, as expressed in Martin Buber's famous "I-Thou relationship"—"All real living is meeting." Most speech is not dialogue in this sense, and genuine dialogue may be silent as well as spoken.

What I mean by "dialogical approach," however, is broader than just Martin Buber's philosophy of dialogue. As I use it here, it encompasses all the elements that I have discussed in Part One, "Foundations." Biblical, existential, and relational trust (Chapter 1) are inherently dialogical. The *emunah* of the Hebrew Bible, indeed, is perhaps the most important traditional basis for that meeting or reciprocal dialogue that informs this book. Hasidism, too, the eighteenth-century communal mysticism of Eastern European Jewry, is thoroughly dialogical and is a major source for both Buber's and my own dialogical approach. It is also a major source for an understanding of the meeting of religion and psychology, even if couched in different metaphors and myths than either of these fields would use today. Hence the presentation of Hasidic hallowing in Chapter 2 is coupled with a presentation of Hasidic helping and healing, drawing on the wealth of Hasidic tales that give us our best glimpse into the actual life of the Hasidim.

Chapter 3 combines Buber's philosophy of dialogue with dialogical psychotherapy, which is not simply "Buberian," as one might speak of Freudian, Rogerian, or Jungian therapy, but has appeared, sometimes under Buber's influence and sometimes independently, in representatives of many different schools of therapy, as I demonstrate at length in the first part of my book *The Healing Dialogue in Psychotherapy* (1985). Although we do not call dialogical psychotherapy a school, therefore, it is today a movement the mainstream of which has been developed over the last half century in the writings of Hans Trüb, Leslie H. Farber, Ivan Boszormenyi-Nagy, myself, Barbara Krasner, Richard Hycner, and Aleene Friedman and continues to develop through the Institute of Dialogical Psychotherapy and the institutes of Contextual Therapy that are found in Philadelphia and Boston. Chapter 4 lays the groundwork for our understanding of the meeting of religion and psychology and the issues that rise from that meeting. Even here the two approaches that are used—my own philosophies of touchstones of reality and of images of the human—are dialogical in the broadest sense of the term—not as an extension of Buber's philosophy of dialogue but as a recognition that both touchstones and human images are the product of the meeting between ourselves and others, ourselves and the world.

My dedication needs a special word of explanation. Hans Trüb was for ten years a disciple of Jung and member of Jung's inner circle. After a personal and professional crisis of guilt in which he saw he had sacrificed ethical responsibility to "the spiritual," he found his way to that "healing through meeting," which is the title of his posthumous book and did so not just in theory but in his therapeutic practice. Ivan Boszormenyi-Nagy and following him Barbara Krasner have established in America and Europe a form of therapy that is called "contextual," because even when it deals with individuals it is oriented toward intergenerational family therapy. Ivan Boszormenyi-Nagy, although originally Catholic, does not think of himself as a religious person or a religious thinker. Barbara Krasner was raised as a Jew and has deepened her commitment to Judaism and made it living in social action and therapy. Both are friends of many years, Ivan as colleague and occasionally co-therapist in family therapy, Barbara as my student in the Ph.D. Program that I founded and directed in Religion and Psychology at Temple University from 1969 to 1973, as coworker in social action, and as an ever dearer and more respected friend. If I also include them in my dedication, it is not only because of this shared friendship and my great indebtedness to both of them, but also because they do indeed embody for me the meeting of religion and psychology in the fullest sense of the term. Their contextual therapy is based on Martin Buber's philosophical anthropology and his philosophy of dialogue, as I have shown at length in an article in *Psychotherapy*.[1] Buber's life of dialogue is based, in turn, on a profound religious understanding. Equally important, in their emphasis upon restoring relational trust and trustworthiness, Nagy and Krasner converge with that existential trust that is central for both Buber's thought and my own. This dedication in no way implies a negative estimate of all the other thinkers with whom I deal in this book, each of whom has made a contribution in his own way to the meeting between religion and psychology.

1. Maurice Friedman, "Martin Buber and Ivan Boszormenyi-Nagy: The Role of Dialogue in Contextual Therapy," *Psychotherapy*, Vol. XXVI, Fall 1989, No. 3, pp. 402–409.

I must in conclusion acknowledge my incalculable debt to my former wife and still close friend, Eugenia Friedman, for reading and responding to the first draft of this book and struggling with me over the central issues, which she understands in depth from her own experience and from the many years we have shared in common. No one else could have given me the help that she has in bringing *Religion and Psychology: A Dialogical Approach* to its true form.

Maurice Friedman
San Diego State University
June 1991

Part One

FOUNDATIONS

Chapter 1

BIBLICAL, RELATIONAL, AND EXISTENTIAL TRUST

THERE IS A BASIC TRUST in Hinduism, Buddhism, and Taoism—a trust that says that this world is not a place in which we are hopelessly lost. But there is a special emphasis on trust in the Hebrew Bible—a trust or faithfulness, *emunah*—that does not necessarily have a faith content. This trust does not mean security. The "happy man" in Psalm I is not assured of immortality in the world to come or of many sheep, goats, and camels in this life. He is compared to a tree planted by streams of water that brings forth fruit in its season. He has found a true existence that the sinner, however wealthy and prosperous, does not have. That is why the latter is compared to "chaff blown by the wind": dry and rootless, he loses his way; he has no way.

Thus at the center of faith of biblical Judaism stands not belief, in the ordinary sense of the term, but trust—a trust that no exile from the presence of God is permanent, that each man and each generation is able to come into contact with reality. In the life of individual man, as of generations of men, it is the movement of time—the facts of change and death—that most threatens this trust. Every great religion, culture, and philosophy has observed that "all is flux" and that man himself is a part

3

of this flux. The conclusions that have been drawn from this fact, however, are as different as the world views of those who have drawn the conclusions. The response of biblical man has not taken the form of a cyclical order of time or an unchanging absolute, like the Greek, nor of the dismissal of time and change as *maya*, or illusion, like the Hindu, nor of the notion that one may flow with time, like the Taoist. He stands face to face with the changing creation and receives each new moment as an address of God—the revelation that comes to him through the unique present.

To stand before eternity is to be aware of one's own mortality:

> *For a thousand years in thy sight*
> *are but as yesterday when it is past, . . .*
> *men . . . are like a dream, like grass . . .*
> *in the morning it flourishes and is renewed;*
> *in the evening it fades and withers. . . .*
> *our years come to an end like a sigh. . . .*
> *yet their span is but toil and trouble;*
> *they are soon gone, and we fly away.*

> (Psalm 90:4-10)

This is the universal human condition—a condition that has tempted some to see existence as unreal or as an ephemeral reflection of reality and others to "eat, drink, and be merry, for tomorrow we die." The psalmist, in contrast, prays that he may withstand this reality and heighten it, that he may make his existence real by meeting each new moment with the wholeness of his being:

> *So teach us to number our days*
> *That we may get a heart of wisdom*

> (Psalm 90:12)

In the beautiful poem of Ecclesiastes from the later Wisdom literature, time has become the cycle that goes round and round and will not reach a meaning. Even when at the end of the poem we are told to remember the Creator in the days of our youth, there is still no suggestion that we shall find meaning here, in the actual flow of time, but only somewhere above. But in the Psalms and in the Book of Job there is a wrestling for meaning despite the passage of time.

It is not only man's mortality, however, but the suffering of the innocent and the prosperity of the wicked that lead to the tempering of trust in Job and in the Psalms. The reaffirmation of trust takes place out of an immediate sense of exile. When God no longer prepares a table for the good man in the presence of his enemies; when the good man sees not the recompense of the wicked, but their prosperity and their arrogance, his trust is shaken. He cannot bear the fact that the presence of God is emptied out of the world, that the sinners who cannot stand in the judgment are nonetheless confirmed by the congregation, and divine and social reality are split asunder. The world is not built in such a way that the natural and moral order correspond. Neither the author of the Book of Job nor of Psalms 73 and 82 can say with the earlier Psalmist, "I am old and I have been young, and never yet have I seen the righteous begging for bread." It is not true. The righteous suffer and the wicked prosper. It is out of this situation that Job cries out and contends with a strength perhaps unequalled in any of the world's religious scriptures.

The basic paradox of the Hebrew Bible is the dialogue between eternal God and mortal man, between the imageless Absolute and man who is created in God's "image." If that dialogue is to take place, it must take place not in eternity but in the present—in the unique situation of a limited man who was born yesterday and will die tomorrow. Jacob wrestles with the angel, and Job wrestles with God to receive the blessing of this dialogue on which the very meaning of their existence depends.

Job wanted a dialogue with God, but when this dialogue comes it dismays him by forcing him to recognize that the partner with whom he speaks is the Creator who at each moment creates the ground of existence and transcends it.

> *Where were you when I laid the foundation of the earth?*
> *Tell me, if you have understanding . . .*
> *when the morning stars sang together,*
> *and all the sons of God shouted for joy?*

> (Job 38:37)

The reality of creation is the reality of the otherness that man cannot remove into his rational comprehension of the world. We seek to anthropomorphize creation—to rationalize reality to fit the moral conceptions of man. Despite our power to "comprehend" the world, it has a reality independent of us. The real God is not the God whom man removes into the sphere of his own spirit and thought, but the creator who speaks to man through creatures that exist for their own sake and not just for human purposes.[1]

What Job asks for he does receive: not an explanation as to why he suffers, but at least this God who has become far from him comes to him, speaks to him out of the whirlwind and says, "Now I will speak and you reply." Then Job says, "Before I had heard of you with the hearing of the ear, but now my eye sees you." When Job earlier makes the statement, "I know that my redeemer lives," he couples it with the statement, "And I will see him, even out of my flesh"—when my skin is stripped away by disease—I will see him, "my eyes and not another." This is what does happen to Job at the end. Had Job *not* contended, had he followed the advice of his friends and accepted his suffering humbly as his due or God's will, he would not have known the terrible and blessed experience of God coming to meet him as he went forth to meet God.

The meaning of the biblical dialogue is not what we get from God— whether it be "peace of mind," "peace of soul," "successful living," or "positive thinking"—but our walking with God on this earth. The trust at the heart of this walking with God is tried, and man is exiled by the facts of the passage of time, sickness and death, and by the very social order that man builds. There is the possibility of renewing his trust, but only if we can bring the exile into the dialogue with God, not if we turn away from the exile or overlook it. What happened to Job can and does happen, in more or less concentrated form, to any man. Instead of turning Job's situation into the abstract metaphysical problem of evil, we should encounter it as a touchstone of reality. For the real question—the question that lies at the inmost core of our very existence—is not Why? but How? How can we live in a world in which Auschwitz and Hiroshima happen? How can we find the resources once more to go out to a meeting with anyone or anything?

Although "biblical trust" is "Western," it is still based on the paradox that transcends Aristotle's law of contradiction, i.e., that a thing is either A or not-A. If we speak of God creating the world and yet remaining in relationship with it, we have already gone beyond this law. Even if we speak of two people talking with each other, we imply an interhuman reality incomprehensible in terms of Aristotle's logic. If they were entirely other than each other, they could not talk, and if they were the same, they would not need to talk. Nor is it the sameness in each other that speaks but one whole person to another, really other, whole person. Starting with trust as grounded in this paradoxical combination of separateness and relationship—arrows going apart and arrows coming together—we must recognize exile as inevitable.

In biblical Judaism, trust and exile are inseparably coupled with rebellion. The story of Adam and Eve is not, as Nietzsche thought, "slavish Semitic obedience." On the contrary, the very meaning of the story is that man becomes man in rebelling against God, in ceasing to be a child and eating of the fruit of the tree of the knowledge of good and evil. Similarly the most famous statement of trust in the Book of Job— "He may slay me. I await it."—is followed by the statement, "But I will argue my ways to his face. This is my comfort, that a hypocrite cannot come before him." To bring each new situation into the dialogue with God means both faithfulness and contending. There can be no question here of "blind faith." When Kierkegaard made the story of Abraham's temptation to sacrifice Isaac the very paradigm of unquestioning obedience, he disregarded the story that appears just two chapters earlier in Genesis. Abraham not only pleads for the people of Sodom lest the innocent be destroyed with the guilty, but he contends with the Lord and demands that he be faithful to his own way of justice: "I who am dust and ashes have taken it upon myself to argue with the Lord. Will the Lord of justice not do justice?"

The focal need of our age is not faith as a specific intellectual or religious belief but a general attitude of trust—a sense of being at home in the universe. People today live in growing fear and insecurity, for they do not really believe that the leaders of the nations will be able to find those means of unity that will stave off the destruction that each country is preparing for its neighbors. The leaders themselves are in the clutch of a fear and distrust, which are more powerful than all the rational arguments that show the need of finding peaceful solutions to international problems. Thus we are caught in a vicious circle. Unsatisfactory political, economic, and social conditions create insecurity, which in turn prevents that cooperation and trust that might make possible the solution of these problems.

The term "existential trust" grows out of the basic trust that concerned me in my youth, the basic attitude of trust in the world religions that I have been in dialogue with, and the *emunah*, or unconditional trust in relation, of the Hebrew Bible.

It is our existential trust that ultimately gives actuality and continuity to our discontinuous and often merely potential relationships to our human partners. And it is this trust, too, that gives continuity and reality to our own existence as persons; for in itself personality is neither continuous nor always actual. If it is the confirmation of others and our own self-confirmation that gets us over the gaps and breaks in the first instance, it is our existential trust that enables this individual course to become a personal direction rather than a meaningless flux.

Trust accepts the facts that a genuine relationship is two-sided and therefore beyond the control of our will. The question again and again arises in our lives, "Why should I go out to meet this person unless I am sure that he will move to meet me?" Many people hold back for fear of being hurt. But this is true in our relationship with God as well. In 1898, William James said in his essay "The Will to Believe": "For the religious person, the universe is not an It but a Thou, and every relationship that is possible between persons is possible with the universe." The situation is comparable, said James, to a man who has joined a club. If he will not go halfway to meet the other members of the club, they will not come halfway to meet him. What can be known in this situation can be known only by taking the risk of entering the relationship. This is a real risk, without guarantees of any sort, for you may find a response and you may not. Therefore, trust must never be understood as trust that in this particular occasion I know that there will be a response. Genuine trust is the exact opposite of this. It is a readiness to go forth on this occasion with such resources as you have, and, if you do not receive any response, to be ready another time to go out to the meeting. Many people imagine that they are justified in a settled mistrust or even despair because once or twice they ventured forth and encountered a stone wall or a cold shoulder. After this they anticipate rejection and even bring it about, or they protect themselves from it by never risking themselves. The genuine freedom of both sides of the dialogue means that there can be no guarantees written in the heart of the universe, no ontological ground that assures us that this or that is the nature of the universe.

Existential trust cannot be inculcated by autosuggestion. Yet we do not have so much ground for mistrust as we usually think. We cut the ground from beneath our feet by a self-fulfilling prophecy. We were confirmed so little as children, perhaps, that we are used to living with just the crumbs from the table. Therefore, we already know in advance that nothing really joyful can happen to us, and we make sure that nothing joyful does happen. We impoverish our lives a great deal more than they need to be because we live on a scarcity economy in which we exclude *a priori* much of the grace that is waiting to come to us if we are really open, and we imagine our resources to be far less than they are. We are not able, we are not even willing to understand that new resources come to us all the time as we move into the situation that awaits us. It is said that the Red Sea would not open for the Israelites to cross until the first Israelite had put his foot in the sea. We wait on the bank, demanding that the river open before we venture forth.

The real courage that is asked of us is the courage to respond, the courage to go out to meet the reality given in this moment, whatever its form. My trust is not that this reality will be such as I might wish it to be, but only that here and here only is meaning accessible to me, even if not without horror, suffering, and evil. This is what it means to walk life's way step by step. Moment by moment, day by day, we are placed before the question, "Do I have the courage to go out to meet and respond to what comes?" This includes the courage *not* to speak out and *not* to respond when we cannot do so in this situation as a whole person in a meaningful way. Our response ought not be triggered off—that is merely a reaction. We ought not to respond to what we know somewhere in our being is not a true address. "Because of impatience we were driven out of the Garden of Eden," says Kafka, "and because of impatience we are prevented from returning to it."

If it is important not to allow ourselves to be "triggered off," it is equally essential not to withhold ourselves. One of the forms we have of withholding ourselves is that protective silence that makes us feel we never have to speak out, that we are merely observers in the group, that nothing is demanded of us. Another of the forms of withholding ourselves, however, is that anxious verbosity that overwhelms the situation so that we are not present and we do not allow anyone else to be present either. Still another form of withholding ourselves is substituting technique for trust.

Many encounter groups operate on the naive but widespread assumption that the mere expression of hostility is therapeutic under any circumstances. The operating principle of such groups is not that you should not withhold your *self* but that you should not withhold your surface feelings, especially the type of feelings that the group wants and expects, such as anger and hostility. Trust in technique is essentially irreligious. This does not mean that we should not structure a situation. But it is vital that the structure be one within which spontaneity can come into being. When we reach the place where we are expecting and looking for a certain result, then we have traded in trust for arbitrariness, and willfulness has replaced genuine will. Among those whose whole lifework is concerned with freeing others to their potentiality are some of the worst manipulators, some of the most authoritarian figures I have ever met. That is because they cannot trust but have to be sure they get the result they want. Other people join in this spirit, and all members of the "sensitivity awareness" group become amateur manipulators who tend, as a result, to become more and more insensitive to the unique and concrete happenings *between* members of the group.

We address others not by conscious mind or will but by what we are. We address them with more than we know, and they respond—if they really respond—with more than they know. Address and response can never be identified merely with conscious intent or even with "intentionality." Our resources have to do with what calls us and with the way in which we bring or do not bring ourselves into wholeness in response to this call. The courage to address and respond sees life as a giving and a receiving, but it does not mean a "trust that" life will always be a flowing, even in Lao-tzu's sense. The courage to respond is not the courage of blind faith but the courage of really entering again into relationship.

A newspaper story that has continued to make a deep impression upon me is that of a flood in which a car was washed over the bridge. The husband drowned, but the wife clung for eight hours to a telephone pole.

Several boats put out to try to save her, but they were capsized in their turn and the would-be rescuers drowned. Finally, at the end of the eight hours, she was torn away with a shriek into the flood. There are many situations in life where there is a hand reaching out to help and the person in need tries to but cannot quite reach it. It seems as if it is too much to demand of oneself, too much to hope for, too much to ask—too much pain to open oneself again to the possibility of really living, of reentering the dialogue. The last moment with a sigh the person lets go of the hand that is reaching for him and falls. He may commit suicide, but more often he simply gives up ever again trying really to go beyond himself, ever again risking pain and suffering to discover whether there is something there to meet. He prefers to say, "No, I have been through this before. I am not going to expose myself. I prefer to call it all negative rather than move off my base without a guarantee of response." And he is right, in his terms; for there can be no such guarantee.

I shall never forget a rabbinical student of mine—the class wit whose humor excelled all would-be competitors. Once when he had invited my wife and me over for dinner, he was walking around the living room with his two-year-old son on his shoulders. Suddenly he stopped and said to me, "I wish I could trust in God the way that little boy trusts in me."

What is it to trust in God? If it is anything, it is like personal trust rather than an attempt to pin down who or what God is or who or what we are. The true trust of a person is not that you already know all about him before you meet him. That is simply defining and delimiting an object. True trust is the readiness to find out where he is moment by moment through address and response. The same holds for our relationship to God. The meaning of the imagelessness of God is that you have no conception, no definition of God, no assurance that he will be merciful but not terrible. Trust in God, like existential trust, is not trust in what God will do for you but simply that unconditional trust that enables one, as long as one has strength to do so, to go forth to meet what comes. It is only trust that gives us the real resources to keep going. It is very much like a man who has a direction and who starts walking in that direction. He is knocked down and the breath is knocked out of him, but when he gets his breath back he gets up and starts walking again in the same direction. Your resources are those that you find at a given moment. Except for freedom from false notions of unfreedom, they do not depend on any conceptions of "God." Trust in God and existential trust are identical.

Existential trust does not mean trust *in* existence as being constituted in one particular way. It cannot be attained by "positive thinking," and it does not lead to "peace of mind" or "peace of soul." It is not inconsonant with pain, grief, anxiety, and least of all with vulnerability. Where it does not exist, one no longer goes forth to meet others: "The broken heart kens nae second spring again, thae the waeful nae cease frae their greeting." There are some people who continue to live, yet never really go out again as a whole being to meet anyone. Our desire for security leads some of us to see ourselves as forsaken simply because life does not comport itself as we think it should. We wish to prescribe what will come to us and, like Kafka's mole, construct a burrow that will make it sure that nothing reaches us except what we want to reach us. Our views of existence are based upon our disappointments, upon the shattering of trust that every child experiences no matter how confirming his parents are. Every child experiences separation and betrayal. On growing up and first entering into romantic relations with the opposite sex, he is already expecting rejection and hurt—the repetition of his early experiences. Time and time again we think that we have "had it"; yet at another moment we are able, like a character in Samuel Beckett's novels, to get up and go on. More than we can conceive, we are sustained from within ourselves, from what comes to meet us, and from the meeting itself. We are not sustained in smooth continuity, to be sure. Yet our existence is given back to us, we are renewed. Moment by moment we are carried, day by day we are given back our ground and our freedom. The smog of existential mistrust through which we move need not prevent our making ever-new contact with reality.

"Ours is the Age of Suspicion," wrote the great Jewish religious philosopher Abraham Joshua Heschel, "and its golden rule is 'Suspect Thy Neighbor as Thyself'!" In his bitter ironic novel *The Confidence Man*, Herman Melville foresaw the existential trust that has come to plague our time. "From what you say," an old man says to the Confidence Man, "I see you are something of my way of thinking—you think that to distrust the creature is a kind of distrusting of the Creator." These are indeed corollaries—to trust in the human being one must trust in existence and vice versa. The Confidence Man himself explicitly draws the connection between misanthropy and existential mistrust:

> "You rather jumble together misanthropy and infidelity." "I do not jumble them: they are co-ordinates. For misanthropy, springing from the same root with disbelief of religion, is twin with that . . . Set aside materialism and what is an atheist but one who does not, or will not, see in the universe a ruling principle of love: and what a misanthrope, but one who does not, or will not, see in man a ruling principle of kindness? . . . In either case the vice consists in a want of confidence."[2]

A century later Martin Buber described the modern "eclipse of God" in precisely these terms. The waning of genuine dialogue between person and person is the symptom, writes Buber, but a pervasive "existential mistrust," such as has never before existed, is the disease itself:

> The existential mistrust is indeed basically no longer, like the old kind, a mistrust of my fellowman. It is rather the destruction of confidence in existence in general . . . At its core the conflict between mistrust and trust of man conceals the conflict between the mistrust and trust of eternity.[3]

It is no accident that Martin Buber wrote that he knew no such deep-reaching and comprehensive crisis in history as ours, and that he called our crisis "the crisis of confidence." The split between id and superego that Sigmund Freud advanced as basic to human nature as such Buber saw as a specific illness of modern man arising from just that crisis of confidence.

> Where confidence reigns man must often, indeed, adapt his wishes to the commands of his community but . . . only if the organic community disintegrates from within and mistrust becomes life's basic note does the repression acquire its dominating importance. The unaffectedness of wishing is stifled by mistrust, everything around is hostile or can become hostile, agreement between one's own and the other's desire ceases, for there is no true coalescence or reconciliation with what is necessary to a sustaining community, and the dulled wishes creep hopelessly into the recesses of the soul . . . Now there is no longer a human wholeness with the force and courage to manifest itself. For spirit to arise the energy of the repressed instincts must mostly first be "subliminated," the traces of

its origin cling to the spirit and it can mostly assert itself against the instincts only by convulsive alienation. The divorce between spirit and instincts is here, as often, the consequence of the divorce between man and man.[4]

Why is relational trust central to human existence, as I have claimed? Because we become human beings and persons through "confirmation," through being confirmed by others in our uniqueness as potential partners in dialogue. Mutual confirmation is essential to becoming a self—a person who realizes his or her uniqueness precisely through relation to other selves whose distance from one is completed by one's distance from them. True confirmation means that I confirm my partner as this existing being living face to face with me even while I oppose her. I legitimize her over against me as the one with whom I have to do in real dialogue. This mutual confirmation takes place through the event of making the other present and being made present by the other. This making present, in turn, occurs through what Buber calls "inclusion," or "imagining the real." To imagine the real means to imagine quite concretely what another person is wishing, feeling, perceiving, and thinking. This is no empathy or intuitive perception, but a bold swinging into the other that demands the intensest action of one's being in order to make the other present in his wholeness, unity, and uniqueness. One can do this only as a partner, standing in a common situation with the other. To become aware of a person means to perceive the dynamic center, which stamps on all that person's utterances, actions, and attitudes the recognizable sign of uniqueness. Such an awareness is impossible if, and as long as, the other is for me the detached object of my observation; for the other will not thus yield her wholeness and its center. It is possible only when the other becomes present for me.

If the perception of the other's wholeness, unity, and uniqueness is only possible when I step into an elemental relation with her and make her present as a person, then by the same token the analytical, reductive, and deriving look that predominates between person and person today stands in the way of this perception, as Martin Buber points out.

This look is a reductive one, because it tries to contract the manifold person, who is nourished by the microcosmic richness of the possible, to some schematically surveyable and recurrent structures. And this look is a deriving one, because it supposes it can grasp what a man has become, or even is becoming, in genetic formulae, and it thinks that even the dynamic central principle of the individual in this becoming can be represented by a general concept. An effort is being made today radically to destroy the mystery between man and man. The personal life, the ever-near mystery, once the source of the stillest enthusiasms, is levelled down.[5]

The person of existential trust is able to accept the unique that is present in each new situation, despite all resemblance to the past. Real presentness means presence—being open to what the present brings by bringing oneself to the present, allowing the future to come as it comes, rather than attempting to turn it into a predictable replica of the past. This means meeting others *and* holding one's ground when one meets them. Real, uncurtailed, personal existence begins not when one says to the other, "I am you," but when one says, "I accept you as you are," in your otherness and uniqueness. The typical mark of the inauthentic person of today is that she does not really *hear*, she does not really *listen* to another. In so doing, she becomes guilty not just to the other but to the common world that we are building together, to the common We. "In our age," writes Buber, "in which the true meaning of every word is encompassed by delusion and falsehood and the original intention of the human glance is stifled by tenacious mistrust, it is of decisive importance to find again the genuineness of speech and existence as We."[6]

Existence as We can never mean that the individual merely conforms to society or subordinates his or her own self to the collectivity. It means that each contributes to the common order from where and from what he or she is. Buber sees marriage as the exemplary bond; for marriage means that I can share in real existence only if I take seriously the fact that the other *is*, answering her address and answering for her as one entrusted to me. Through marriage, I enter into relation with otherness, "and the basic structure of otherness, in many ways uncanny but never quite unholy or incapable of being hallowed, in which I and the others who meet me in my life are inwoven, is the body politic." Real marriage leads to "vital acknowledgment of many-surfaced otherness—even in the contradiction and conflict with it." By its crises and the overcoming of them in the organic depths, marriage teaches us that the person with whom we have to do "does not have merely a different mind, or way of thinking or feeling, or a different conviction or attitude, but has also a different perception of the world, a different recognition and order of meaning, a different touch from the regions of existence, a different faith, a different soil."[7] Buber carries this experiencing of the otherness in marriage into the sexual act itself, where a quite concrete two-sided sensation makes the other person present for all time, after which a mere elaboration of subjectivity is never again possible or tolerable. True lovers have a bipolar experience, a contemporaneity at rest. They receive the common event from both sides at once "and thus for the first time understand in a bodily way what an event is." This is the otherness of the other who lives with me as Thou, who faces me as partner, who affirms and contends with me, but vows me faithfully to being as I vow her.

Sex, which should be the crown of the interhuman, often in our culture becomes the opposite—the mark of its inauthenticity. A great many persons are inclined to distrust themselves, and they are inclined to mistrust one another. This mistrust arises in part because of the popular Freudian view of the person as a two-layered being whose instincts are likely at any moment to take over control from the rational mind. That ancient dualism in which the body and sex are regarded as evil has been modernized in no less puritanical form by those popular Freudians who tell us that our conscious thoughts and feelings are rationalizations for the drive toward fulfillment of libidinal urges that we cannot admit directly to ourselves. If we cannot join Freud in making the conscious mind so much the superstructure determined by and reflecting our unconscious motivations, we can certainly assert that relating to the other as an It and relating to the other as a Thou are nowhere so completely and confusedly intermingled as in sex and love. That would be no problem if the It were transformed by and taken up into the Thou. Often, however, we do not know which is in the service of which. Even if we could rid ourselves of the tenacious notion that sex is something innately evil, we would still have the problem of when it is a healing through meeting and when it is a still further wounding through mismeeting.

If we approach sex in terms of the ontology of the between, this means that it must be seen within the context of interhuman relationships, including love. This does not imply some naive rationalism that ignores the dark swirling forces in the human being that have been uncovered by the romantics and by depth psychology. It means, rather, that human existence can never be reduced to a psychological state, a pure content of feeling, minus the attitude that the person has to that state of feeling and the relation that the person has to other persons. We are not to turn away from what attracts our hearts but to find mutual contact with it by making our relationship to it real. We are not necessarily torn between a cruel id and a cruel superego. Where some degree of trust and relationship exists, we may bring our passions into unification with a personal wholeness that is itself a by-product of the ever-renewed act of entering into dialogue. Martin Buber calls this shaping of the chaos of matter into the cosmos of personal existence "a cruelly hazardous enterprise." It is, nonetheless, an enterprise that we can and must undertake.

Chapter 2

HASIDIC HALLOWING, HELPING, AND HEALING[1]

A PARTICULARLY RICH SOURCE for the understanding of the issues that arise from the meeting of psychology and religion is found in the implications of the Tales of the Hasidim for healing and helping. Hasidism is the popular mystical movement of East European Jewry in the eighteenth and nineteenth centuries. The Hebrew word *hasid* means "pious." It is derived from the noun *hesed*, meaning loving-kindness, mercy, or grace. The Hasidic movement arose in Poland in the eighteenth century, and, despite bitter persecution at the hands of traditional rabbinism, spread rapidly among the Jews of Eastern Europe until it included almost half of them in its ranks. Hasidism is really a continuation in many senses of biblical and rabbinical Judaism. While it is not an historical continuation of Christianity, many people have been startled by the resemblances between Hasidism and early Christianity, in particular between the founder of Hasidism—the Baal Shem Tov, or Good Master of the Name of God—and Jesus. Both spoke to the common, the ordinary folk; both represented something of a revolt against the overemphasis on learning; both tried to renew the spirit from within the tradition rather than destroying, cutting off, and radically changing the tradition.

18

The Hasidim founded real communities, each with its own rebbe. The rebbe, the leader of the community, was also called the Zaddik, the righteous or justified person. "The world stands because of the zaddik," says the Talmud, and in Jewish legend this has grown into the myth of the thirty-six hidden zaddikim of each generation—*the lamedvovnikim*—without whom the world could not stand. Each one of these zaddikim had his own unique teaching that he gave to his community. Originally as it was passed down from generation to generation, the leadership devolved not so much on those who could receive a doctrine on those who could embody a way of life. Thus the first effect of the zaddik was to bring the people to immediacy in relationship to God. Later, when hereditary dynasties of Hasidim arose and the rebbes lived in great palaces and were surrounded by awe and superstition, the zaddik became almost a mediator between the people and God—the very opposite of his original function.

Hasidism speaks in compelling accents of a wholehearted service of God that does not mean turning away from one's fellows and from the world. All that is asked is to do everything one does with one's whole strength—not the denial of self and the extirpation of the passions but the fulfillment of self and the direction of passion in a communal mysticism of humility, love, prayer, and joy. In the end, the most important heritage that Hasidism has bequeathed us is not its doctrine and teachings but its image of the human—the image of the Besht, the Maggid of Mezritch, Levi Yitzhak of Berditchev, Nachman of Bratzlav, Shneur Zalman of Ladi, the "Yehudi" of Pshysha, and a host of other zaddikim, each with a unique relationship to God and to his particular community.

THE WAY OF MAN

Martin Buber's most concentrated image of the human is his classic little book, *The Way of Man According to the Teachings of the Hasidim*. On the basis of Hasidic tales, Buber expounds six stages that point the way to authentic personal existence and to the life of dialogue. In the first, "heart-searching," God's "Where art thou, Adam?" is seen as the question which breaks in on every person who has turned her life into a system of hideouts, the question that asks her where she is in her life.

Only when she has begun to respond to this question with her existence will her life become a way. But this question is not introspection of any sort. On the contrary, it is the voice of otherness that brings the self-encapsulated person back into dialogue. There is a demonic question that says, "From where you have got to, there is no way out." This is a sterile heart-searching "which leads to nothing but self-torture, despair and still deeper enmeshment." The true heart-searching, in contrast, means that response to the address of the other that helps one find one's particular way. "If a man does not judge himself," says Rabbi Nachman of Bratzlav, "all things judge him." This means that anything may stand in that relation of otherness that will call one to account by enabling one to see one's own life from a perspective outside oneself. And he adds: "All things are messengers of God to him." All things in "judging" us can call us back to genuine dialogical existence.

The second stage is "the particular way," that unique task that every person has and that no one else will ever have. "When I get to heaven, they will not ask me, 'Why were you not Moses?' " said Rabbi Zusya, "but 'Why were you not Zusya?' " Why did you not become what only you were called to become? Without the image of the human, without Moses, he could not have become Zusya, but he could never become Zusya by merely imitating Moses. He had to respond to this image of the human in his unique way. One's very existence as a person places on one the demand to authenticate one's life. If we recognize this, we are still left with the all-important question of how we discover "what we truly are." Buber answers that one knows one's particular way through that knowledge of one's essential quality and inclination which is revealed to one by one's "central wish, that in him which stirs his inmost being." This is no romanticism of emotion, rather the recognition that only the wholeness that includes the "central wish" can lead to the recognition of one's unique task. Often, this recognition comes only in the form of the "evil" urge that seeks to lead one astray; for one has gotten so out of touch with one's own strongest feelings that one knows them only in the guise of what seems to be tripping one up on one's path to success.

The third stage is that resolution that seeks personal unity through doing whatever one does "all of a piece" and not "patchwork," until one attains a steadier unity than before and can maintain one's wholeness with a "relaxed vigilance." The fourth stage is "to begin with oneself," to recognize that in conflicts with others, it is our own inner contradictions that again and again foster misunderstanding and mistrust. The cause of conflict between myself and my fellows, says Buber, is that I do not say what I mean and that I do not do what I say. This is another way of saying that I do not respond as a whole person, that I am not really present, really responsible, really "there." As a result, I lead people to expect something, which later I am quite unwilling to follow through on. This is not a matter of sticking to a rigid external code, but of a spontaneity that is not mere fragmented impulse, but the expression of my wholeness as a person. It is that which places the stamp of personal uniqueness on all my utterances, gestures, and actions. Though my actions cannot be predicted even by those who stand in the closest relationship to me, through these gestures and actions I may be recognized ever again and ever more strongly as the unique person that I am.

Though one begins with oneself, one does not end with oneself, Buber points out in the fifth stage. One does not aim at oneself, but at the task that one has to fulfill. One comprehends oneself, including one's resources as a person that enable one to transform relationships by bringing a new response to them, but one is not preoccupied with oneself—neither with one's salvation nor with one's guilt and one's neurosis, neither with one's genius nor with one's frustrations and grievances. "True, each is to know itself, purify itself, perfect itself, but not for the sake of its temporal happiness nor for that of its eternal bliss—but for the sake of the work which it is destined to perform upon the world."

Buber calls the sixth and final stage "Here Where One Stands." The culmination of all the other stages is the return to the lived concrete, the hallowing of the everyday. We all feel at times as if true existence has passed us by, says Buber, and so we search for it somewhere, anywhere but where we are. But the treasure is buried under our own hearth. The true names of all the paradises that people seek by chemical, or other means, writes Buber in his criticism of Aldous Huxley's advocacy of mescalin, is situationlessness. One may stand in one's situation, one may resist it, one may change it if need be, "but situationlessness is no true business of man." Here where you stand is your situation, that which addresses and claims you.

The environment which I feel to be the natural one, the situation which has
been assigned to me as my fate, the things that happen to me day after day,
the things that claim me day after day—these contain my essential task
and such fulfillment of existence as is open to me.[2]

In my own closely related presentation of Hasidism, also based on
Hasidic tales, I have singled out, for our purposes, uniqueness, serving
God with the "evil" urge, *kavana*, or inner intention, overcoming
dualism, and love and community.

UNIQUENESS

Hasidism emphasizes the uniqueness of each person. We are called to
become what we in our created uniqueness can become—not just
to fulfill our social duty or actualize our talent or potentialities, but to
become the unique person we are called to be. This is not an already
existing uniqueness that we can fulfill through "self-expression" or
"self-realization." We have to realize our uniqueness in response to the
world. "Why did you not become what only you could become?" does
not mean, "Why were you not *different* from others," but "Why did you
not fulfill the creative task you have become aware of as yours alone?"
The "different" is merely a term of comparison. The unique is something valued in and for itself. This is very important; for the search for
originality, which is so strong in our day, usually takes the form of a
different twist or a new wrinkle. What we ought to be concerned about is
our faithful response. If we respond really faithfully, this will bring out
our own uniqueness.

Hasidism is like Hinduism in not having any one way that a person
should walk. But the way for the Hasid is not a matter of one's caste duty,
or even one's dharma or karma, but of one's personal uniqueness, one's
"I" in the deepest sense of that term. To speak of the heart drawing us
does not mean the facile impulse of the moment. Our "I" is not our
image of ourselves but the deepest stirring within ourselves. That
stirring, in its response, becomes our way.

This emphasis on uniqueness also means, of course, that we must
stand our ground and witness for that unique creation that we are. This
balance—neither affirming ourself absolutely nor denying ourself abso-

lutely but recognizing that we have been given a created ground on which to stand and from which to move to meet the world—is the true humility of Hasidism.

Uniqueness does not preclude dialogue. On the contrary, it is precisely through each standing his or her own ground and yet moving to meet the other that genuine dialogue from ground to ground takes place. For a person for whom there is no dialogue, even the ground of life itself crumbles away.

SERVING GOD WITH THE "EVIL" URGE

Only if we carefully listen to what way our heart draws us can we discover our unique way and follow it with all our strength. Yet often we are cut off from the awareness of our own deepest self and do not hear the call of the heart. That is why the "evil" urge is so important to Hasidism.

The "evil" urge is not evil in itself. It is evil only when it is not given direction. It is evil only when it is not given the personal meaning of our unique response to the situation. It is needed for our service. The person who succeeds in being "good" by repressing the "evil" urge is not serving God with all his or her heart, soul, and might. The "evil" urge is the passion, the power that is given us to serve God. We cannot extirpate it or do away with it. When it seems to make us fail, it does so because we have tried to impose upon ourselves and our environment what we willfully will to be.

The "evil" urge is that something more in us that taps us on the shoulder and recalls us to ourselves. Often we have so lost touch with ourselves that we do not know which way our heart draws us. It is then that precisely the "evil" urge, which seems to wish to lead us astray, comes to our rescue. By its very tempting of us, it tells us that we have left ourselves out of our own projects, that our deepest passion has not been given direction, that our decisions have not been made with our whole being.

Passion means that one does not suppress one's humanity before bringing oneself into relation with others, but, on the contrary, directs one's "evil" urge into that relationship in such a way that, without losing its force, it ceases to be evil. It is in this sense that Hasidism represents a

sanctification of the profane in which every natural urge is waiting to be
hallowed and the profane itself just a name for what has not yet become
open to the holy. So often the religious is conceived of as putting aside
the extraneous and the profane and turning to the holy and the pure. But
in Hasidism the extraneous is precisely that which has something to ask
of us.

Jesus offered his disciples a counsel of perfection—"But I say unto
you that he who looks at a woman to lust after her in his heart has
already committed adultery." Paul, in contrast, saw not only temptation
but sin as inevitable—"Of myself [in my flesh] I can do no good thing."
"The evil that I would not do I do." In between the teaching that one can
overcome temptation altogether and become "pure in heart" and that
which sees one as naturally sinful is the teaching, already present in the
Hebrew Bible and the Talmud, but given strongest emphasis and exem-
plification in Hasidism, that the daily renewal of creation also means the
daily renewal of temptation, and with it the strength and the grace to
direct that temptation into the service of God through an essential and
meaningful relation with the world.

Hasidism offers a teaching that rejects both the radical separation of
good and evil and the confusion of the two. But this teaching can only
become ours if it is lifted out of the realm of spiritual inspiration and
realized concretely in our interhuman relationships. Although Hasidism
stands squarely on the doctrines of both the *Zohar* and the Lurianic
kabbalah, it shapes their attitudes toward bodily life into a pervasive,
practical teaching of the sanctifying of the profane and the "hallowing
of the everyday."

> By no means . . . can it be our true task, in the world into which we have
> been set, to turn away from the things and beings that we meet on our way
> and that attract our hearts; our task is precisely to get in touch, by
> hallowing our relationship with them, with what manifests itself in them
> as beauty, pleasure, enjoyment. Hasidism teaches that rejoicing in the
> world, if we hallow it with our whole being, leads to rejoicing in God . . .
> Any natural act, if hallowed, leads to God, and nature needs man for what
> no angel can perform on it, namely, its hallowing.[3]

We human beings have been placed in the world that we may raise the
dust to the spirit. Our task, as long as we live, is to "struggle with the

extraneous and uplift and fit it into the divine Name." All sacraments have at their core a natural activity taken from the natural course of life that is consecrated in them. But the heart of the sacrament is equally that it does not level the event down to a symbolic gesture or mystically exalt it to "an exuberantly heartfelt point," but that it "includes an elementary, life-claiming and life-determining experience of the *other*, the otherness, as of something coming to meet one and acting toward one." Therefore, it is not merely "celebrated" or "experienced." It seizes and claims the human being in the core of one's wholeness and needs nothing less than one's wholeness in order to endure it. This otherness with which one comes into contact is a material or corporeal one; for "there is no rung of human life on which we cannot find the holiness of God everywhere and at all times."⁴ Not only sin, evil, and the extraneous can be sanctified, but also the neutral, the banal, the seemingly indifferent, the everyday.

In contrast to other religions, and even to many Kabbalists, for whom asceticism is considered a goal in itself, for Hasidism it is never more than a means whereby some persons achieve liberation from their enslavement to the world, deepest heart-searching, and ultimate communion with the Absolute. "Never should asceticism gain mastery over a man's life. A man may only detach himself from nature in order to revert to it again and, in hallowed contact with it, find his way back to God."

KAVANA

How does one serve God with the "evil" urge? Not through turning away from everyday life in the world, but through bringing right dedication—*kavana*—to everything one does, through responding with one's whole being to the unique claim of unique situations. This means bringing all of one's passion into meaningful relationship with the people one meets and the situations one encounters. *Kavana* does not mean that what is important is "purity of heart," but that one must bring oneself with all one's possibility of response into every action. This is the Hasidic image of the human. This bringing oneself is no once-and-for-all-commitment, but an ever-renewed finding of direction, a responding to the call in each new hour.

The Lurian kabbalah taught that originally there were vessels so full

of grace that they burst and sparks of light descended into the darkness
and were covered with shells. We can help restore these sparks to their
divine source and thus take part in the Messianic restoration of the
exiled Shekinah to God. To the Lurian Kabbalist, and to many of the
zaddikim who came after the Baal Shem, this act of *tikkun*, or restoration, was made possible through special magical and mystical intentions
(*kavanot*). To the Baal Shem and those zaddikim who remained faithful
to his tradition, the *kavanot* were less important than *kavana*, the
consecration and dedication of the whole being that comes in the turning
to God (*teshuvah*).

One thing Hasidism, Zen Buddhism, Sufi mysticism, and the Catholic Franciscans have in common, as Martin Buber has pointed out, is
that in all of them there prevailed the hallowing of life through devotion
to the divine. In Hasidism and in Hasidism alone, however, it is not the
life of monks that is reported, but that of spiritual leaders who are
married and produce children and who stand at the head of communities
composed of families. "In Hasidism the hallowing extends fundamentally to the natural and social life. Here alone the whole man, as God has
created him, enters into the hallowing."

> This is the ultimate purpose: to let God in. But we can let him in only
> where we really stand, where we live, where we live a true life. If we
> maintain holy intercourse with the little world entrusted to us, if we help
> the holy spiritual substance to accomplish itself in that section of Creation
> in which we are living, then we are establishing, in this our place, a
> dwelling for the Divine Presence.[5]

> "Ye shall be holy men unto me" really means "Ye shall be holy unto me,
> but as men, ye shall be humanly holy unto me." Man cannot approach the
> divine by reaching beyond the human: He can approach Him through
> becoming human. To become human is what he, this individual man, has
> been created for. This, so it seems to me, is the eternal core of Hasidic life
> and of Hasidic teaching.[6]

Early Christianity regarded the world as a place of sin and temptation
and called the Devil the Prince of this World. The attitude of the
zaddikim, as reflected in their tales, is quite different. Whether the
world is good or evil depends on our relationship to it. When Rabbi

Pinhas heard of the great misery among the needy, he listened, sunk in grief, then cried, "Let us draw God into the world, and all need will be quenched."

> God's grace consists precisely in this, that He wants to let Himself be won by man, that He places Himself, so to speak, into man's hands. God wants to come to His world, but He wants to come to it through man. This is the mystery of our existence, the superhuman chance of mankind.[7]

OVERCOMING DUALISM

The Hasidic demand that we discover and perform our own created task, that we channel the passion of the "evil" urge into the realization of our personal uniqueness, that we act and love with *kavana*, or inner intention, implies the strongest possible rejection of all those ways whereby we divide our lives into airtight compartments and escape becoming whole. Becoming whole does not mean "spiritual" wholeness, or the wholeness of the individuated Self within the unconscious (to use the language of Jung); it means that personal wholeness the necessary corollary of which is the wholeness of our lives. Our true wholeness is not the perfection of our "immortal soul" but the fulfillment of our created task. Only the latter brings our personal uniqueness into being in integral relation with the creation over against which we are set. Our existence does not take place *within* ourselves but in *relationship* to what is *not* ourselves. To make our goal spiritual perfection, consequently, means a foreshortening of our personal existence.

To be humanly holy in the measure and manner of our personal resources is actually a harder demand than perfection; for it asks you to do what you really *can* do, rather than despair over what you cannot. To open our lives to the holy does not mean to rise above our situation. It means to bring our situation into dialogue with God. The openness to the holy does not mean leaving the everyday for a higher spiritual sphere, but hallowing the everyday through a genuine openness to what meets you. "Whoever says that the words of the Torah are one thing and the words of the world another," said Rabbi Pinhas of Koretz, "must be regarded as a man who denies God."

Although Kierkegaard and Marx already pointed to the crisis and alienation of modern man a century ago, and the psychoanalysts did the same at the turn of the century, only now can we really understand this crisis in its true depth and take the injured wholeness of the human upon us. We no longer know the holy face to face, but we know its heir, the "spiritual": We "recognize" it without allowing it to determine our life in any way. We take culture and ideas with grim seriousness: We place them on golden thrones to which their limbs are chained, but any claim of the spirit on personal existence is warded off through a comprehensive apparatus. "No false piety has ever attained this concentrated degree of inauthenticity."

To this behavior of the present-day human who has got rid of the command of hallowing, "Hasidism sets the simple truth that the wretchedness of our world is grounded in its resistance to the entrance of the holy into lived life." "A life that does not seek to realize what the living person, in the ground of his self-awareness, understands or glimpses as the right is not merely unworthy of the spirit; it is also unworthy of life."[8] What underlay this seemingly harsh judgment was Buber's recognition that what was in question was not some separate sphere of the religious or holy, but the quality of life itself, its call to become "humanly holy" in the measure and manner of our personal existence.

Our age is dominated, perhaps more than any before, by a dualism in which people live in one world and have their ideals and symbols in another. Our alternatives seem increasingly to be reality divested of symbols, or symbols divested of reality. It is we who decide on each new battlefield whether the prevailing direction of religion and our lives is toward a dualism in which the spirit has no binding claim upon life and life falls apart into unhallowed segments, or toward the continual overcoming of that dualism by taking up again and again the task of hallowing the creation that has been given to us. Every rung of human existence can be a ground of hallowing if we put off the habitual. We can overcome this dualism by the insistence, in each human and social sphere anew, that the spirit be relevant to life and that life be open to the demand of the spirit. We meet God not in the structures of the theologians and the concepts of the philosophers, but in the events and meetings of concrete life.

LOVE AND COMMUNITY

In consonance to all that we have said above, the love of Hasidism is not a spiritualized love, but a love involving the whole person. By the same token, it is not a purely forgiving love, but one that places a real demand upon the other—the demand of the relationship itself. The hallowing of the everyday means making the concrete relations of one's life essential, and a real relationship includes both mutuality and passion. Mutuality means that love does not simply flow forth from the loving person to others; rather it moves back and forth within the dialogue between them as the fullest expression of that dialogue.

Hallowing the everyday and going out to meet the world with one's whole being meant, to the Hasidim, loving one's fellows. All Hasidic life takes place within community, and community is both matrix and product of love. Even the most exalted zaddik is bound to the community. There is no room here for the lonely anchorite or hermit living in seclusion in the desert or the saint living on top of his pillar. "One of the great principles of Hasidism," writes Buber, "is that the zaddik and the people are dependent on one another." The zaddik guides not just through his teaching but also and even more through his day-by-day existence, "unemphatic, undeliberate, unconscious . . . the complete human being with his whole worldly life in which the completeness of the human being is tested. As a zaddik once said: 'I learned the Torah from all the limbs of my teacher.' " The zaddik helps and guides, but the disciples help the zaddik in his hours of desolation and light his life with the flame he has kindled.

The mutuality of Hasidic life has never been expressed better than in Rabbi Yitzhak Eisik of Zhydatchov's saying, "The motto of life is 'give and take.' Everyone must be both a giver and a receiver. He who is not both is as a barren tree." The person who tries to help others without receiving is like the famous "Giving Tree" in the children's story of that name which ends up a mere stump. That is because we do not exist fundamentally as role to role but as person to person. What we need from each other is not Martin Heidegger's "solicitude" but love.

The Hasidic community was a genuine caring community. This caring did not stop at the border of the particular Hasidic community, or even at the border of all the people of Israel. "Save the Jews," one zaddik prayed to God, "and if you cannot do that, save the goyim, and soon." Rabbi Mikhal of Zlotchov commanded his sons to pray for their enemies that all might be well with them and assured them that, more than all prayers, this is, indeed, the service of God.

Beginning with the paradox of how the therapist "climbs down" to where the client is and yet retains the resources to help lift himself and the client "up to the light," the rest of this chapter uses Hasidic tales to illuminate such therapeutic issues as the problematic of mutuality, "inclusion," or "imagining the real," whether the therapist responds to the conscious intention of the client or the whole person, the contrast between Hasidic teachings and psychoanalysis, the contrast between *professional accountability* and *personal responsibility*, and the limits of the responsibility of the helper in the therapy relationships.

CLIMBING DOWN

> Rabbi Shelomo said: "If you want to raise a man from mud and filth, do not think it is enough to keep standing on top and reaching down to him with a helping hand. You must go all the way down yourself, down into mud and filth. Then take hold of him with strong hands and pull him and yourself out into the light."[9]

This Hasidic story has always seemed to me to express in a nutshell the paradox of all healing and helping. If we ask why it is not enough to stand above and reach down a helping hand, the answer is clearly that a person who sees you standing above him will not believe you can understand his problem well enough to help him. Once Rabbi Meier, who was an opponent of Rabbi Bunam, compelled two of his Hasidim to insult Bunam by asking how it was possible that he could be a rabbi when he spent his youth selling lumber in Danzig. Rabbi Meier, who does not know how to sin, cannot know what is wrong with the people who seek him out," Rabbi Bunam pointed out to his disciples. "I was in Danzig and in the theaters, and know what sinning is like—and ever since then I have known how to straighten out a young tree that is growing crooked."

Once when we were discussing "Climbing Down" in a group, a

psychologist objected that he was not going to go out to where other people were. They had to come to his office. Present also was a doctoral tutee of his and mine who had been seventeen years in Alcoholics Anonymous. I asked him whether what AA calls the "twelfth step" was not just such a climbing down. The twelfth step involves going out to try to rescue someone whose sobriety is threatened and who wants you, a more seasoned recovered or recovering alcoholic, to help him or her resist the temptation. Our tutee confirmed in the strongest possible terms that it did involve just that and described some really hair-raising situations into which he had had to go.

The risk, of course, is that the more seasoned recovered alcoholic will also lose his or her sobriety in the process of trying to help the endangered comrade. This brings us to the other part of the paradox. How does one avoid sinking into the "mud and filth" with the person one is trying to help or even pulling that person down with you? How does one get the resources to go down into the pit and yet "take hold of him with strong hands and pull him and yourself out into the light"? "Healing," Buber suggests in the Postscript to *I and Thou*, "is only possible to the one who lives over against the other, and yet is detached." Only the zaddik whose soul is unified can descend into the whirlpool, Buber pointed out in an early Hasidic book. The "bold faced," said Rabbi Zusya, "may roam about in alleys and marketplaces and need not fear evil." That is because they have relatively greater wholeness than the one who comes to them for help. Rabbi Bunam went to the theater, but he did not himself become a great sinner. Later, when he became the wise rabbi to whom people came for healing and help, he brought with him his earlier insight into the secular world that he had known. The Baal Shem, the founder of Hasidism, once said to a zaddik who used to preach admonishing sermons: "What do you know about admonishing! You yourself have remained unacquainted with sin all the days of your life, and you have had nothing to do with the people around you—how should you know what sinning is!"

THE ZADDIK'S HEALING

The healing performed by the zaddik rests upon the Hasidic attitude toward the unity of body and soul. The unity of the body depends, Martin Buber suggests, on the unity of the soul:

The relation of the soul to its organic life depends on the degree of its wholeness and unity. The more dissociated the soul, the more it is at the mercy of its sicknesses and attacks, the more concentrated it is, the more it is able to master them. It is not as if it conquers the body; rather through its unity it ever again saves and protects the unity of the body.

The healing of the body takes place, accordingly, at the point where a crystallization and unification take place in a dispersed soul; for here "there takes place rapidly and visibly . . . what otherwise only grows in vegetative darkness, the 'healing.' " Occasionally such an elemental moment of healing can come to a person from himself, but more often it is through the zaddik, the whole soul that comes to the aid of the dispersed one. This is what Martin Buber in a 1921 essay called "psychosynthesis" in contrast to Freudian psychoanalysis:

> Through nothing else can this process be effected so simply and directly as through the psychosynthetic appearance of a whole, united soul laying hold of the dispersed soul, agitating it on all sides, and demanding the event of crystallization. It does not "suggest"; it fashions in the fellow-soul by which it is called, a ground and center, and the more genuinely and fully, the more it is concerned that the appealing soul that calls it does not remain dependent on it: the helper establishes ground and center not in order that he might install his own image in the soul that is to be rebuilt, but in order that it might look through him, as through a glass, into being and now discover being in itself and let it be empowered as the core of living unity.[10]

A striking example of this type of healing is the story in which the Baal Shem read aloud a passage from the Scriptures with the assistance of Rabbi Nahum of Tchernobil, who was at that time sickly and plagued with all manner of aches and pains. "When the Baal Shem began to read, Rabbi Nahum felt pain leave one of his limbs after another with each successive part of the passage, and when the reading was over, he was rid of all his complaints: sound and well."

If the soul which is relatively whole can save and protect the unity of the body whereas the dissociated soul is at the mercy of its sicknesses, as Buber suggested, then it also follows that the healer whose soul is relatively more whole than that of the one to be healed can help the latter if he or she can give the person helped something of the personal wholeness that he or she lacks. We cannot demand of the contemporary healer that he or she be a zaddik, but we can expect that the healer have achieved a greater degree of personal wholeness than the one healed so that we can speak of the former as one who, relatively speaking, has attained being and the latter as one who is in the process of becoming.

Once Rabbi Zusya of Hanipol came to an inn where he saw long years of sin on the forehead of the innkeeper. Alone in his room he was overcome by "the shudder of vicarious experience" so that in the midst of singing psalms, he cried aloud, "Zusya, you wicked man! There is no lie that failed to tempt you, and no crime you have not committed," after which he enumerated the sins of the innkeeper as if they were his own, sobbing the while. The innkeeper, who had followed him, was at first seized with dull dismay. "But then penitence and grace were lit within him, and he woke to God." Zusya's experience was vicarious, but it was at the same time real. He did not play act or try to work some technique. He really relived the sins as his own, and only through this "shudder" was he able to help the innkeeper.

Another time, confronted by a person who refused to do penance, Zusya "climbed down all the rungs" until he was with the man and could bind the root of his own soul to that of the other. But then the other had no choice but to do penance along with Zusya, and it was very great and terrible penance. When the man had stopped screaming, however, Zusya lifted him up and said, "Thine iniquity is taken away and thy sin expiated."

One zaddik did not want the Messiah to come because he did not want to give up as lost all the souls that he might help through "climbing down" to where they were: "I stake my whole self for everyone, even the most unfaithful, and probe down to the root of his apostasy where wickedness can be recognized as need and lust. And if I get that far, I can pull him out all right!" A disciple of the great Maggid of Mezritch told that all the desires of the disciples were fulfilled the moment they were within the limits of the town or at least as soon as they entered the house of the maggid. But if there was one among them whose soul was still churned up with wanting—he was at peace when he looked into the face of the maggid.

"SHOCK THERAPY"

A more active form of help, not unlike a psychological shock therapy,
was reported when the Maggid of Mezritch once laughed at every line of
a list of sins written down by an old man who asked him to impose a
penance. The shocked rav who witnessed this later understood what
happened through a saying of the Baal Shem:

> It is well-known that no one commits a sin unless the spirit of folly
> possesses him. But what does the sage do if a fool comes to him? He
> laughs at all this folly, and while he laughs, a breath of gentleness is
> wafted through the world. What was rigid, thaws, and what was a burden
> becomes light.[11]

A striking clinical example of this laughter therapy was related to me
by the Jerusalem psychologist Tamar Kron. An attractive forty-year-old
woman came to see her after having had therapy with a man who
practiced "mirror-like impassivity." The woman used to enter Dr. Kron's
room with a sad countenance, mouth pulled down and whiny voice, and
weep from the moment she sat on her chair until the end of the session.
Although Dr. Kron found this somewhat irritating, she offered her the
acceptance and support due to a depressed patient. But in one session
when the patient, in her usual tearful and quivering voice, related an
encounter she had had with her boss, her therapist found the situation so
funny that, despite herself, she burst out laughing. The patient was so
taken aback that she stopped crying and stared at Dr. Kron. Then she
started laughing too, and they both laughed till tears rolled down their
eyes. When they were able to stop laughing, they looked into each
other's eyes. The patient confessed that she had always thought that she
was supposed to bring only her problems to the therapist and was not
allowed to joke and laugh. Actually she had a good sense of humor and
loved to laugh, but the serious expression of her former therapist had
reinforced her depressive mood. She now felt relieved and relaxed, her
natural attractiveness came to the surface, and from then on she enter-
tained her therapist with jokes even while she brought herself to the
therapy more as a whole person.[12]

Another example of "shock therapy" is the story of Rabbi Hayke, a devout and learned man who lived as a hermit and mortified his flesh. Rabbi Aaron, a disciple of the Great Maggid, heard of him and preached so forcibly in the town near him that the hermit was drawn to come hear his sermon. But all that he said was: "If a man does not grow better, he grows worse." These words bit into the mind of the ascetic "like a poison which rouses the very core of life against itself." When he begged Rabbi Aaron to help him out of the maze of error in which he had lost his way, Rabbi Aaron sent him to his own teacher, the Maggid of Mezritch, with a letter. The maggid opened the letter and read aloud its contents: The man who was delivering the letter did not have a particle of sound goodness in him.

> Rabbi Hayke burst into tears. "Now, now," said the maggid. "Does what the Lithuanian writes really matter so much to you?"
> "Is it true or isn't it?" asked the other.
> "Well," said the maggid, "if the Lithuanian says so, it is, very probably, true."
> "Then heal me, rabbi!" the ascetic begged him.
> For a whole year, the maggid worked over him and healed him. Later, Rabbi Hayke became one of the great men of his generation.[13]

A similar story is that of Rabbi David of Lelov who had done great penance for twelve years, fasting from one sabbath to the next and subjecting himself to all manner of rigid discipline. When he went at the end of this time to visit Rabbi Elimelekh, the healer of souls, to discover what he must do to attain perfection, Rabbi Elimelekh twice ignored him, not even shaking hands with him when he shook hands with everyone else. David of Lelov wept all night, and in the morning, despite himself, crept to the window and heard Rabbi Elimelekh preach of those who fast and torment themselves for a dozen years and then come to him to ask him to supply the little they still lack.

> But the truth of the matter is that all their discipline and all their pains are less than a drop in the sea, and what's more: all that service of theirs does not rise to God, but to the idol of their pride. Such people must turn to God by turning utterly from all they have been doing, and begin to serve from the bottom up and with a truthful heart.[14]

Rabbi David was so moved by these words that he almost lost consciousness. Trembling and sobbing, he ventured onto the threshold, at which point Rabbi Elimelekh ran up to him, embracing and blessing him. When the zaddik's son protested that this was the very man whom he had twice ignored, Elimelekh answered, "No, indeed! That was an entirely different person! Don't you see that this is our dear Rabbi David!"

An even stranger story is that of young Jacob Yitzhak, later the Seer of Lublin, who, when visiting a little town, heard the rav of the place recite the Morning Prayer with deep fervor and later found that same fervor in all he did. When the rav told him he had never served a zaddik, Jacob Yitzhak was surprised; "for the *way* cannot be learned out of a book, or from hearsay, but can only be communicated from person to person." When he took the rav to see his own teacher, Rabbi Elimelekh, the latter turned to his window and paid no attention to his visitors. Jacob Yitzhak took the violently excited rav to the inn and returned alone. "What struck you, my friend, to bring with you a man in whose face I can see the tainted image of God?" Elimelekh asked him, and explained that there is a place, lit by the planet Venus, where good and evil are blended. When ulterior motives and pride enter into a person's service of God, he comes to live in that dim place and does not even know it. He is even able to exert great fervor by fetching his blaze from the place of the impure fire and kindling his service with it. When the stranger was told these words, he recognized the truth in them, turned to God, ran weeping to the master and was given help that enabled him to find the way.

What is striking about this story is that at first glance it would appear that the stranger was doing the very thing that Hasidism most exalts: serving God with the "evil" urge. Yet the motive, the *kavana*, of the service is tainted and the result is a "sublimation" that contains too much of the sphere of the planet Venus (one thinks of Wagner's Tannhäuser!) The result is "patchwork" at best. "From every deed an angel is born, a good angel or a bad one," wrote Buber in "The Life of the Hasidim." "But from half-hearted and confused deeds which are without meaning or without power angels are born with twisted limbs or without a head or hands or feet."

THE TANGLE OF OPPRESSIVE IMPULSES

In interesting contrast to this story stands the one of Rabbi Shelomo of Karlin who while reciting psalms was visited by "a man whose soul had become enmeshed in a tangle of oppressive impulses." When Rabbi Shelomo came to the words "and hath delivered us from our oppressors," he turned to his guest, patted him on the shoulder, and asked: "Do you believe that God can wrest us from all oppression?" "I believe," said the man, and from then on all disturbing impulses left him. At first glance this seems to be a story of faith healing, or more precisely of being healed through one's own faith, as when Jesus said to the woman who touched his garment without his knowing it and was healed of an issue of blood, "Thy faith hath made thee whole." To me, the heart of the tale lies elsewhere. What imprisons us all too often in the tangle of evil urges that oppress us is our guilt—our feeling of responsibility for having such impulses and an accompanying feeling of helplessness that becomes stronger in proportion to our guilt. Rabbi Shelomo of Karlin has suggested instead that we should look on them as something that oppresses us just as external tyranny and misfortune do. It is such a radical change in the way of looking at his disturbing impulses that enables the man to ascend to the faith that this oppression too might be wrested from him by God. The faith is there, to be sure, but only after a genuine *metanoia*, a total change in the way of seeing one's existence.

Sometimes Hasidic healing was physical and spiritual together, as when Rabbi Moshe Leib performed a dance of healing for his friend the rabbi of Berditchev when he learned that the latter had fallen ill. After his prayer for the zaddik's recovery, he put on his new shoes made of morocco leather and danced with such powerful mystery that "an unfamiliar light suffused the house, and everyone watching saw the heavenly hosts join in his dance."

"INCLUSION"

Another form of healing comes from that intuition that Martin Buber describes as "inclusion," imagining the real or experiencing the other side of the relationship. In contrast to both empathy and identification, inclusion means a bold imaginative swinging "with the intensest stirring of one's being" into the life of the other so that one can to some extent concretely imagine what the other person is thinking, willing, and feeling. This means seeing through the eyes of the other and experiencing the other's side of the relationship *without* ceasing to experience the relationship from one's own side. Rabbi Mordecai of Neskhizh said to his son, "He who does not feel the pains of a woman giving birth within a circuit of fifty miles, who does not suffer with her, and pray that her suffering may be assuaged, is not worthy to be called a zaddik." When Rabbi Bunam's wife informed him that a whole carriage-load of Hasidim had come to see him, he exclaimed, "What are you thinking of? You know that that's not my business." But an hour later, after they had all left, he confessed, "I can't hold out against it any longer. The moment they came in, I knew the needs and wishes of every one of them."

A humorous story about "inclusion" is told of Yehiel Mikhal of Zlotchov. Once when he visited a city for the first time and was called on by prominent members of the congregation, he fixed a long gaze on each person's forehead and then told him the flaws in his soul and what he could do to heal them. The news of this got around, and the next visitors pulled their hats down to their noses to prevent his seeing the quality of their souls through looking at their foreheads. "You are mistaken," Rabbi Mikhal said to them. "An eye which can see through the flesh, can certainly see through the hat."

I quoted this story in my book *The Healing Dialogue in Psychotherapy* and commented:

> Some people think of such gifts of seeing as magic powers. I rather think of them as being in touch—as touching, contact, a "dialogue of touchstones." If we keep in view the concrete reality of the between that underlies such intuition, we shall not be tempted to think of ourselves as *possessing* unusual powers. Those who feel they possess intuition sometimes try to use it for the spiritual or psychological domination of others. If we take seriously the "partnership of existence," the between, we shall not imagine that it is *our* power. What we contribute to the event is that we allow the intuition to happen between us and the other rather than preventing it from happening by blocking it from our awareness, as is usually the case. But we cannot take credit for it. If the other person does not want to

reveal him or herself to us at all, then this inclusive intuition will not take place. We cannot force the other to reveal himself.[15]

At first glance, the story appears to contradict what I have said. Rabbi Mikhal's second group of visitors did not want him to read their souls; yet he seemed ready to do so without their consent. Total mutuality in the process of therapy is neither possible nor desirable. Yet the zaddik often seems to arrive at his task of healing from such an exalted place that we might fairly wonder whether he has in fact climbed down into the mud and filth with the person he is helping. There is no gainsaying the great reverence in which the Hasidim held the zaddik nor the fact that that reverence undoubtedly contributed to the effectiveness of the healing. But precisely the fact that something must come first from the Hasid shows that there is after all an element of mutuality even in what Martin Buber properly describes, not only for pastoral care but for teaching and psychotherapy, as a "normative limitation of mutuality." In the story in question, the visitors came of their own volition to see Rabbi Kikhal, and this coming, we may surmise, placed a demand on him other than any they consciously had in mind.

The healer and helper cannot remain above in lofty isolation but must, like Rabbi Elimelekh, who was sometimes accused of aloofness, be ready to go to the threshold to embrace "dear Rabbi David." At the same time, the healer brings what, relatively speaking, we can call a "whole soul" to the encounter with one whose soul (and body) is not whole. And the healer and helper practices "inclusion," imagines the real, as the person who is helped cannot be expected to do for the healer.

HOW ONE CAN HELP ONESELF

Yet, as Martin Buber emphasized, the healer does not want the person being helped to become dependent but to find his or her own unique way through turning to a genuine relationship to being. It is not surprising, therefore, that a whole group of tales have no actual healer but only the example and advice of the zaddik as to how one can help oneself.

One of the most interesting of these is Rabbi Pinhas of Koretz's advice concerning anger. Rabbi Pinhas once said to a Hasid that anger not only makes one's soul impure but transfers impurity to the souls of those with whom one is angry. Yet another time he said, "Since I have tamed my anger I keep it in my pocket. When I need it, I take it out." At first glance these two sayings appear contradictory. One warns against anger; the other implies that anger is sometimes needed. The key here is the difference between untamed anger and tamed anger. Untamed anger that tears through one, especially suppressed anger that comes out as rage, makes one less of a person, and it also makes those who are attacked less, whether they express their own anger in turn or repress it. When one has reached a great personal integration, anger may be a legitimate expression of one's person, which enhances rather than diminishes it. I do not mean by this that self-righteous anger in which one indulges when one imagines one is wholly in the right and the other wholly in the wrong. I mean anger as a demand placed upon the other in relationship *for the sake of the relationship.* This is not an anger that destroys. On the contrary, it confirms the other and is, when it is true, an expression of love for the other.

Rabbi Zusya taught that when God says to us as to Abraham, "Get you out of your country," God means the dimness we have inflicted on ourselves, and when God says get out of our birthplace, he means the dimness our mother inflicted on us, and out of our father's house, the dimness our father inflicted on us. We are afflicted with a dimness, which it is our life task to remove, whether it be our own hand that shuts out the wonders and mysteries of life or our lack of awareness, our obtuseness, our insensitivity, our callousness toward what Abraham Joshua Heschel calls "radical amazement" and "the awareness of the ineffable." In any case, dimness is something that stands between us and our own life path.

But the other thing that is striking about this teaching suggests a contrast with psychoanalysis: One does not begin by getting rid of the dimness that one's mother and father imposed on one but of the dimness that one has imposed on oneself. Like existential psychotherapy, this teaching recognizes that it is the attitude that we bring to what our mother and father "did" to us that imprisons us quite as much or more than our parents' actions or omissions themselves.

What is true of sickness is also true of healing. Our own attitude is even more important in our being healed than the gifts and good will of the healer. Rabbi Shelomo of Karlin once said to a man, "I have no key to open you," at which the man cried out, "Then pry me open with a nail!" From then on, Rabbi Shelomo always warmly praised him.

THE LIMITS OF RESPONSIBILITY OF THE HEALER

In the Ph.D. program in Religion and Psychology that I directed at Temple University, one of the issues that I regularly stressed as arising from the meeting of religion and psychology was that of the limits of responsibility of the healer and helper in the therapy relationship. By responsibility I mean not only professional but personal responsibility, not only accountability but one's ability and one's duty to respond as a person in a mutual, though not fully mutual, situation. This is a topic on which many Hasidic tales touch in one way or another.

As we have already seen, because the zaddik does not want his Hasidim to become permanently dependent on him, he calls on them to help themselves. One New Year's Eve Menahem Mendel of Rymanov entered the House of Prayer and surveyed the many people who had come together from near and far. "A fine crowd!" he called out to them. "But I want you to know that I cannot carry you all on my shoulders. Every one of you must work for himself." On New Year's day before the blowing of the ram's horn the rabbi of Kobryn used to call out: "Little brothers, do not depend upon me! Everyone had better take his own part." In contrast to those zaddikim who prayed that those in need of help might come to them and find help through their prayers, Rabbi Naftali of Roptchitz prayed that those in need of help might find it in their own homes and not have to go to Roptchiz and be deluded into thinking that the rabbi had helped them.

THE LIMITS OF THE POWER OF THE HELPER

A part of the realism of the zaddikim was their recognition of the limits in those they wished to help. The Baal Shem expounded the statement that the Truth goes over all the world to mean that Truth is driven out of one place after another, and must wander on and on! The Seer of Lublin said that he loved the wicked who knew they were wicked more than the righteous who knew they were righteous. "But concerning the wicked who consider themselves righteous, it is said: 'They do not turn even on the threshold of Hell.' For they think they are being sent to Hell to redeem the souls of others." One wonders to how many do-gooders and members of the helping professions these words apply!

An equally important realism was the zaddik's recognition of the limits of his own power to help. Rabbi Israel of Rizhyn said of Rabbi Barukh of Mezbizh, "When a wise man went to the Rabbi Reb Barukh, he could spoon up the fear of God with a ladle, but the fool who visited him became much more of a fool." "This," Buber comments, "does not hold for this one zaddik alone." The way in which persons limit the help they might receive is expressed by the Baal Shem in the allegorical tale of "The Deaf Man":

> Once a fiddler played so sweetly that all who heard him began to dance, and whoever came near enough to hear joined in the dance. Then a deaf man who knew nothing of music, happened along, and to him all he saw seemed the action of madmen—senseless and in bad taste.[16]

Rabbi Pinhas of Koretz remarked that the people who came to hear his words of teaching were full of fervor on the sabbath but as soon as the holiness of the sabbath was over, they were a thousand miles away from it. "It is as when a madman recovers: he is unable to remember what happened in the days of his madness." The Seer of Lublin in marked contrast recognized that there was something that ten Hasidim could accomplish that the zaddik himself could not. Once a group of Hasidim took up a man who had been moaning on the bench and drank merrily with him until morning, as a result of which they averted the fate that the Seer had accepted that he should die on the sabbath. A very different note is sounded in the story of the man who came to the Seer for help against alien thoughts that intruded while he prayed. The Seer told him what to do, but the man kept pestering him. Finally the Seer said: "I don't know why you keep complaining to me of alien thoughts. To him who has holy thoughts, an impure thought comes at times, and such a thought is called 'alien.' But you—you have just your own usual thoughts. To whom do you want to ascribe them?"

THE SHORTCOMINGS OF THE HELPER

In the above tales the zaddik's power to help is limited by his Hasidim. In some cases, however, it is limited by his own lacks or shortcomings.

Martin Buber suggests that the turning point in the life of Abraham Yehoshua Heschel, the rabbi of Apt, came when a respected woman came to ask his advice. The instant the Apter rebbe set eyes on her he shouted: "Adulteress! You sinned only a short while ago, and yet now you have the insolence to step into this pure house!" Then from the depths of her heart the woman replied:

> The Lord of the world has patience with the wicked. He is in no hurry to make them pay their debts and he does not disclose their secret to any creature, lest they be ashamed to turn to him. Nor does he hide his face from them. But the rabbi of Apt sits there in his chair and cannot resist revealing at once what the Creator has covered."[17]

From that time on the rabbi of Apt used to say, "No one ever got the better of me except once—and then it was a woman." In his Introduction to *The Later Masters*, Buber describes this turning point as learning that human justice fails when it attempts to exceed the province of a just social order and encroaches on that of direct human relationships: "Man should be just within the bounds of his social order, but when he ventures beyond it on the high seas of human relationships, he is sure to be shipwrecked and then all he can do is to save himself by clinging to love."

There is a story of how the Baal Shem spoke to a number of persons and each was sure that he alone was addressed. In a later generation Rabbi Simha Bunam of Pshysha was very aware that he did not have this gift. "When my room is full of people, it is difficult for me to 'say Torah,' " he remarked once. "For each person requires his own Torah, and each wishes to find his own perfection. And so what I give to all I withhold from each."

"BURNOUT" OF THE HEALER

There are more somber notes still sounded by the zaddikim, notes that suggest that they too experienced what we describe as "burnout," when in their very desire to help they depleted their own resources. One such story is that of the Seer of Lublin who once remarked: "How strange! People come to me weighted down with melancholy, and when they leave, their spirit is lighter." "But I myself," he added, and started to say, "am melancholy" but paused and continued instead: "am dark and do not shine."

The most enigmatic and troubling of such stories is that told about Menahem Mendel of Kotzk, the famous Kotzker rebbe who spent the last twenty years of his life in seclusion. He was sometimes visited by his friend Rabbi Yitzhak of Vorki, one of the very few admitted to him during the period when he kept away from the world. Once after a long absence, Yitzhak of Vorki entered Mendel's room with the greeting, "Peace be with you, Rabbi." "Why do you call me rabbi?" the Kotzker Rebbe grumbled. "Don't you recognize me? I'm the sacred goat:

> An old Jew once lost his snuffbox made of horn, on his way to the House of Study. He wailed: "Just as if the dreadful exile weren't enough, this must happen to me! Oh me, oh my, I've lost my snuffbox made of horn!" And then he came upon the sacred goat. The sacred goat was pacing the earth, and the tips of his black horns touched the stars. When he heard the old Jew lamenting, he leaned down to him, and said: "Cut a piece from my horns, whatever you need to make a new snuffbox." The old Jew did this, made a new snuffbox, and filled it with tobacco. Then he went to the House of Study and offered everyone a pinch. They snuffed and snuffed, and everyone who snuffed it cried: "Oh, what wonderful tobacco! It must be because of the box. Oh, what a wonderful box! Wherever did you get it?" So the old man told them about the good sacred goat. And then one after the other they went out on the street and looked for the sacred goat. The sacred goat was pacing the earth and the tips of his black horns touched the stars. One after another they went up to him and begged permission to cut off a bit of his horns. Time after time the sacred goat leaned down to grant the request. Box after box was made and filled with tobacco. The fame of the boxes spread far and wide. At every step he took the sacred goat met someone who asked for a piece of his horns.
>
> Now the sacred goat still paces the earth—but he has no horns. [18]

If the sacred goat no longer has horns, then the tips of his horns no longer touch the sky and the connection between heaven and earth is broken. This is what the Kotzker rebbe implied had happened to him. If we take the story out of the humorous form of the snuffbox, we can assume that what Menahem Mendel really meant was that his Hasidim came to him with all the petty cares and burdens of their daily lives and that in the course of helping them, he lost his own connection with God or, even more important for him, was not able to work toward the reunification of God with his exiled Shekinah, the indwelling Glory or Presence of God which, according to the Lurian Kabbalah, needs to be reunited with the En Sof, the infinite Godhead, for redemption to come. If we follow this line of thinking, we shall conclude not only that Menahem Mendel of Kotzk was "burnt out" by his years of service but also that he did not see the possibility of redeeming the world— reuniting God and his exiled Shekinah—through helping his followers raise the sparks fallen after the breaking of the vessels of light and surrounded by shells of darkness. If this is so, then "hallowing the everyday" could not for the Kotzker, Martin Buber to the contrary, lead to that restoration of the sparks (*tikkun*) that presages redemption. We may wonder legitimately whether Menahem Mendel made himself too available to his community and not enough to his own needs, whether his image of himself as zaddik and person led him to overextend himself, or whether his congregants disappointed him by not caring enough for the redemption of the Shekinah from its exile.

The Kotzker's withdrawal raises a profound question about the relationship between zaddik and hasid and the help that the former can give to the latter. In some mysterious way the healing process can be transformed into its opposite, and the one who is trying to heal may be lamed in that very process. I have always been enormously struck by the pathos of this story of "The Sacred Goat." Perhaps more than any other it illustrates both the meeting and the mismeeting of religion and psychology. It not only touches on the limits of the responsibility of the helper and the "burnout" that is so common an experience to pastors, therapists, and all persons in the helping professions. It also raises the question of whether Menahem Mendel of Kotzk was not in need of a therapist himself. But along with that question comes the recognition of the tragic limitations of resources and situation. Who could have been a therapist to him, and, given his position in the community, who would have presumed to approach him offering such help? Yet the answer that all too many rabbis, ministers, and priests have offered over the ages— "Take your troubles to God"—is no answer either for those who need that healing through meeting that, like confirmation itself, can only come from person to person. When that does happen, we know the true meaning of existential grace.

When one person is singing and cannot lift his voice, and another comes and sings with him, another who can lift his voice, then the first will be able to lift his voice. That is the secret of the bond between spirit and spirit.[19]

Chapter 3

MARTIN BUBER'S PHILOSOPHY OF DIALOGUE AND DIALOGICAL PSYCHOTHERAPY

In spite of all similarities every living situation has, like a newborn child, a new face that has never been before and will never come again. It demands of you a reaction which cannot be prepared beforehand. It demands nothing of what is past. It demands presence, responsibility; it demands you. I call a great character one who by his actions and attitudes satisfies the claim of situations out of deep readiness to respond with his whole life, and in such a way that the sum of his actions and attitudes expresses at the same time the unity of his being in its willingness to accept responsibility.[1]

RESPONSIBILITY, TO MARTIN BUBER, means response, the response of the whole person to what addresses her in the lived concrete. The "ought" must be brought back to lived life, says Buber, from where it swings in the empty air. Therefore, there can be no moral code that is valid in advance of particular situations. Rather, one moves from the concrete situation and the deep-seated attitudes that one brings to that situation to the decision and response that produces the moral action.

"The true norm demands not our obedience but ourselves." It does not want us to repress one part of ourselves in order to obey with the other, but to respond with all that we are, our passions and our reason, our sensing and our intuiting. No one has ever understood the Ten Commandments, Buber has said, unless he has heard the Thou of the command as addressing oneself in one's particular situation.

Buber's classic presentation of his philosophy of dialogue is his poetic book *I and Thou*. Here he distinguishes between the "I-Thou" relationship that is direct, mutual, present, and open, and the "I-It," or, subject-object, relation in which one relates to the other only indirectly and non-mutually, knowing and using the other. The I-Thou relationship is the only one in which I know the other in her uniqueness, for it is the only one in which I can perceive her in her wholeness and as of value in herself. The difference between these two relationships is not the object to which one relates: One can relate to a cat, a tree, or a painting as one's Thou, and one can and often does relate to a human being as an It. What is decisive is the relationship itself—whether it is sharing or possessing, imposing on the other or helping her to unfold, valuing the relationship in itself or valuing it only as a means to an end. Persevering in an unbroken I-Thou relationship is impossible: Rather, the I-Thou and the I-It should alternate in such a way that ever more of the world of It is brought into the world of Thou. The I-Thou is the basic relationship for Buber, for through it one becomes truly human. But its authentication would not be possible were it not for the civilized structure and ordering of the world of It. Without the world of It one cannot live, says Buber, but if one lives in this world alone, one is not truly human. I-It is not evil in itself, but its predominance prevents the return to the Thou and leads to meaninglessness, evil, or even insanity.

The I-Thou philosophy is concerned with the difference between mere existence and authentic existence, between being human at all and being more fully human, between remaining fragmented and bringing the conflicting parts of oneself into an active unity, between partial and fuller relationships with others. No one ever becomes a "whole person." But one may move in the direction of greater wholeness through greater awareness and fuller response in each new situation. By the same token, no one can say that you "ought" to have an I-Thou relationship in every situation. The "ought" for Buber is the *quantum satis*—the sufficient amount of your resources in this situation. This "ought" recognizes the practical limitation of your resources from moment to moment as opposed to any general doctrine of original sin or of the death instinct. It also recognizes the practical, and sometimes tragic, limitations of the situation. These, however, cannot be known in advance. "I cannot know how much justice is possible in a given situation," Buber once wrote me, "unless I go on until my head hits the wall and hurts."

The psychological is only the accompaniment of the dialogue between person and person. What is essential is not what goes on within the minds of the partners in a relationship but what happens *between* them. For this reason, Buber is unalterably opposed to that psychologism that wishes to remove the reality of relationship into the separate psyches of the participants. "The inmost growth of the self does not take place, as people like to suppose today," writes Buber, "through our relationship to ourselves, but through being made present by the other and knowing that we are made present by him." Being made present as a person is the heart of what Buber calls confirmation.

Confirmation is interhuman, but it is not simply social or interpersonal; for unless one is confirmed in one's uniqueness as the person one can become, one is only seemingly confirmed. The confirmation of the other must include an actual experiencing of the other side of the relationship so that one can imagine quite concretely what another is feeling, thinking, and knowing without falling into that empathy, in the narrow sense of the term, which leads one to leave one's own ground and lose sight of one's own side of the relationship. This "inclusion," or imagining the real does not abolish the basic distance between oneself and the other. It is rather a bold swinging over into the life of the person one confronts, through which alone I can make her present in her wholeness, unity, and uniqueness.

This experiencing of the other side is essential to the distinction that Buber makes between "dialogue," in which I open myself to the otherness of the person I meet, and "monologue," in which, even when I converse with her at length, I allow her to exist only as a content of my experience. Wherever one lets the other exist only as part of oneself, "dialogue becomes a fiction, the mysterious intercourse between two human worlds only a game, and in the rejection of the real life confronting him the essence of all reality begins to disintegrate."

Real love is not constituted by feelings, not even the most intense and sincere feelings, for real love takes place *between* I and Thou. It is the responsibility of an I for a Thou, of which feelings are only the accompaniment. One cannot enter genuine dialogue unless one is a real person. "Dialogue between mere individuals is only a sketch." But in contrast to Jung, Buber sees dialogue as the goal and individuation as the stepping stone and the by-product. When one becomes integrated, it is so one may go forth to meeting. If one falls back instead on the enjoyment of one's wholeness, then even that wholeness disintegrates. What is more, the way to the personal wholeness that makes possible real dialogue is dialogue itself. "By what could a man from being an individual so really become a person as by the strict and sweet experiences of dialogue which teach him the boundless content of the boundary?"

Buber cannot follow George Herbert Mead in seeing the self as "an eddy in the social current." "What is said here is the real contrary of the cry, heard at times in twilight ages, for universal unreserve. He who can be unreserved with each passerby has no substance to lose." But Buber objects with equal vigor to Kierkegaard's advice to "be chary in having to do with the other." "He who cannot stand in a direct relation to each one who meets him has a fullness which is futile." Kierkegaard's notion that in order to come to God he had "to remove the object," namely his fiancée, Regina Olsen, Buber considers a sublime misunderstanding of God.

> Creation is not a hurdle on the road to God, it is the road itself. We are created along with one another and directed to a life with one another. Creatures are placed in my way so that I, their fellow creature, by means of them and with them find the way to God. . . . God wants us to come to him by means of the Reginas he has created and not by renunciation of them. . . . The real God lets no shorter line reach him than each man's longest, which is the line embracing the world that is accessible to this man.[2]

Kierkegaard wishes to reach God by joining hands with him *above* the world, writes Buber, whereas we wish to reach him by joining hands with him *around* the world.

Buber holds "that there resides in every man the possibility of attain-

ing authentic human existence in the special way peculiar to him."
Individuation is "the indispensable personal stamp of all realization of
human existence." But in contrast to Fromm, Buber holds that the goal
is not self-realization, but the meaning that arises in the fulfillment of
one's created task, one's response to that part of creation in which one
is set:

> The self as such is not ultimately the essential, but the meaning of human
> existence given in creation again and again fulfills itself as self. The help
> that men give each other in becoming a self leads the life between men to
> its height. The dynamic glory of the being of man is first bodily present in
> the relation between two men each of whom in meaning the other also
> means the highest to which this person is called, and serves the self-
> realization of this human life as one true to creation without wishing to
> impose on the other anything of his own realization.[3]

Only one finds meaning who no longer aims at happiness, or at meaning
for that matter, but forgets oneself in the response to what calls one out in
the deepest level of one's being.

> That meaning is open and accessible in the actual lived concrete does not
> mean it is to be won and possessed through any type of analytical or
> synthetic investigation or through any type of reflection upon the lived
> concrete. Meaning is to be experienced in living action and suffering
> itself, in the unreduced immediacy of the moment. Of course, he who
> aims at the experiencing of experience will necessarily miss the meaning,
> for he destroys the spontaneity of the mystery. Only he reaches the
> meaning who stands firm, without holding back or reservation, before the
> whole might of reality and answers it in a living way. He is ready to
> confirm with his life the meaning which he has attained.[4]

Good to Buber is only that which is done with the whole being. Evil is
passion without direction, or action without passion, both of which
mean lack of true decision. True decision does not mean that one *is*
whole; it means that one is moving toward wholeness through genuine
response in dialogue.

> It is a cruelly hazardous enterprise, this becoming a whole, becoming a
> form, of crystallization of the soul. Everything in the nature of inclina-

tions, of indolence, of habits, of fondness for possibilities which has been swashbuckling within us, must be overcome, and overcome, not by elimination, by suppression, for genuine wholeness can never be achieved like that, never a wholeness where downtrodden appetites lurk in the corners. Rather must all these mobile or static forces, seized by the soul's rapture, plunge of their own accord, as it were, into the mightiness of decision and dissolve within it.[5]

Largely on the foundations Buber has laid in his philosophy of dialogue and his philosophical anthropology has grown "dialogical psychotherapy." By dialogical psychotherapy we mean a therapy that is centered on the *meeting* between the therapist and his or her client or family as the central healing mode, whatever analysis, role playing, or other therapeutic techniques or activities may also enter in. It is more of an approach than a school of psychotherapy because it belongs to no one school and has had its representatives and pioneers in many major schools of psychotherapy, some of whom have not been influenced directly by Buber but have moved in a comparable direction.

That psychotherapist who above all others made his lifework and his lifeway that of the life of dialogue and who as a result stands as the fountainhead of "dialogical psychotherapy" is the Swiss psychiatrist Hans Trüb. What had the greatest influence on Trüb was not Buber's doctrine, but the meeting with him as person to person, and it is from this meeting that the revolutionary change in Trüb's method of psychotherapy proceeded. Trüb tells of how the closed circle of the self was again and again forced outward toward relationship through those times when, despite his will, he found himself confronting his patient not as an analyst but as human being to human being. From these experiences, he came to understand the full meaning of the analyst's responsibility. The analyst takes responsibility for lost and forgotten things, and with the aid of his psychology he helps to bring them to light. But he knows in the depths of his self that the secret meaning of these things that have been brought to consciousness first reveals itself *in the outgoing to the other.*

The psychotherapist in his work with the ill is *essentially a human being.* . . . Therefore he seeks and loves the human being in his patients and allows it . . . to come to him ever again.[6]

The personal experience that caused Trüb to move from the dialectical psychology of Jung to "healing through meeting" was, he tells us, an overwhelming sense of guilt. This guilt was no longer such as could be explained away or removed, for it was subjectively experienced as the guilt of a person who had stepped out of real relationship to the world and tried to live in a spiritual world above reality. It is just here, in the real guilt of the person who has not responded to the legitimate claim and address of the world that the possibility of transformation and healing lies. Guilt does not reside in the person, says Buber. Rather, one stands, in the most realistic sense, in the guilt that envelops one. Similarly, the repression of guilt and the neuroses which result from this repression are not merely psychological phenomena, but real events between persons.

A significant extension of the life of dialogue and of dialogical psychotherapy is the theory of "will and willfulness" developed under Buber's influence by the Sullivanian psychoanalyst Leslie H. Farber. Farber sees genuine will as an expression of real dialogue, arbitrary willfulness as a product of the absence of dialogue. The proper setting of wholeness is dialogue. When this setting eludes us, "we turn wildly to will, ready to grasp at any illusion of wholeness (however mindless or grotesque) the will conjures up for our reassurance." This is a vicious circle, for the more dependent a person becomes on the illusion of wholeness, the less she is able to experience true wholeness in dialogue. "At the point where he is no longer capable of dialogue he can be said to be *addicted* to his will." Willfulness then is nothing other than the attempt of will to make up for the absence of dialogue by handling both sides of the no longer mutual situation. No longer in encounter with another self, one fills the emptiness with one's own self, and even that self is only a partial one, its wholeness having disappeared with the disappearance of meeting. "This feverish figure, endlessly assaulting the company, seeking to wrench the moment to some pretense of dialogue, is . . . the figure of man's separated will posing as his total self."

We experience "a mounting hunger for a sovereign and irreducible will, so wedded to our reason, our emotions, our imagination, our intentions, our bodies, that only after a given enterprise has come to an end can we retrospectively infer that will was present at all." This is the will of the whole being rather than of isolated willfulness, of freedom rather than bondage, of dialogue rather than monologue. One way out of the impasses of the disordered will may be despair, Farber suggests. Despair may provide "the very conditions of seriousness and urgency which bring a man to ask those wholly authentic—we might call them tragic—questions about his own life and the meaning and measure of his particular humanness." When despair is repudiated, these questions will not be asked. The failure to confront these questions may mark the turning to the inauthentic.[7]

The next major step in the movement of dialogical psychotherapy is my own book *The Healing Dialogue in Psychotherapy*.[8] In Part I, "Dialogue in the Schools of Psychotherapy," I present roughly in chronological order therapists within a variety of different and even incompatible schools who in one way or another impinge on or illuminate healing through meeting and confirmation. I do not in any way claim that all these are "dialogical psychotherapists" (Three of them, in fact, are, namely, Hans Trüb and Leslie H. Farber, whom we have discussed above, and Ivan Boszormenyi-Nagy, whom we shall discuss below in Chapter 13.). Thus, under "Freudians" I deal with Sigmund Freud and Robert Langs, under "Jungians" Carl Jung, James Hillman, Edward Whitmont, Arie Sborowitz, and Hans Trüb, under "The Interpersonal Approach" George Herbert Mead, Alfred Adler, Harry Stack Sullivan, Erich Fromm, and Frieda romm-Reichmann, under "Humanistic Client-Centered Therapy" Carl Rogers, under "Object Relations and Self-Psychology" Melanie Klein, W. R. D. Fairbairn, Heinz Kohut, and Harry Guntrip, under "Existential Therapists" Viktor von Weizsäcker, J. L. Moreno, Rollo May, Medard Boss, and Leslie Farber, under "Gestalt Therapists" Fritz and Laura Perls and Erving and Miriam Polster, and under "Family Therapists" Lyman Wynne and Ivan Boszormenyi-Nagy.

In Part II of this book I deal with confirmation and the development of the person, disconfirmation and "mental illness," confirmation in therapy, the unconscious as the ground of the physical and the psychic, dialogue with dreams, paradoxes of guilt, the problematic of mutuality, empathy, identification, inclusion, and intuition, and the "dialogue of touchstones." A discussion of these themes appears in Chapters 12, 14, and 15 of this book.

In his book *Between Person and Person: Toward a Dialogical Psycho-*

therapy[9] Richard Hycner builds on the foundation I laid in *The Healing Dialogue in Psychotherapy* and carries it further. In contrast to my book, Hycner's thoughts are a direct outgrowth of his years of study and clinical practice as well as of his dialogue with the writings of Buber, Trüb, Farber, and myself. *Between Person and Person* deals vividly with many elements of dialogical psychotherapy, beautifully integrates them with a variety of other concepts, and applies them concretely to therapeutic practice. Taken altogether it is a compelling presentation of dialogical psychotherapy that marks this movement's coming of age— along with the Institute for Dialogical Psychotherapy, co-directed by Richard Hycner, James DeLeo, and myself, which for the past eight years has operated as an educational and for the last three years in addition as a training center in San Diego.

In my Preface to Hycner's *Between Person and Person*, I list ten elements of dialogical psychotherapy that may help the reader of this book. The first is "the between"—the recognition of an ontological dimension in the meeting between persons, or the "interhuman," that is usually overlooked because of our tendency to divide our existences into inner and outer, subjective and objective. The second is the recognition of the dialogical—"All real living is meeting"—as the essential element of human existence in which we relate to others in their uniqueness and otherness and not just as a content of our experience. From this standpoint the psychological is only the accompaniment of the dialogical and not, as so many psychologists, even humanistic ones, tend to see it, the touchstone of reality in itself. The third element is the recognition that underlying the I-Thou, as also the I-It relations, is that twofold movement of setting at a distance and entering into relationship that Buber makes the foundation of his philosophical anthropology.[10]

All of the foregoing lead to the fourth element—the recognition that the basic element of healing, when it is a question not of some repair work but restoring the atrophied personal center, is "Healing through meeting." This is so because of the fifth element—the unconscious seen, as Buber saw it, as the wholeness of the person before the differentiation and elaboration into psychic and physical, inner and outer. This applies to dreams too, which from this standpoint are never just the raw material of the unconscious but, upon being remembered, have already entered into the dialogue between therapist and client and between the client and others. The result of this approach is the possibility of having dialogues with our dreams themselves, as with any other person or thing that comes to meet us.

Guilt, correspondingly, is not seen from this standpoint as basically inner or only neurotic but as an event of the "between," something that arises from the sickness between person and person and that can be healed only through illuminating the guilt, persevering in that illumination, and repairing the injured order of existence through an active devotion to it. This implies going from the ruptured dialogue to the resumption of dialogue.

Therapy too rests upon the I-Thou relationship of openness, mutuality, presence, and directness. Yet it can never be fully mutual. There is mutual contact, mutual trust, and mutual concern with a common problem but not mutual inclusion. The therapist can and must be on the patient's side too and, in a bipolar relationship, imagine quite concretely what the patient is thinking, feeling, and willing. But the therapist cannot expect or demand that the patient practice such inclusion with him. Yet there *is* mutuality, including the therapist sharing personally with the client when that seems helpful.

Inclusion itself is the eighth element of dialogical psychotherapy. Inclusion, or "imagining the real, must be distinguished from that empathy that goes to the other side of the relationship and leaves out one's own side and that identification that remains on one's own side and cannot go over to the other. Only the two together can produce the ninth element—that confirmation from the therapist that begins to replace the disconfirmation that the patient has experienced in family and community. This confirmation comes from understanding the patient from within and by going beyond this, as Trüb suggests, to that second stage when the demand of the community is placed on the patient. This demand enables the patient to go back into dialogue with those from whom he or she has been cut off.

The tenth and last element, the "dialogue of touchstones," really includes all the others, and in particular inclusion and confirmation. Through his or her greater experience in inclusion and imagining the real, the therapist enables the patient to go beyond the terrible either/or of remaining true to one's touchstones of reality at the cost of being cut off from the community or of entering into relation with the community at the cost of denying one's touchstones. The therapist must help the patient bring his or her touchstones of reality into dialogue with other persons, beginning with the therapist himself.

Chapter 4

THE MEETING OF RELIGION AND PSYCHOLOGY: TOUCHSTONES OF REALITY AND IMAGES OF THE HUMAN

"It cannot be supported for a moment," writes Freud, that there can be some other way of regarding man aside from the scientific. The result of Freud's application of the science of psychoanalysis to the region of the mind was the unmasking of religion, conscience, and morality as mere products of the economy of the libido in the interaction of ego, superego, and id. Religion, to Freud, is an illusion, and one that has no future.

> The final judgment of science on the religious *Weltanschauung*, then, runs as follows. While the different religions wrangle with one another as to which of them is in possession of the truth, in our view the truth of religion may be altogether disregarded. . . . Its doctrines carry with them the stamp of the times in which they originated, the ignorant childhood days of the human race. Its consolations deserve no trust. Experience teaches us that the world is not a nursery.[1]

58

Even odder than that reality should correspond to our wishes, writes Freud in *The Future of an Illusion*, would be the notion that "our poor, ignorant, enslaved ancestors had succeeded in solving all these difficult riddles of the universe." In the end Freud not only allows for no *meeting* between religion and psychology but does away with any reality transcending man or beyond the reaches of exact science: "No, science is no illusion. But it would be an illusion to suppose that we could get anywhere else what it cannot give us."[2]

In the "Philosophy of Life" chapter of his *New Introductory Lectures*, Freud declares that there can be no way of regarding man other than the scientific:

> For the spirit and the mind of man is a subject of investigation in exactly the same way as any nonhuman entity. The contribution of the science of psychoanalysis consists precisely in having extended research to the region of the mind. Any other . . . view of the mind has a purely emotional basis.[3]

Freud does not deny that other views of the mind and of its relation to man might exist as an emotional need on the part of mankind, but he insists that we cannot admit them to real knowledge in any sense of the term.

> Science does well to distinguish carefully between illusion, the result of emotional demands of that kind, and knowledge. It is inadmissible to declare that science is one field of intellectual activity, and religion and philosophy another and . . . that they all have an equal claim to truth. . . . Scientific research looks on the whole field of human activity as its own and must adopt an uncompromisingly critical attitude toward any other power that seeks to usurp any part of its province.[4]

Freud sets out to show, on the one hand, that the origin of all ego-ideals is in a repression of the Oedipus complex that is at the same time its heir. On the other hand, Freud rejects as unjust the accusation that psychoanalysis ignores "the higher, moral, spiritual side of human nature." Freud asserts, on the contrary, "that the ego-ideal answers in every way to what is expected of the higher nature of man." As "a substitute for the longing for the father, it contains the germ from which

all religions have evolved" and the sense of worthlessness with which
the believer judges himself. Similarly, social feelings rest on the basis of
a common ego-ideal with the result that "the tension between the
demands of conscience and the actual attainments of the ego is experienced as a sense of guilt."5

Freud has taken seventeenth-century mechanism, eighteenth-century
rationalism, nineteenth-century economics and biology, ancient Greek
myths, an emergent philosophy of the unconscious, and a touch of
mysticism and forged them into a new and powerful image of the human
that has cast its shadow on our age as no other. It is not surprising,
therefore, that many people, like Freud, deny categorically that religion
and psychology can meet at all, especially if psychology is seen as a
hard science and religion as a set of beliefs taken on faith or as the
corollary of some church whose prescriptions must be followed in holy
obedience under threat of hell. Yet from the time of Blake, Kierkegaard,
Nietzsche, and Dostoevsky in Europe and of William James and James
Henry Leuba in America, there has been an ever-growing insight into
the relation between them. Actually, if we take psychology back to its
root—the study of the soul—the connection between religion and psychology is as old as human history itself, whether in the form of myth
and tale, aphorism and parable, or the teachings of Jesus, Socrates, the
Bhagavad Gita, and the Buddha.

This being so, it will help us to make some distinctions that are not
usually made. The progress of the soul, whether it be tracked in religion
or psychology or together in some book such as Søren Kierkegaard's
Concept of Anxiety, is more properly called "religious psychology." On
the other hand, that study that takes religion as its subject matter and
applies psychological categories to it is properly called "psychology of
religion." This is so whether those categories are themselves fairly
external to religion, as in Freud's Future of an Illusion, or are drawn
from within religion itself through sympathetic phenomenology, as in
William James' great classic Varieties of Religious Experience, or represent a mixture of sympathetic insight and external category, as in the
works of C. G. Jung and Erich Fromm.

Still a third variety of the mix of religion and psychology is that field
known as "pastoral psychology" and associated with Seward Hiltner
among others. This field has grown up in the last fifty years and is

represented by numerous schools of pastoral psychology, usually associated with a seminary, several journals of pastoral psychology, and a general awareness that ministers, priests, and rabbis are likely to be called upon for personal counseling and should have at least minimal training for so doing. Some pastors even set themselves up as professionals and charge their parishioners. More often, it is considered a service that goes with the church or synagogue, and not infrequently the church or synagogue will enlist the services of someone with training to help in such counseling. Actually the pastor has probably always performed some such functions. The difference now is that there is greater awareness of psychological problems per se and of the desirability of the pastor having some education and even professional training in psychology to aid in working with such problems.

Although this book will touch on subjects that have great relevance for religious psychology, psychology of religion, and pastoral psychology as we have defined them above, it is not centrally concerned with any of these. Rather it is concerned with the *meeting* of religion and psychology and the issues that grow out of such meeting. We are using "meeting" here almost in the way we might speak of the meeting between one person and another. Only in this case it is metaphorical. The similarity is that there must be a real meeting with otherness from both sides and a real understanding about the problems with which each side must deal. The difference is that not only are religion and psychology not persons, they are not even entities of the same order. Psychology is a field of study and, in clinical psychology, a field of practice when its theories are extended into psychotherapy of one form or another. Religion is variously understood as an institution, a social group, or a fellowship; a ritual, a set of prescribed or spontaneous actions, and a way of being together; a creed, theology, myth, or other form of doctrine, and in most cases is something of all three.

As my teacher Joachim Wach expounded religion, it always includes a doctrinal, a practical, and a social dimension. Moreover, as I myself have often pointed out, these in turn must rest on some prior encounter—what I have called in two of my books "touchstones of reality."[6] This encounter can never be grasped as an entity in itself but only in terms of its residue—in memory, in tradition, in celebrations and mournings.

Nonetheless, despite these fundamental dissimilarities, there is great significance in the meeting of psychology and religion when it is seen as a meeting on equal terms rather than as one in which one side or the other dominates and uses its counterpart simply as grist for its mill. Psychology is a body of knowledge within the structure of a science whereas religion is a body of tradition, ritual, history, and experience accessible in parts to many sciences and as a whole to none. Yet the meeting of the two can bring to light issues that cannot arise from the consideration of psychology of religion, religious psychology, or pastoral psychology taken by themselves. Indeed, the full dynamic of this meeting brings to light aspects of both subjects that might remain hidden when they are considered only by themselves. That is why I have found this topic an ever-challenging one from my teaching days in my Ph.D. program in Religion and Psychology at Temple University till the present when I have taught "The Human Dimension of Religion and Psychology" some dozen times at San Diego State University.

There is not simply one religion but a multiplicity. Nor, for that matter, is there one psychology but many. In speaking of the meeting of psychology and religion, therefore, we need to make clear *what* psychology and *what* religion we are talking about. No book could claim to cover all religions or all psychologies, much less a meeting between all of the one and all of the other. Biblical trust, Hasidic hallowing, and dialogical psychotherapy are expounded in the above chapters because they represent necessary foundations for our "dialogical approach." Yet we shall also touch upon aspects of other religions and of the various psychologies that illuminate the issues with which we shall deal without pretending that in so doing we are doing justice to all of them or ignoring the fact that every selection is necessarily idiosyncratic.

In this book we shall deal with religion not in terms of its phenomenological manifestations in creed, cult, and sect but in terms of what underlies this: the basic human attitudes that religion tends to embody, corresponding to my own definition of religion and the "religious" in *The Human Way*:

> Religion, for me, is neither an objective philosophy nor a subjective experience. It is a lived reality that is ontologically prior to its expression in creed, ritual, and group. At the same time it is inseparable from these

expressions and cannot be distilled out and objectified. The *religious* at this deepest level might be described as a basic *attitude* or relationship arising in the encounter with the whole reality directly given to one in one's existence.[7]

[Religion] expresses itself, to be sure, in doctrinal forms such as myth, creed, theology, and metaphysics, in practical forms such as liturgy, ritual, prayer, and in social forms such as fellowships, churches, sects, and denominations. For all that, we cannot reduce religion to any one of these expressions or even to all of them taken together and their interrelations. The matrix of all of these expressions is our ultimate meeting itself, and this is not in itself directly expressible. What is more, the expressions of religion inevitably come loose from their mooring, become detached and independent. When this happens, it is necessary to return to the original immediacy, to reestablish the ultimate meeting that creed, ritual, and social form no longer lead us back to.[8]

If the results of such an approach to religion cannot claim universal validity, neither is it in any way parochial, i.e., merely to be understood in terms of Judaism or Christianity or even Western religions. It is, rather, an approach that can be applied by anyone to whatever particular meeting of psychology and religion is important to him or her. Here again we may be helped by a quotation from *The Human Way*:

The great error is to see religion as proof of the existence of God or as a description of God's nature or attributes. Religion is the way that one walks. It is a commitment, a life-stance. It is one's basic response to life whether or not one affirms the existence of God. Our dialogue with religions is not a search for *the* truth, accordingly—either Plato's absolute or the one true religion or the "perennial philosophy." Each religion speaks of its uniqueness, and each says something to us about our life as humankind and as the unique persons we are. The answer to the dilemma of religious particularism versus religious universalism, consequently, is the *mutually confirming pluralism of touchstones of reality.*[9]

For the past dozen years as I have said, I have taught a course entitled "The Human Dimension of Religion and Psychology." What *is* the human dimension? Is it the image of the human, the wholeness of the person, or both? What enables religion and psychology to meet? There are two approaches to human existence and meaning that I have developed independently of each other—that of the *image of man* or, as I now call it, the *human image*, and that of *touchstones of reality*. They are not synonymous, yet both are ways of "meeting the nameless Meeter," both claim that "meaning is accessible in the lived concrete," as Martin Buber puts it. As such, both are ways of speaking of the central biblical paradox that we are created in the image of an imageless God whom we cannot define or describe, imitate, or model ourselves after yet can relate to meet, "know" in the direct, unmediated knowing of mutual contact in the events of our lives. All religion is found on the basic trust that this world is not a place in which we are hopelessly lost, that evil or illusory as the world may be, and sinful or ignorant as we are, there is a way, a path, that leads from darkness to light, from lostness to salvation, from evil to redemption.

"Touchstones of reality," as I use that phrase in my book of that title, is not a definition: It is a metaphor. I use this metaphor in conscious contrast to all those ways of thinking that try to deal with reality in objective terms: metaphysics, philosophy of religion, theology. But I also use it in contrast to the subjective approaches that explain "reality" away, whether in terms of Freudian psychology, or Sartrian existentialism of choice—the invention of values—or the linguistic analyst who says this is what you prefer or postulate and the rest is just an unwarranted inference from your emotions, or any of the other cultural relativizing or subjectivizing approaches. In contrast to both the objective and the subjective, I claim that in our lives we do have certain events that become for us touchstones of reality, and that we bring them with us into other life events so that they affect the way we enter these life events, and are themselves modified in the process. A touchstone of reality could be like Pascal's ecstatic experience when he sewed the word "fire" into his coat. But it could also be for someone else the sense of sharing in a group, like the social psychologist who told us that his touchstone of reality was taking part in a football team. While I cannot define what reality is apart from our touching, in touching we do come in contact with something really "other" than ourselves, with some otherness that has its unique impact upon us. I do not mean by touchstones of reality merely subjective experience, therefore, but what transcends our subjective experience even though we are fully part of it.

If religion derives from and rests upon our touchstones of reality, it also embodies and expresses our image of the human, our image not only of what human life is but also of what it can and ought to be. The image of the human means a meaningful personal and social direction that gives us some guidance in choosing between our potentialities and finding a way forward in the present that leads organically into the future.

What does this have to do with religious life? Just everything. Whatever may be the case with "religion," the religious person has always been aware of the central importance of the image of the human. This is because the religious life is not in the first instance philosophy or gnosis—an attempt to know *about* the world or God—but a way that we walk *with* God, a flowing with the Tao, a discovery of "the action that is in inaction, the inaction that is in action" (the central statement of the *Bhagavad Gita*). For the religious person, it is not enough to have a "philosophy of life": One must live one's philosophy. Rabbi Leib, son of Sara, went to the great Hasidic leader the Maggid of Mezritch not to hear him say Torah but to watch him lace and unlace his felt boots. "Not to say Torah but to be Torah"—this is the existential demand that all religion ultimately places on us.

Philosophies of religion are ultimately meaningless abstractions if one divorces them from the living Buddha, Lao-tzu, Confucius, Jesus, Mohammed, Moses, St. Francis, or the Baal-Shem-Tov. When Swami Prabhavananda and Christopher Isherwood claim in their introduction to the *Bhagavad Gita* that it does not matter whether Christ or Krishna really lived since we have their teachings and they are universal, they miss the central reality from which all religious teachings spring and to which they again and again point back: the image of the human.

The human dimension of religion and psychology is *both* the image of the human and personal wholeness. The two are mutually entailed if we understand the image of the human aright—not as some universal model or ideal that we all can or ought to adopt but as a highly personal unique life-stance that every one of us chooses again and again as *our* personal way of being human. It is the expression of what we are in our uniqueness *and* in our humanity. The universality that is talked of here is one that exists only in and through the concrete, the particular, the unique.

I cannot here reproduce all the nuances of the image of the human that I depict in the first chapter of my book *To Deny Our Nothingness*, but I can give some hint of why the image of the human means both the universally human and the unique at once:

> The pole of the unique and the pole of the human stand in fruitful tension with each other: in each situation I must be concerned with what is authentic *human* existence and what is authentic existence for me in particular. These two can never be divided from each other, nor can they be identified. What we mean by . . . "human" is at once something we take for granted and something we do not know and must constantly discover and rediscover. That we are all "human" is the commonest presupposition of social intercourse. What the human is, can be, and ought to become is continually changing, however, not only with each new culture and period of history, but also with each new individual. It is precisely in one's uniqueness, and not in what one has in common with others, that each person realizes what the *human* can become in one. . . . The image of the human is an embodiment of an attitude and a response. Whether it is an image shared by only one person or by a society as a whole, the individual stands in a unique personal relation to it. One's image of the human is not some objective, universal Saint Francis, but the Saint Francis who emerges from one's own meeting with this historical and legendary figure.[10]

Our image of the human and our personal wholeness go together not only because each person's image of the human is unique but also because our wholeness as persons is inseparable from the unique direction that we take, the attitude and life-stance that we bring to our response to the demand placed on us by the persons and world with which we stand in dialogue. Thus our individuation and our integration cannot be an end in itself, divorced from the unique direction that our image of the human and our touchstones of reality embody. These images and touchstones are our way of going out to meet what comes to meet us. We cannot use everything else merely as a means to the end of our personal integration, as sometimes seems to be the goal of Jungian therapy, or "follow our bliss" without concern for the partnership of existence.

Personal wholeness is not the ultimate goal or end of our existence but a stage from which we go out to the meeting. But it *is* important as a stage. What is more, it is a stage that is not easily reached. Our passion needs direction, our excitement needs containment; our moments of ecstasy must alternate with moments of simple calm. The right rhythm of alternation between one and the other differs from person to person and situation to situation. "It is impossible to tell persons what way they should take," said the Seer of Lublin. "For one way to serve God is through teaching, another through prayer, another fasting, and still another through eating." Yet there is a way the individual person can discover one's unique path. That is by listening to the call of one's own heart: "Everyone should carefully observe what way one's heart draws one to, and then choose this way with all one's strength."

Unfortunately, many substitute social awareness for the awareness of their centralmost wish—that calling and drawing of the heart that, if anything, gives us our profoundest glimpse into the meaning of the "I." But even where one does not turn away to the oldest tradition or the latest fad for guidance, the heart itself often seems to offer promptings that are confused and contradictory. The subjective world to which we refer ourselves is not seldom as perplexing and misleading as the objective. One answer to this perplexity is implicit in the Seer's statement, namely, the distinction between the many impulses that throng and crowd one another, each calling for attention and gratification, and the powerful innermost wish that calls the heart itself.

What we mean by the *heart* is the wholeness of the person, and here too one can be mistaken. Human history is littered with sad exemplars of mistaking intensity, logic, emotion, or inspiration for human wholeness. One of the reasons such a mistake is made is that we tend to trust one of our faculties more than another and wish to identify the *I* with that faculty preeminently. For many persons, this expresses itself as a trust in reason as objective and a mistrust of emotions or feelings as subjective. In our day, on the other hand, some correctives to this tendency have swung us so far in the other direction that intuitions and feelings are given our sole confidence, and reason and logic are depreciated and looked down upon.

It takes a great deal of listening to allow what happens to come forth spontaneously—not inhibited by an image of oneself that tells one in advance what one's strengths and weaknesses are supposed to be, but

also not inhibited by the group pressure to express the emotions approved of, expected, and even demanded by the group. We would like to
live more intensely, more vitally, more fully. We would like to share love
and joy. But the more we aim at this goal, the more one part of us will be
looking on from the sidelines, anticipating and measuring results, and
for that very reason not living fully in the present, not being whole. One
of the forms of lack of personal wholeness is that endless self-
preoccupation that splits us into two parts, one of which is the observer
and the other the actor who is being observed. This bifurcation of
consciousness prevents us from having any sort of spontaneous response, from ever really going outside of ourselves.

Our problem is that we are divided within ourselves, that we are not in
genuine dialogue with one another, and that we live immersed in a deep
existential mistrust. These sicknesses of our human condition cannot be
overcome simply by the will to wholeness, openness, and trust or by the
magic of technique.

True self-awareness does not turn us into objects through reflection
and analysis. Rather, it is an intuitive awareness of ourselves that grows
in listening and responding if we use ourselves as a radar screen: hearing
not just how the other responds but also how we ourselves respond to the
other. "Our wholeness is most there when we have forgotten ourselves,
responding fully to what is not ourselves," I wrote in *Touchstones of
Reality*:

> Any genuine wholehearted response—"When the music is heard so
> deeply that you are the music while the music lasts"—can bring us to this
> immediacy. Our self-consciousness returns when we go back, as we must,
> from immediacy to mediacy. Yet even it need not get in the way as much
> as we usually suppose. The fact that we are reflective can be handled
> lightly instead of heavily, especially if we do not make the mistake of
> identifying our "I" with that reflective consciousness and regarding the
> rest as just the objects that the "I" looks at.[11]

What are some of the issues that arise through the meeting between
psychology and religion? One is the limits of the psyche as touchstone of
reality. Another the question as to what extent religious experience can
be explained by psychological categories. Or, to turn the tables, is
psychology for many just a modern-day substitute for religion? Are

religious motives one thing and psychological ones another? What is the difference and the relation between neurotic guilt and existential guilt?

These are some of the general questions that arise. There are also a set of questions that have to do with the implication for psychotherapy of the meeting between psychology and religion: What are the limits of the responsibility of the helper? To what extent is the therapist cause and the patient effect? To what extent is it a matter of what Buber calls the "between"? What is the difference and the relation between the professional accountability and the personal responsibility of the therapist? Is the therapist responsible only for the "presenting problem" of the patient or for all the client's problems when the client is not aware of them?

We deal with these issues in Parts III and IV of this book. Before we do this, however, we shall look in Part II at some of the attempts in our time to approach our topic through one or another psychology of religion.

Part Two

A CRITIQUE OF SOME PSYCHOLOGIES OF RELIGION

Chapter 5

RELIGION AS ARCHETYPES: C. G. JUNG'S ANALYTICAL PSYCHOLOGY

CARL JUNG IS OF PARTICULAR INTEREST for the meeting of religion and psychology since he is at one and the same time one of the foremost modern psychologists and what I call in my book *To Deny Our Nothingness* a "Modern Gnostic."

The Gnostic was a member of an ancient sect that believed in salvation through an esoteric knowledge or revelatory vision open only to the few who knew they did not feel at home in an evil creation. Hans Jonas singles our radical dualism as the cardinal feature of Gnostic thought. This dualism expresses itself in every sphere—God and the world, spirit and matter, soul and body, light and darkness, good and evil, life and death. Its root is the belief that God is so transcendent that he has nothing to do with the world, and that it is an evil creator god, or demiurgos, who has created and rules over the cosmos. Correspondingly, the divine aspect of man—the pneuma, or spirit—has nothing to do with the body and the soul or with the world. But man does not know that this essential aspect of himself is alien to the world, and therefore he must have knowledge of God (gnosis) before he can be transformed and thereby saved.

Gnosticism recurs in the history of the world's religions as a recognizable type with infinite variations. It has an equally deep and perennial hold on mythology and has again and again entered into the mainstream of intellectual history and even philosophy. In contemporary culture, too, it has often recurred, even if frequently in a mixed form.

Within the category of the Modern Gnostic, we must distinguish between those who directly follow the ancient Gnostics' emphasis on the transcendent God unconnected with the world and hidden from man, and those who replace this transcendent God with an emphasis on the divinity found within the self. This second type is not found as such in ancient Gnosticism, but two of its most important elements are. One of these is the focus on the knowledge of the divinity of the inner self. Another is antinomianism (rejection of any law). The Gnostic hostility toward the world led to two seemingly opposed forms of Gnostic morality: the ascetic and the libertine. Actually, both are consistent in that both hold the world to be either a negative obstacle to salvation or something that must be used as a mere means to the end of salvation. In practice, it was often the majority of the adherents who were ascetics while an élite of *pneumatics*, or "the perfect," took part in evil and deliberately inverted the old morality. The basis for this antinomianism was the belief that they were essentially holy regardless of their actions and that whatever contact they had with the world and with sin was necessarily a redeeming one.

The Modern Gnostic is neither libertine nor consciously antinomian, for he no longer thinks of "evil" as really evil. In his view the old moral conceptions of good and evil are relativized in favor of a new conception of good as the integration, or individuation, of the person and real evil as anything that stands in the way.

The chief representative of this type of Modern Gnostic is the Swiss psychiatrist Carl Jung. Jung is, of course, the founder of one of the most important schools of psychoanalysis, and he cannot be properly understood outside of the context of the development of psychoanalysis in our century. Yet he was also explicitly concerned with Gnosticism from his early youth, and he consciously endeavored in his psychology to create a Modern Gnostic mythology that would recapture the psychic wisdom of the ancient Gnostics. This mythology includes a terminology essentially original to Jung: the "anima" and the "animus" as feminine and masculine parts of the soul, the "shadow" as the suppressed, irrational, and therefore negative part of the soul, the distinction between the personal unconscious and the collective unconscious, which latter contains the great psychological archetypes that Jung sees as universals, and the process of individuation as the shaping of an autonomous center in the unconscious through which the numinous contents of the collective unconscious can be integrated into a personal, if still largely unconscious, wholeness. Even this terminology, especially the anima, Jung freely admits to be Gnostic, though he claims that it is empirically supported by his experiences. But above and beyond this, in volume after volume, he richly documents his view of the individuation of the Self from Gnostic sources and from medieval alchemy, which he sees as a link between the Gnostics and modern psychology. It would be a mistake to look on Jung as metaphysician or theologian, as he himself never tires of telling us. He does not "believe" in these Gnostic myths, as did the Gnostics themselves, but accepts them as symbols of unconscious psychic processes. On the other hand, it would be equally erroneous to accept Jung's view that he is simply being empirical since, *Modern* Gnostic that he is, he turns to the unconscious with the same expectation of saving knowledge as the ancient Gnostic turned to the demiurge and the hidden God.

The naiveté of Jung's distinction between the "metaphysical" and the "empirical" is made possible by a simplicistic theory of knowledge that elevates the psyche from an indispensable corollary of knowledge to being both the creator of what is known and itself the highest reality. Man "himself is the second creator of the world, who alone has given to the world its objective existence." The understanding of "the empirical nature of the psyche" is "a matter of the highest importance and the very foundation of . . . reality" to the man of the twentieth century, writes Jung, "because he has recognized once and for all that without an observer there is no world and consequently no truth, for there would be nobody to register it." Jung complains that people criticize him as a Gnostic and ignore the facts from which he proceeds—facts which are of prime importance to him and which others are at liberty to verify. What he does not recognize is that the "facts" that he cites illustrate abundance (of square or circular mandalas, for example) but not universality, resemblance but not necessarily affinity, coincidence but not necessarily meaning. Moreover, the overwhelming mass of "facts" that he brings from ancient scripts, so far from leading to a cautious, empirical temper, avalanche into highly speculative conclusions, which, if they are not precisely "metaphysical" postulates, are also anything but the "auxiliary concepts, hypotheses, and models" that he claims they are. They are, rather, the Modern Gnostic mythology that he himself explicitly aims at creating, but that he also forgets at the time when he wishes to fall back on the security of being "a doctor and scientist."[1] This syncretism of science and mythology is itself a typically modern response to the problem of a contemporary image of man. Jung tries to deduce secondary meaning from the quasi-universality of enormous numbers of myths and symbols taken in and out of context.

Jung may be characterized as a Modern Gnostic—*Gnostic* in his concern for saving knowledge, in his attitude toward the unification of good and evil, in his pointing toward an élite of those who have attained individuation and got beyond the relativity of good and evil; *Modern* in the fact that none of the Gnostic symbols Jung uses have the transcendent value that they originally had, but all stand for transformations and processes within the psyche, shading as that does, for Jung, into a vast, collective, and essentially autonomous area that is reached through, but is not dependent on, the individual conscious ego. These two senses of Modern and Gnostic are put together for us by Jung himself in "The Spiritual Problem of Modern Man." He characterizes the widespread interest in all sorts of psychic phenomena in the modern world as comparable to and having a deep affinity with Gnosticism. He recognizes, quite rightly, that even Theosophy and Anthroposophy "are pure Gnosticism in a Hindu dress." But the significance of this spiritual interest Jung sees as lying exclusively within the psyche and in psychic energy. If the Christian symbol is Gnosis and the compensation of the unconscious still more so, Gnosis itself is rooted in the psyche, and it is psychic experience that is expressed in Jung's Gnostic myth. This concern with having psychic experience Jung labels "Gnostic."

Modern man, in contrast to his nineteenth-century brother, turns his attention to the psyche with very great expectations; and . . . he does so without reference to any traditional creed, but rather in the Gnostic sense of religious experience. . . . The modern man abhors dogmatic postulates taken on faith and the religions based upon them. He holds them valid only insofar as their knowledge-content seems to accord with his own experience of the deeps of psychic life.[2]

Jung's equation of gnosis with psychic experience is typical of modern man. But in contrast to other modern advocates of "experience," Jung does not value all experiences, but only those found within, and particularly within the unconscious. Like the ancient Gnostic, he sees the outer world as evil, and even the inner world that is accessible to man becomes good only when it comes into touch with that hidden divinity within the soul—the unconscious. The spiritual change that has come over modern man has put such an ugly face on the world "that no one can love it any longer—we cannot even love ourselves—and in the end there is nothing in the outer world to draw us away from the reality of the life within."[3] But this "life within" is not simply *experienced*, as Jung suggests: it is *known*, and that precisely in the Gnostic sense. Jung's equation of ancient Gnosticism with modern psychic experience makes sense, for what he is really talking about is the gnosis that he brings to this experience. This gnosis, so far from leading Jung to abandon himself to the uniqueness and concrete immediacy of any given experience, leads him to seek for the "universal meaning" in it, that is, the meaning that fits his own theories.

Jung looks upon his psychology as satisfying "the need for mythic statements" by a world view "which fits man meaningfully into the scheme of creation, and at the same time confers meaning upon it." Like other contemporary interpreters of myth, he fails to recognize the difference between the dramatic immediacy of myth and the reflective mediacy of *Weltanschauung*. On the contrary, he clearly sees his own "myth" as a saving gnosis for contemporary man that would take the place of the no longer efficacious myth of Christianity. It is "the myth of the necessary incarnation of God"—"man's creative confrontation with the opposites and their synthesis in the self, the wholeness of his personality." "That is the goal," the "explanatory myth which has slowly taken shape within me in the course of the decades."

Jung's autobiography *Memories, Dreams, Reflections* abounds with

Modern Gnostic motifs: Jung's early certainty that his first task was not to establish a relationship *with* God, but to know more *about* him; the view of God as wishing "to evoke not only man's bright and positive side but also his darkness and ungodliness"; the "cure" of a neurosis in one week through Jung's dream that his patient was meant to be a saint; sexuality as the expression of the chthonic, or earth, spirit, that Jung equates with "the 'other face of God,' the dark side of the God-image"; the confession that between 1918 and 1926 he "had seriously studied the Gnostic writers, for they too had been confronted with the primal world of the unconscious and had dealt with its contents, with images that were obviously contaminated with the world of instinct"; the testimony that it was the "comparison with alchemy, and the uninterrupted intellectual chain back to Gnosticism," that gave substance to his psychology; the emphasis on liberation not through imagelessness and emptiness, like the Hindus, but through active participation in every part of the psyche; the relativization of good and evil that converts both into "halves of a paradoxical whole"; the equation of "the wholeness of the self" brought about in the depths of the unconscious with "the divinity incarnate in man"; the equation of God with "a *complexio oppositorum*" for which "truth and delusion, good and evil, are equally possible." These motifs are capped by two quintessentially Gnostic statements. The first deals with the radical dualism between good and evil, dark and light: "The sole purpose of human existence is to kindle a light in the darkness of mere being"—through making the unconscious conscious. In the second, Jung puts forward gnosis as the saving goal of his personal existence:

> My life has been permeated and held together by one idea and one goal: namely, *to penetrate into the secret of the personality*. Everything can be explained from this central point, and all my works relate to this one theme.[4]

Jung's Gnostic myth is given significant, further extension in such works as *Psychology and Alchemy* and *Aion: Researches into the Phenomenology of the Self*. The concern of the psychotherapist, he tells us in the former work, is not what the patient does but how he does it, and this makes good and evil "ultimately nothing but ideal extensions and abstractions of doing," which "both belong to the chiaroscuro of life." Jung sees Christ as not only not *condemning* the sinner, but *espousing* him. The medieval alchemists preferred "to seek through knowledge rather than to find through faith," and in this "they were in much the same position as modern man, who prefers immediate personal experience to belief in traditional ideas." If Jung here again equates knowledge with personal experience, he is still more modern in asserting that "the central ideas of Christianity are rooted in Gnostic philosophy, which, in accordance with psychological laws, simply *had* to grow up at a time when the classical religions had become obsolete."[5] Jesus becomes the great prototype of the Modern Gnostic—the hero of a new "perennial philosophy":

> There have always been people who, not satisfied with the dominants of conscious life, set forth . . . to seek direct experience of the eternal roots, and, following the lure of the restless unconscious psyche, find themselves in the wilderness where, like Jesus, they come up against the son of darkness, an *antimimon pneuma*.[6]

In *Aion*, Jung asserts that the totality of the self is indistinguishable from the God image, while identifying the devil that the modern Jesus encounters with "the post-Christian spirit" of today. The end result of Christian consciousness through the centuries, writes Jung, "is a true *antimimon pneuma*, a false spirit of arrogance, hysteria, woolly-mindedness, criminal amorality, and doctrinaire fanaticism, a purveyor of shoddy spiritual goods, spurious art, philosophical stutterings and Utopian humbug, fit only to be fed wholesale to the mass man of today."[7] What splits the world into irreconcilable halves today is modern man's lack of personal wholeness, and this Jung sees as remediable only through taking Christ as a symbol of the self. At the same time, Jung substitutes for Christ's teaching of *perfection* the archetypal teaching of *completeness*, which he identifies with Paul's confession, "I find then a law, that, when I would do good, evil is present with me." What Paul lamented, Jung affirms—namely, the experience of evil within oneself:

> Only the "complete" person knows how unbearable man is to himself. So far as I can see, no relevant objection could be raised from the Christian point of view against anyone accepting the task of individuation

imposed on us by nature, and the recognition of our wholeness or completeness, as a binding personal commitment.[8]

Gnostic salvation of the soul in relation to the transcendent God is now equated with bringing the warring opposites of the conscious and unconscious into "a healthier and quieter state (salvation)." Though the history of the Gnostic symbol of the *anima mundi* or Original Man "shows that it was always used as a God image," we may assume, says Jung, "that some kind of psychic wholeness is meant (for instance, conscious + unconscious)." "I have not done violence to anything," Jung finds it necessary to explain. Psychology establishes "that the symbolism of psychic wholeness coincide with the God image." The Gnostics possessed the idea of an unconscious—the same knowledge as Jung's, "formulated differently to suit the age they lived in." To say that "each new image is simply another aspect of the divine mystery immanent in all creatures" is, to Jung, absolutely synonymous with saying that "all these images are found, empirically, to be expressions for the unified wholeness of man." What clinches this equation for Jung is his experience that the mandala structures that he finds in Gnosticism as elsewhere have in the dreams of his patients "the meaning and function of a centre of the unconscious personality."[9] No ancient Gnostic could have had such a one-dimensional psychological view of religious symbols! But Jung, in all innocence, converts gnosis into his psychology, even as he converts his psychology into gnosis:

> Gnosis is undoubtedly a psychological knowledge whose contents derive from the unconscious. It reached its insights by concentrating on the "subjective factor," which consists empirically in the demonstrable influence that the collective unconscious exerts on the conscious mind. This would explain the astonishing parallelism between Gnostic symbolism and the findings of the psychology of the unconscious.[10]

Instead of seeing the Gnostics as they for the most part were— enormously abstruse system-builders and mythicizers—Jung turns them into modern thinkers, "theologians who, unlike the more orthodox ones, allowed themselves to be influenced in large measure by natural inner experience." The Gnostic dissolution of Christ's personality into symbols for the Kingdom of God is praised by Jung as representing "an assimilation and integration of Christ into the human psyche," through which human personality grows and consciousness develops. These achievements Jung sees as "gravely threatened in our anti-Christian age" (no longer, it seems, merely post-Christian!) "not only by the sociopolitical delusional systems" ("the murderous upsurge of bolshevistic ideas," as Jung puts it in another place) "but above all by the rationalistic hubris which is tearing our consciousness from its transcendent roots and holding before it immanent goals."[11] Thus, Jung sees Gnosticism as both the antidote for and the natural expression of modern man.

Jung is not entirely unaware, however, that even as far as the content of the symbols is concerned he is a *Modern* Gnostic and not just a Gnostic. He consciously modifies the Gnostic systems, even as he modifies the Christian Trinity, to include a "Shadow Quaternio," an image of the hidden, dark, unconscious, irrational, evil side of man. This transition from the Anthropos, the divine image of man, to the Shadow was already prefigured, Jung claims, in the "historical development which led, in the eleventh century, to a widespread recognition of the evil principle as the world creator"—a typical expression of radical Gnostic dualism. But the need to balance the upward orientation of the psyche "by an equally strong consciousness of the lower man" is seen by Jung as "a specifically modern state of affairs and, in the context of Gnostic thinking, an obnoxious anachronism that puts man in the centre of the field of consciousness where he had never consciously stood before." Even this awareness of the difference between the ancient and the Modern Gnostic Jung quickly loses when he claims that "by making the person of Christ the object of his devotions he [man] gradually came to acquire Christ's position as mediator."[12]

In his discussion of "The Development of Personality," Jung sets the true person, who has attained individuation, in contrast to convention, conformity, and the collective. Although he sees convention as a necessary stopgap, he leaves no question in our minds that the great person, the image of man for all men, is the one who defies convention for the sake of his own inner vocation and his own inner destiny. Of these great persons, Jung cannot speak highly enough. They are the heroes, leaders, saviors who discover "a new way to greater certainty"; they are the ones who achieve the "perfect realization of the meaning of existence innate in all things."

> These personalities are as a rule the legendary heroes of mankind, the very ones who are looked up to, loved, and worshipped, the true sons of God whose names perish not. They are the flower and the fruit, the ever fertile seeds of the tree of humanity. . . . They towered up like mountain peaks above the mass that still clung to its collective fears, its beliefs, laws, and systems, and boldly chose their own way.[13]

Here we have reached the very heart of Jung's image of the human. To assess it as a direction for contemporary man we must ask what specific indications he offers as to what this "wholeness of the self" concretely means and implies. To be a person is to have a vocation, he writes, and "the original meaning of 'to have a vocation' is 'to be addressed by a voice.' " "The clearest examples of this," he adds, "are to be found in the avowals of the Old Testament prophets." But the "still small voice" or roaring lion that the prophets heard was always taken by them as an Other, as the address of God that came to them in the events and situations of their lives. Jung's conception of voice and vocation is quite different. He sees the true personality as trusting in his voice "as in God," but the voice comes not from God but from himself, his own inner destiny: "He *must* obey his own laws, as if it were a daimon whispering to him of new and wonderful paths. Anyone with a vocation hears the voice of the inner man: he is *called*." This does not mean, of course, that he consciously addresses himself. Rather, just as Jung saw himself as split into two personalities, so he sees man in general as split into a conscious ego and an unconscious ground which is the potential arena of the true Self. He leaves us no doubt as to which of these two is the dominant reality: "Only the tiniest fraction of the psyche is identical with the conscious mind and its box of magic tricks, while for much the greater part it is sheer unconscious *fact*, hard and immitigable as granite, immovable, inaccessible, yet ready at any time to come crashing down upon us at the behest of unseen powers."[14] He also leaves us in no doubt as to which of these is the source of value: It is the unconscious that calls and guides, the conscious which listens and obeys, or, if it fails to obey, pays the price of neuroticism:

The neurosis is thus a defense against the objective, inner activity of the psyche, or an attempt, somewhat dearly paid for, to escape from the inner voice and hence from the vocation. For this "growth" is the objective activity of the psyche, which, *independently of conscious volition*, is trying to speak to the conscious mind through the inner voice and lead him towards wholeness. Behind the neurotic perversion is concealed his vocation, his destiny: the growth of personality, the full realization of the life-will that is born with the individual.[15]

In this statement, we have the curious doctrine of a "life-will" which is realized "independently of conscious volition," which means independently of the will. For this to make any sense at all, Jung must be positing another "will" in the depths of the unconscious psyche, and in effect this is just what he does. In *Memories, Dreams, Reflections*, he attributes the fact that he could not be really interested in other people to his *daimon*, his guiding genius, while speaking of himself as the helpless victim. However much Jung may set the impersonal, collective unconscious in contrast to the modern collective as that which is realized only by the liberated, individuated person, it is curiously like totalitarianism in its reference of reality and value to a universal that allows room for individuality but not for true uniqueness:

The psychic substratum upon which the individual consciousness is based is universally the same, otherwise people could never reach a common understanding. So in this sense, personality and its peculiar psychic makeup are not something absolutely unique. The uniqueness holds only for the individual nature of the personality.[16]

"The inner voice is the voice of a fuller life, of a wider, more comprehensive consciousness," wrote Jung. Only through responding to this law of one's being and rising to personality does one attain to one's life's meaning. But if one only becomes a personality through consciously assenting to the power of the inner voice, this assent still means the sacrifice of oneself to one's vocation. "That," says Jung, "is the great and liberating thing about any genuine personality."[17] This means again that one must choose between one's conscious will and one's unconscious will, and the latter, the voice of the unconscious, Jung freely identifies with "the will of God." He sees this obedience as a necessity, rather than as the free response or failure to respond of the Bible, and he sees the group as bound to another type of iron necessity, the laws of nature.

How can psychic experience take the place of the traditional God as a voice, an address, a guidance when God is consistently identified by Jung with individuated man, and the new mystery that he proclaims is the mystery of God become man?

A modern mandala is an involuntary confession of a peculiar mental condition. There is no deity in the mandala, nor is there any submission or reconciliation to a deity. *The place of the deity seems to be taken by the wholeness of man.*

If we want to know what happens when the idea of God is no longer projected as an autonomous entity, this is the answer of the unconscious psyche. *The unconscious produces the idea of a deified or divine man.*

The goal of psychological, as of biological, development is self-realization, or individuation. But since man knows himself only as an ego, and the self, as a totality, is indescribable and indistinguishable from a God-image, self-realization—to put it in religious or metaphysical terms—*amounts to God's incarnation.*[18]

The remarkable thing about these statements is that Jung sees no essential difference between modern man's relation to the inner self and ancient man's relation to the divine Other. Jung ascribes certain qualities of otherness to the archetypal unconscious, to be sure, in particular that sense of numinous awe of which Rudolph Otto has spoken. But he has robbed his commanding voice of its essential otherness by identifying it with one's own destiny, one's law, one's daimon, one's creativity, one's true self, one's life will. "Self-realization" is not the terminus for the contemporary image of man; it is at best the starting point. The word in itself carries no meaning, for we do not know what our true self is; we do not know the direction in which we must authenticate our existence in order to "realize" our selves. This is all the more the case when "self" is identified not with the whole body-soul person in his active relations with the world and other persons but with the "inner man," the self within, the unconscious center of "personal wholeness." The indications that Jung gives all seem to imply that the task of authenticating one's concrete existence in the world is merely secondary and instrumental to realizing an inner wholeness in which both good and evil, authentic and inauthentic are relativized. "The vast majority needs authority, guidance, law," says Jung. But the pneumatic, or perfect man, the Gnostic élite, is able to put aside the law in favor of his own inner wholeness, his "soul":

> Mankind is, in essentials, psychologically still in a state of childhood—a stage that cannot be skipped. . . . The Pauline overcoming of the law falls only to the man who knows how to put his soul in the place of conscience. Very few are capable of this ("Many are called, but few are chosen"). And these few tread this path only from inner necessity, not to say suffering, for it is sharp as the edge of a razor. [19]

Whatever else "conscience" is, it has always been held to be the voice that prompted one to distinguish intrinsic right from wrong in concrete situations. Now this voice is put aside, along with the elemental seriousness of those situations and of one's desire to respond to them in the right way. In their place is the "inner necessity," which need not take either conscience or the situation seriously since both belong to the relatively less real and less valuable world of one's relations to others. Yet man's existence is, in important part, made up of these very relations. To make them extrinsic and instrumental inevitably means to destroy man's personal wholeness by dividing him into an essential inner self and an inessential social self. Submission *to* and deliverance *from* convention are an either/or for Jung that admits of no third alternative. One who at the same time tries to follow one's own way and adjust to the group inevitably becomes neurotic. The "wholeness of self" that the individuated man attains is the integration of the inner self, a wholeness that reduces the person in his relation to other persons to a mere *persona*, a mask, or social role, with at best only secondary significance. Thus, in his teaching as in his life, Jung is not really able to unite "inner" and "outer" and overcome the conflict between them. Instead, he demands a fundamental choice between them that makes the "outer" the instrument and material for the "inner."

Much of Jung's Modern Gnosticism is presented in scholarly guise. His *Answer to Job*, in contrast, is an explicitly personal statement. Like many ancient Gnostics, he begins by distorting the imageless God of the

Old Testament into the evil creator god. Only a Modern Gnostic, however, could hold this god to be a projection of the collective unconscious of mankind, as Jung does, and yet rant at it in a highly personal manner. Indeed, the resentment that Jung gives vent to in his diatribe against God might lead one to think that he projects his own father into the empty skies, à la Freud.

God, to Jung, is not conscious, and is therefore not man. Yet he is seen by Jung as conscious enough to be aware that he is inferior to man and at the same time human enough to be personally jealous! Like the evil, Gnostic creator god, the God of the Book of Job is only to be feared, and not to be loved or trusted. The two central motifs of the Bible and of the Book of Job—the wholehearted love of God and the unconditional trust in the relationship with God—are entirely absent in Jung's treatment of Job. In their place is a caricature of a wrathful, malicious deity that seems almost willfully projected into the text:

> One can submit to such a God only with fear and trembling, and can try indirectly to propitiate the despot with unctuous praises and ostentatious obedience. But a relationship of trust seems completely out of the question to our modern way of thinking. Nor can moral satisfaction be expected from *an unconscious nature* god of this kind. . . . Yahweh's allocutions have the unthinking yet nonetheless transparent purpose of showing Job *the brutal power of the demiurge.*[20]

Jung's Job, in short, "is set up as a judge over God himself." The central meaning of the whole book, which upholds Job's trust and his contending, but censures his gnosis—the desire of the creature to comprehend within his limited reason the creation that transcends him—is lost.[21] Jung's contending knows no trust and his gnosis no limits.

The very meaning of religion is changed by Jung from the direct dialogue between Job and God, which refuses to leave the ground of the immediate and the concrete, to a universal myth which has no concern for the unique and none for Job himself.

> Religion means, if anything at all, precisely that function which links us back to the eternal myth. . . . I would even go so far as to say that the

mythical character of a life is just what expresses its universal human validity.[22]

This turning away from the existential immediacy of lived life to "universal human validity" has the inevitable effect of depersonalizing man, of removing that freedom and that stamp of personal wholeness that make him a person. The very next sentence after the passage quoted above affirms: "It is perfectly possible psychologically for the unconscious or an archetype to take complete possession of a man and to determine his fate down to the smallest detail." Not only does Jung see God as acting out of the unconscious of man, but as *forcing* him "to harmonize and unite the opposite influences to which his mind is exposed from the unconscious."[23]

> Whatever man's wholeness, or the self, may mean *per se*, empirically it is an image of the goal of life spontaneously produced by the unconscious, *irrespective of the wishes and fears of the conscious mind*. It stands for the goal of the total man, for the realization of his wholeness and individuality *with or without the consent of his will*.[24]

How there can be any personal wholeness, individuality, or spontaneity in the face of a conscious self taken over and compelled by the unconscious is incomprehensible to me. Only an attitude such as this could lead Jung to ignore Job's deeply personal plea, "Thou shalt seek me and I will not be," in favor of the "answer to Job" that he finds in the historical development of the collective unconscious. "Job," I have said in *Problematic Rebel*, "is the true existentialist." Jung is anything but!

God for Jung is the "loving Father" who is unmasked as dangerous, unpredictable, unreliable, unjust, and cruel, in short, "an insufferable incongruity which modern man can no longer swallow." Here, as in the modern mandalas, the place of God is gradually taken by deified man. Consciousness separates man from his instincts and makes him prone to error, but man's instincts themselves "give him an inkling of the hidden wisdom of God." Jung exalts the instincts themselves; this exaltation means "the inclusion of evil." The more consciousness lays claim to moral authority, says Jung, "the more the self will appear as something dark and menacing."[25] One would think from this that the "evil" of the shadow lay only in the fact that it was suppressed, that the unconscious was not given its full due in the *complexio oppositorum* of the self. But, in fact, Jung again and again refers *all* moral valuation to the unconscious and leaves the conscious only the task of obeying.

The essential content of the unconscious, writes Jung, is "the idea of the *higher man* by whom Yahweh was morally defeated and who he was later to become." Man not only judges God, in Jung's reading; he ultimately replaces him. The apocalyptic writers such as Ezekiel foresee "what is going to happen, through the transformation and humanization of God, not only to God's son as foreseen from all eternity, but to man as such." The incarnation of God in Christ is not enough; for Christ is perfect man, but not complete, i.e., sinful man. The new incarnation will be that of God in sinful man. *"God will be begotten in creaturely man."* This, Jung quite rightly remarks, "implies a tremendous change in man's status, for he is now raised to sonship and almost to the position of a man-god." The deification of man as "man-god" that Dostoevsky foresaw as the abysmal consequence of "the death of God" is now openly hailed by Jung. *"God wanted to become man and still wants to."* [26]

> From the promise of the Paraclete we may conclude that God wants to become *wholly* man; in other words, to reproduce himself in his own dark creature (man not redeemed from original sin).
>
> God . . . wants to become man, and for that purpose he has chosen, through the Holy Ghost, the creaturely man filled with darkness—the natural man who is tainted with original sin and who learnt the divine arts and sciences from the fallen angels. The guilty man is eminently suitable and is therefore chosen to become the vessel for the continuing incarnation, not the guiltless one who holds aloof from the world and refuses to pay his tribute to life, for in him the dark God would find no room. [27]

The uniting of God's antinomy must take place in man, says Jung, and "this involves man in a new responsibility." Man "has been granted an almost godlike power": He must know God's nature "if he is to understand himself and thereby achieve gnosis of the Divine." [28]

Never has Jung's radical antinomian Gnosticism received clearer expression. Never has he stated so openly his goal of substituting for the Christian God-man the Modern Gnostic man-god who will achieve gnosis of the Divine through understanding himself. This does not mean a deification of the conscious ego. Jung warns again and again against the danger of the "inflation" to which the ordinary mortal, not freed from original sin, would instantly succumb if he saw himself as Christ, or as a complete God-man.

> Even the enlightened person remains what he is, and is never more than his own limited ego before the One who dwells within him, whose form has no knowable boundaries, who encompasses him on all sides, fathomless as the abysms of the earth and vast as the sky.[29]

In other words, there is for Jung a transcendence within in relation to which the conscious "I" knows its limits and its limitedness. This is of great significance for avoiding the inflation of the conscious by the archetypal materials of the unconscious that leads the Simon Magi of every age to suicidal self-absolutization. But there is another, even greater danger, which Jung does not warn us of, and that is the danger of a divinization of the unconscious that leaves man at the mercy of the dark, irrational forces Jung worships as the dark side of God. Jung sees no middle ground between sinless man and sinful man, no possibility of sinful man's transforming and hallowing his instincts rather than simply celebrating them. By identifying the real "self" with the autonomous center in the unconscious, Jung is in danger of taking his own inner knowledge for the will of God and imposing it on others.[30]

It is to Jung's great credit that his psychology of religion raises profound questions for the meeting between psychology and religion—questions that cannot simply be answered but must be lived and struggled with until they yield ever new insight.

One of these questions is whether including evil is positive and necessary for psychotherapy? The answer to this must clearly be yes, in part. We must take seriously what Jung calls the "shadow," or our psychology and psychotherapy will remain only on the surface. This does not necessarily mean taking part in evil or embracing the instinctual in the way Jung suggests. But it does mean that we can avoid evil only at our peril. If we do take evil seriously, does that alter our view of religion? Is there a dark, diabolical side of God? This is a question of utmost profundity that has occupied human beings in all ages and will continue to do so, especially in an age such as ours when evil has manifested itself in a cruel nakedness as never before.

Another question Jung's psychology of religion raises is whether God is just a function of the personal or collective unconscious. Can psychic experience take the place of the address of God? A corollary of these questions is whether to get to religious and mythical truth we have to venture into the unconscious depths that overwhelm the psychotic? Jung, of course, advocates an individuation or integration in the depths which is the very contrary of psychosis. But even so we have to ask whether religious truth is to be found only in the unconscious?

A question which may be asked today more insistently than a few years ago is whether Jung's psychology encourages narcissism. In the last two decades our time has been called the age of narcissism. The current popularity of the Jungian mythologist Joseph Campbell and his watchword "Follow your bliss" give further testimony to the validity of this characterization. Jung was very much aware of the danger of inflation and certainly had little time for the individual ego. Nonetheless, by encouraging people to focus on archetypal depths that can be reached only through the individual psyche Jung has also encouraged a turning away from equal concern with the beings to whom one stands in relation.

A more basic question that we can raise about Jung's psychology is that of his touchstone of reality. Should our goal be liberation from or completion of existence? The corollary of this question is, Is the task of authenticating one's concrete existence in the world made secondary by Jung to the task of achieving inner wholeness? Does Jung's emphasis on individuation as the goal make conscience and situation instrumental and thus destroy the wholeness of the person who lives in the context of interhuman, family, and group relations?

One final question that we need to look at at greater length is whether Jung oversteps the boundaries of psychology as a science by proclaiming what Martin Buber described as "the religion of pure psychic immanence." What Buber criticized Jung for is that, for all his disclaimers, "He oversteps with sovereign license the boundaries of psychology" by defining religion as "a living relation to psychical events which. . . . take place . . . in the darkness of the psychical hinterland" and conceives of God in general as an "autonomous psychic content."

That these are not merely psychological statements, as Jung would claim, but metaphysical ones, Buber showed by quoting Jung's statements that otherwise "God is indeed not real, for then He nowhere impinges upon our lives" and that God is "for our psychology . . . a function of the unconscious" as opposed to the "orthodox conception" according to which God "exists for Himself." This means psychologically "that one is unaware of the fact that the action arises from one's own inner self." Psychology becomes to Jung the only admissible metaphysic while remaining, for Jung, an empirical science. "But it cannot be both at once," Buber commented.[31]

The court of conscience is dispensed with by Jung in favor of the soul which is integrated in the Self as the unification, in an all-encompassing wholeness, of good and evil. Jung sees the Self as including the world, to be sure, but "the others," declared Buber, "are included only as contents of the individual soul that shall, just as an individual soul, attain its perfection through individuation." All beings who are "included" in this way in my self are, in fact, only possessed as an It. "Only then when, having become aware of the unincludable otherness of a being, I renounced all claim to incorporating it in any way within me or making it a part of my soul, does it truly become Thou for me. This holds good for God as for man."[32]

Jung is not a Gnostic, who traditionally believed in a totally transcendent God, but a *Modern* Gnostic, whose touchstone of reality is the collective psyche, or Self. For all the numinous, guiding quality of Jung's collective unconscious, it is still an It and not a Thou. It can neither be addressed as Thou nor can one live in real dialogue and contending with it, as could one with the transcendent yet present God of the Hebrew Bible. It certainly has a quality of overagainstness; it can never be identified with the conscious person or even with the personal unconscious. But there is no mutuality, no give and take, no sense that Jung's God needs us for the very purpose for which he created us. Indeed, Jung's God is not the Creator but a demiurge finding his place within a larger order as Zeus did within the Greek cosmos. Jung's ultimate touchstone of reality is not the autonomous content of the unconscious psyche that he calls Self but the unconscious psyche itself.

The Viennese logotherapist Viktor Frankl makes a similar criticism of Jung's psychology of religion in his early book *The Unconscious God*.

Not only is the unconscious neither divine nor omniscient, but above all man's unconscious relation to God is profoundly personal. The "unconscious God" must not be mistaken as an impersonal force operant in man. This misunderstanding was the great mistake C.G. Jung fell prey to. Jung must be credited with having discovered distinctly religious elements within the unconscious. Yet he misplaced this unconscious religiousness of man, failing to locate the unconscious God in the personal and existential religion. Instead, he allotted it to the region of drives and instincts, where unconscious religiousness no longer remained a matter of choice and decision. According to Jung, something within me . . . drives me to God, but it is not I who makes the choice and takes the responsibility. . . . The spiritual unconscious and, even more, its religious aspects . . . is an existential agent rather than an instinctual factor. . . . Unconscious religiousness stems from the personal center of the individual man rather than an impersonal pool of images shared by mankind.[33]

The placing of the divine in the unconscious, however archetypally and universally conceived, still psychologizes God *and* reality, robbing our meeting with "the things of this world" of any revelatory power other than the mimetic reflection of our forgotten and buried inner truths. If Jung had not asserted the psyche as *the* exclusive touchstone of reality, he could have bestowed great honor upon a realm that undoubtedly has profound meaning, whether that of the shadow, the anima, the animus, the Great Mother or any of the other life-symbols that slumber in our depths, without hypostasizing that realm into an inverted Platonic universal and elevating this larger-than-life-size sphere to the now empty throne of the Absolute.

Chapter 6

AUTHORITARIAN AND HUMANISTIC RELIGION: ERICH FROMM'S PSYCHOLOGY OF FREEDOM AND RELATEDNESS

IN CONTRAST TO Freud's psychology, with its biological individualism and its innate competitiveness and aggression, Fromm sees the key problem of psychology as "that of the specific kind of relatedness of the individual towards the world and not that of the satisfaction or frustration of this or that instinctual need *per se*." Following Karl Marx and Harry Stack Sullivan, Fromm sees man as *primarily* a social being, i.e., social in his very self and not just in his needs. Psychology, as a result, is "psychology of interpersonal relationships." Fromm disagrees emphatically with Freud's view that history is "the result of psychological forces that in themselves are not socially conditioned." But he also disagrees with those theories, "more or less tinged with behaviorist psychology," that assume "that human nature has no dynamism of its own and that psychological changes are to be understood in terms of the development of new 'habits' as an adaptation to new cultural patterns"

(*Escape from Freedom*). Human nature is not infinitely malleable, and the human factor is one of the dynamic elements in the social process.

Fromm sees freedom as a corollary of the wholeness of the personality. "Positive freedom consists in the spontaneous activity of the total, integrated personality." Such spontaneity comes through "the acceptance of the total personality and the elimination of the split between 'reason' and 'nature.' " The foremost component of spontaneity is love—not the dissolution of the self in another person or the possession of another but the spontaneous affirmation of others while preserving the individual self. Love for Fromm means the overcoming of separation without the elimination of otherness. Work, too, is a part of spontaneity—not compulsion or domination of nature, but an act of creation that unites one with nature without dissolving one in it. "The basic dichotomy that is inherent in freedom—the birth of individuality and the pain of aloneness—is dissolved on a higher plane by man's spontaneous action."

Freedom and the organic growth of the self are possible, says Fromm, only if one respects the uniqueness of the self of other persons as well as one's own self. This most valuable achievement of human culture is in danger today, declares Fromm. One may question, however, whether respect for another is as much the achievement of culture as it is of a relation of directness, mutuality, and presentness that enables one to see the other in his concrete uniqueness as of value in himself. One may also question Fromm's definition of "a genuine ideal as any aim which furthers the growth, freedom, and happiness of the self." The very meaning of these terms depends on one's image of the human and one's sense of one's own personal direction. "Life has an inherent tendency to grow, to expand, to express potentialities," writes Fromm, recapitulating Bergson's emphasis on creativity and dynamism. But the question of the image of the human—that of the meaningful direction of this growth and of these potentialities—remains unanswered.

In *Man for Himself* Fromm recognizes that what man *is* cannot be understood without including what man *ought* to be. "It is impossible to understand man and his emotional and mental disturbances without understanding the nature of value and moral conflicts." Yet he joins himself to the Modern Pragmatist in defining the source of values in purely pragmatic terms, the good being that which contributes to the mature and integrated personality, vice being that which destroys it.

> The character structure of the mature and integrated personality, the productive character, constitutes the source and the basis of "virtue." . . . "Vice," in the last analysis, is indifference to one's own self and self-mutilation. Not self-renunciation nor selfishness but self-love, not the negation of the individual but the affirmation of his truly human self, are the supreme values of humanistic ethics. If man is to have confidence in values, he must know himself and the capacity of his nature for goodness and productiveness. [1]

Fromm presents us here with a succession of terms to each of which we have a positive emotional response—"mature," "integrated," "productive," "affirmation of the truly human self"—but to none has he given concrete content. He defines values in terms of "the mature and integrated personality" and "the truly human self," yet these terms themselves imply values and would have to be defined in terms of values. Thus, Fromm offers us one set of explicit, conscious values that are merely instrumental and another of implicit, assumed values the source of which he does not explore. Fromm bifurcates "conscience" into an authoritarian conscience that demands submission out of fear—not too different from Freud's conception of the conscience as the introjection of the censure of the father—and a humanistic conscience that is "the guardian of our integrity." The humanistic conscience "is the voice of our true selves that summons us back to ourselves, to live productively and to develop fully and harmoniously—that is, *to become what we potentially are*." But what is meant by the "true self" and by becoming "what we potentially are?" Fromm knows the beneficial results of authentic existence, but he cannot point to such existence itself.

An important contribution that Fromm does make to the problem of discovering what is authentic is his recognition that pleasure, the subjective experience of satisfaction, is in itself deceptive and not a valid criterion of value. The masochist is only the most striking example of those who take pleasure in what harms them. As one's dreams often reveal, one may think oneself happy and in fact be deeply anxious and wretched underneath. Happiness is more than a state of mind. It is an expression of the total personality. "Happiness is conjunctive with an increase in vitality, intensity of feeling and thinking, and productiveness." It is "the indication that man has found the answer to the problem of human existence; the productive realization of his potentialities." Although Fromm speaks in this book of "existential dichotomies," he seems to ignore the possibility of a tragic conflict between realizing one's potentialities to the full and playing one's part in a historical situation that may call on one to sacrifice this realization, and perhaps life itself. The person who realizes her potentialities productively is one with the world and at the same time preserves the integrity of her self, writes Fromm. Fromm would recognize that such harmony of self and world is not possible in our society, but he seems to assume that all that is needed is a change of social conditions for it to be brought about. The only thing he speaks of as inherently tragic is that one dies without ever having realized all one's potentialities.

Fromm's definition of "a genuine ideal as any aim which furthers the growth, freedom, and happiness of the self" vitiates his emphasis on spontaneous relations to others by making self-realization the goal and relations to others the means to that goal. In contrast to this emphasis on self-realization, Fromm defines love, in *Man for Himself* and in *The Art of Loving*, as "care, responsibility, respect, and knowledge." These terms all imply a mutual relation with others that see the other as of value in himself. Fromm recognizes this explicitly in taking responsibility back to its root meaning of "respond" and in further defining love as "the wish for the other person to grow and develop" and as "the expression of intimacy between two human beings under the condition of the preservation of each other's integrity." The great popularity of psychology, Fromm points out in *The Art of Loving*, indicates an interest in the knowledge of man, but "it also betrays the fundamental lack of love in human relations today. Psychological knowledge thus becomes a substitute for full knowledge in the act of love, instead of being a step toward it." Love, to Fromm, is "a paradoxical two-in-oneness" in which both separateness and togetherness prevail. It means the response to another in his uniqueness, accepting him *as he is*:

> Responsibility could easily deteriorate into domination and possessiveness, were it not for a third component of love, *respect*. Respect is . . . the

ability to see a person as he is, to be aware of his unique individuality. Respect means the concern that the other person should grow and unfold as he is. Respect, thus, implies the absence of exploitation. I want the loved person to grow and unfold for his own sake, and in his own ways, and not for the purpose of serving me.[2]

The knowledge of another in love, similarly, is not that sadism that seeks to know his last secret in order to dominate him, but "the active penetration of the other person," a union in which "I know you, I know myself, I know everybody—and I 'know' nothing." This distinction between knowing an object and knowing in relation takes Fromm beyond *Man for Himself*, where he defines the science of man as observing the reactions of man to various individual and social conditions and from these observations making inferences about man's nature. Now Fromm recognizes that the image of the human is not derived from empirical observation and scientific inference, but from the dialogue between person and person: "In the act of loving, of giving myself, in the act of penetrating the other person, I find myself, I discover myself, I discover us both, I discover man." Fromm does not mean by this knowing in relation a knowledge that can ever be fully objectified. "The only way of full knowledge lies in the *act* of love: this act transcends thought, it transcends words. It is the daring plunge into the experience of union."

In Fromm's discussion of "the objects of love," however, love loses its character as responsibility, respect, care, and knowledge. "Love is not primarily a relationship to a specific person," Fromm writes; "it is an *attitude*, an *orientation of character* which determines the relatedness of a person to the world as a whole." While it may be true that "if I truly love one person, I love all persons, I love the world, I love life," it is not true that one begins with love for all human beings before one is able to love any specific human being. This retreat into the universal destroys the very character of love as a relation to an actual other person. I must love him in his concrete uniqueness, and not as part of a general attitude, if I am to care for him, respect him, respond to him, and truly know him. One may go from particular love to ever-more inclusive love of others. But one cannot go from love of humanity to love of the individual, for the simple reason that love of humanity is an abstract idea or a general emotion that remains essentially within oneself and does not itself imply a relation to any actual other person.

In the end, Fromm sacrifices even the separateness, the paradoxical two-in-oneness on which he had insisted before, in favor of a view of love as an identity of one person with another.

> In essence, all human beings are identical. We are all part of One; we are One. This being so, it should not make any difference whom we love. Love should be essentially an act of will, of decision to commit my life, completely, to that of one other person. . . . All men are part of Adam, and all women part of Eve.[3]

This view is a useful corrective to the romantic notion that love simply *happens* to one—a passive act of falling in love rather than a decision, commitment, an act of will. What is more, Fromm qualifies his statement of identity by the recognition that "We are all One—yet every one of us is a unique, unduplicable entity." He recognizes, as a result, that erotic love is not only an act of love but also an individual attraction between two specific persons. Nonetheless, in his affirmation of identity, which plays an important part in the rest of the book, Fromm leaves his earlier understanding of love for one closer to the Upanishads' "Husband is not dear because of husband but because of the Self within the husband." This means losing sight of the actual person, for the person exists only in uniqueness and not in an identity with all others that is simply complemented by individuality.

The nature of an individual's love for God corresponds to the nature of his love for man, states Fromm. But this is hardly true for Fromm himself, whose usual recognition of the otherness of the other in the healthy, mature relation between man and man entirely disappears in his various discussions of religion. In *Man for Himself*, Fromm postulates a split between man and a cold, meaningless universe. Not only is man *for* himself, as the title of the book suggests, he is also *by* himself. There is only one solution to man's problem, says Fromm:

> to acknowledge his fundamental aloneness and solitude in a universe indifferent to his fate, to recognize that there is no power transcending him which can solve his problem for him. Man must accept the responsibility for himself and the fact that only by using his own powers can he

give meaning to his life. . . . If he faces the truth without panic he will recognize that *there is no meaning to life except the meaning man gives his life by the unfolding of his powers, by living productively*; and that only constant vigilance, activity, and effort can keep us from failing in the one task that matters—the full development of our powers within the limitations set by the laws of our existence.[4]

To know what is meant by living productively and by the full development of one's powers, one must *already* have meaning in life, meaning that can be actualized through the human being's meeting with life, but that cannot be produced from the human side alone. Meaning is a relationship between the human being and the world. By positing that the world is indifferent to the human and that no meaningful relation to it is possible, Fromm has undercut all the ground on which creativity, productivity, and all his other favorite terms rest.

In human relations, Fromm affirms the self *and* the other and denies that one must choose between self-love and love of others. In religion, Fromm posits the self *or* the other, denying a priori the possibility that one may "fulfill oneself" in relation to what transcends one. In both spheres, however, he allows the pragmatic motif to dominate. He defines ethics in terms of what produces a mature, integrated personality, and he defines religion in the same extrinsic way. "Good" or "bad" in religion, as in ethics, is a function of the psychological effect of a type of relationship, rather than of any intrinsic value or disvalue in the relationship itself. What matters to the psychologist, writes Fromm in *Psychoanalysis and Religion*, is what human attitude a religion expresses and what kind of effect it has on man, whether it is good or bad for the development of human powers. Again, we have the curious pragmatic inversion which makes the development of human powers the end, that for which these powers are developed the means.

Fromm's categories of transcendent and immanent are themselves based on and presuppose the values by which he judges some religions as authoritarian, and therefore bad, and others as humanistic, and therefore good. Yet Fromm nowhere adequately deals with the sources of these values that he presupposes. If he refers them back to the human nature, he also defines human nature in terms of these values. This confusion in Fromm's thinking about religion and values is shown most clearly in the ending of *Psychoanalysis and Religion*. Having defined the God of humanistic religion as "the symbol of man's own powers," he now describes the attitude of this religion as the devotion of life to "the aim of becoming what one potentially is, a being made in the likeness of God." If the human being is made in the likeness of God and God is a symbol of human powers, we have a perfect circle! What this contradiction suggests is a still deeper unclarity as to the relation between such essentially instrumental terms as "power," "potentiality," and "creativity" and the values of love, fairness, kindness, and relatedness that Fromm espouses. In *The Art of Loving* God is again created in man's image while values are taken for granted. Thus, the image of the human, which Fromm assumes will emerge into full light through the recovery of our alienated creativity, retreats into still greater darkness.

To recognize oneself as part of humanity, to live according to love, justice, truth, to develop one's powers of love and reason, "to see one's identity with all beings, and to give up the illusion of a separate, indestructible ego," to recognize the equality of all persons in the spiritual realm—these are the ideals that Fromm sets forth as the true religion. By the very fact of being human, man is asked the question of how to overcome the split between himself and the world—through regression to a prehuman form of existence or through full development of his human powers of love and reason "until he reaches a new harmony with his fellowman and with nature." The first answer Fromm sees as inauthentic and destructive, the second as difficult but productive, intensifying man's vital energies in the very effort to reach it. To choose life instead of death, man must enlarge the margin of freedom that is given to him, giving up the quest for ultimate answers in favor of "a degree of intensity, depth and clarity of experience which gives him the strength to live without illusion, and to be free." This path, says Fromm, leads to a "sense of heightened aliveness in which I confirm my powers and my identity." But to reach it, one needs an image of the human, an education that is effective because "the best heritage of the human race" becomes "reality in the person of the teacher and in the practice and structure of society." It is not learning abstract concepts, but responding to an image of the human that produces real change: "Only the idea which has materialized in the flesh can influence man."

What makes the norms that Fromm affirms the universal, productive, primary ones and the ones that he denies the tribal, destructive, secondary ones? Many of us would go along with much that Fromm says and yet be troubled by the vagueness of his image of the human that he threatens to leave either functional or pragmatic or abstractly idealistic. How does one become a "citizen of the world"? How does one get beyond the illusion of one's ego? What makes the universal a value in itself? We may agree that "to risk doing what is right and human, and have faith in the power of the voice of humanity and truth, is more realistic than the so-called realism of opportunism," and not be much clearer as to what direction of movement in any concrete situation is implied by the words "right," "human," and "truth." Fromm recognizes that freedom is more than freedom *from*, it is also freedom *to*, that the capacity to say "no" meaningfully implies the capacity to say "yes" meaningfully. "The 'yes' to man is the 'no' to all those who want to enslave, exploit, and stultify him." Insofar as social injustice is in question, this is evident, and Fromm has stood courageously as a socialist and as a worker for One World who wants to create the new type of human being who can make such a world possible. Insofar as the image of the human is concerned—the direction to authentic personal existence—he has left us with an affirmation of man and of "self-realization" without the direction that would make these terms meaningful.

Throughout most of his writings Fromm talks in terms of the tradition of the Hebrew Bible, according to which man can never overcome the "evil urge" once and for all, although he can direct this urge into the service of God. At other times, however, he falls into a doctrine of perfectionism entirely foreign to the Hebrew Bible. From this latter point of view, he speaks of the "completely free person" not only as loving, productive, and independent but as someone whose character structure is such that he "is not free to choose evil."

Fromm sums up his image of the human in terms of the understanding of evil as "man's loss of himself in the tragic attempt to escape the burden of his humanity." One cannot cease being human even at the most archaic levels of regression, and therefore all evilness is tragic. The degrees of evilness are the same as the degrees of regression—the strivings against life, the love of death, the incestuous-symbiotic striving to return to the womb, the soil, the inorganic, the narcissistic self-immolation that imprisons man in the "hell" of his own ego and makes him an enemy of life. One is free to choose as long as one's inclinations to regress and to move forward are still in some balance. If one heart hardens to such a degree that there is no longer a balance of inclinations, then one is no longer free to choose. But even this hardening of the heart is a specifically human and not a nonhuman phenomenon. To be human is to be faced with the never-ending task of making choices and of recognizing that wrong choices make us incapable of saving ourselves. If one becomes indifferent to life, then there is no longer any hope that one will choose the good.[5]

Chapter 7

RELIGION AS "PEAK
EXPERIENCES": ABRAHAM
MASLOW'S PSYCHOLOGY OF
SELF-ACTUALIZATION

In CONTRAST TO JUNG, the American psychologist Abraham Maslow was, to begin with, not open at all to religion and the religions. Rather he evolved through hard science and empirical methods to the place where he became open to a totally this-worldly, naturalistic mysticism that he placed at the center of his "psychology of being."

Maslow began with Kurt Goldstein's concept of self-actualization. In Goldstein this concept denoted the innate desire or predilection of every organism, including the human being, to achieve its potential. In Maslow, in contrast, self-actualization not only was limited to the human being but to a very special type of human being that Maslow tended to see as exemplary for all mankind.[1] Like Carl Rogers, Maslow meant by self-actualization realization of one's potentialities. But he was open to Viktor Frankl's criticism that self-actualization does not take place in a vacuum. In the introduction to his book *Eupsychian Management*,

Maslow even stated that one does not aim at self-actualization but at one's task, recognizing that self-actualization only comes as a by-product.

Like the present author Maslow began with the awareness of the absence of a contemporary image of the human that might give the human being living today personal and social direction. Maslow saw the self-actualized human being as the model that would fill this gap:

> Every age but ours has had its model, its ideal. All of these have been given up by our culture; the saint, the hero, the gentleman, the knight, the mystic. About all we have left is the well-adjusted man without problems, a very pale and doubtful substitute. Perhaps we shall soon be able to use as our guide and model the fully growing and self-fulfilling human being, the one in whom all his potentialities are coming to full development, the one whose inner nature expresses itself freely, rather than being warped, suppressed, or denied.[2]

Maslow himself points out that his psychology of being is tautologous in so far as it speaks of the fully human person as perceiving the unity of the cosmos and fusing with it and then recognizes that this is, in fact, the very definition of "the fully human person." Similarly, he sees growth as a way of achieving the more defining characteristics of human being and regression and defense as giving up these higher characteristics for the sake of sheer survival.[3]

All of this points us toward the image of the human. What is lacking in it is the recognition that Maslow did not start with a definition of the self-actualized person but with actual persons whom he admired and only then proceeded to abstract his fourteen characteristics of such a person. Even more serious, Maslow, like Rogers and much of the human potential movement, falls short of the image of the human in his failure to recognize that it is not "growth" and realization of potentialities that are crucial but the direction and nature of that growth. Otherwise there is nothing that would entitle us to call one type of growth "higher" than another. Even the word "health" does not really give us a direction but rather presupposes one. The same is true for the word "self-actualization." If I mean by this term being what I already am, then I am that already and the concept is worthless. If I mean by it becoming what I *must* become because of various inner and outer determinants, then the concept is also worthless and there is no such thing as "higher." If it means that I am free to become whatever I wish and whatever I wish is "self-actualization," then the concept is again meaningless.

Maslow, of course, did not leave "self-actualization" an empty term. On the contrary, he filled it with "B-values" ("being values"). Specifically, he sought to supplement Freudian psychoanalysis, which he saw as essentially a system of psychopathology, with a psychology of the higher or spiritual life, "of what the human being should grow *toward*, of what he should become."[4] Maslow followed Fromm in attacking Freud's notion of the superego as authoritarian and relativistic and added to this neurotic conscience, or guilt, an "intrinsic conscience" based upon the unconscious perception of our own nature, destiny, capacities, and "call" in life.[5]

Maslow's terms *self-actualization* and *peak-experience* penetrated the popular vocabulary and helped shape the *Zeitgeist* of 1960s America, as Maslow's biographer Edward Hoffman has pointed out.[6] Since America in the 60s produced a religion-like affirmation of counter-culture values, it is not surprising that Maslow became "an uneasy hero of the counter-culture," as Hoffman puts it, and was a major force in such centers as Esalen Institute at Big Sur, California, and the Western Behavioral Science Institute in La Jolla, California. What is surprising is that this resolute atheist developed a psychology so close to what we are already familiar with from many of the world's mystics. "Self-actualizing people are more able to perceive the world as if it were independent not only of them but also of human beings in general," Maslow claimed, and extended this claim even to "the average human being in his highest moments, i.e., in his peak experiences." The *B-cognizing* and *B-values* of such people make perception richer and brings one wholeness, perfection, completion, justice, aliveness, richness, simplicity, beauty, goodness, uniqueness, effortlessness, playfulness, honesty, and self-sufficiency. What is more, as has been true for mystics everywhere, "the peak-experience is felt as a self-validating, self-justifying moment which carries its own intrinsic value with it." Maslow even went so far in *The Psychology of Being* as to say that the peak-experience is only good and desirable, never evil or undesirable. Furthermore, like the mystics, the peak-experiencer sometimes sees the whole of the world as a single rich entity and at other times perceives eternity in a grain of sand, to use

William Blake's phrase. For the moment, the peak-experience carries with it a complete loss of fear, anxiety, inhibition, defense, and control plus a giving up of renunciation, delay, and restraint. It is no wonder that Maslow characterizes the peak-experiencer as "godlike," "a true integration of the person at *all* levels," and adds to it "the complete, loving, uncondemning, compassionate and perhaps amused acceptance of the world and of the person"![7]

Maslow also characterizes peak-experiences as "acute identity-experiences," bringing both a greater feeling of integration and a greater fusion with the world ("the I-Thou monism"), hence simultaneously greater attainment of identity, autonomy, and selfhood coupled with transcending of oneself, going beyond and above selfhood. Added to this are such qualities as being at the peak of one's powers, fully and effortlessly functioning, spontaneity, innocence, "here-and-now"-ness, and "all there"-ness. Maslow even introduces a dualism that we might expect of Jung but certainly not of him. The person becomes pure psyche and less a thing of the world, determined by intra-psychic laws rather than by the laws of non-psychic reality. Though Maslow hardly seemed capable of this himself, he recognized that expression and communication in the peak-experiences tends to be poetic, mythical, metaphoric, and rhapsodic.[8]

Maslow ends with what he himself recognizes as a paradox, namely, that identity is both an end-goal in itself and a transition along the path to the transcendence of identity.

> If our goal is the Eastern one of ego-transcendence and obliteration, of leaving behind self-consciousness and self-observation, of fusion with the world and identification with it . . . , then it looks as if the best path to this goal for most people is via achieving identity, a strong real self, and via basic-need-gratification rather than via asceticism.[9]

In the second edition of *Toward a Psychology of Being*, Maslow already finds it necessary to make some qualifications in those earlier descriptions of self-actualization that led many to conceive of it as a static, unreal, "perfect" state in which all human problems are transcended. What he claims here, rather, is that self-actualization is a development of personality that frees the person from the deficiency and neurotic problems of youth so that one "is able to face, endure and grapple with the 'real' problems of life (the intrinsically and ultimately human problems, the unavoidable, the 'existential' problems to which there is no perfect solution)." He recognizes, moreover, that *B-cognition* carries with it the danger of making action impossible or at least indecisive and of neglecting that measure of selfishness and self-protectiveness that is necessary for survival. Hence, at least secondarily, fighting, struggle, striving, uncertainty, guilt, and regret must be part of self-actualization, which Maslow now sees as necessarily involving both contemplation and action. Maslow also recognizes that *B-cognition* may make us less responsible in helping others.[10]

It is in *Religion, Values,* and *Peak-Experiences* that Maslow undertakes to apply his insights to what we might call a psychology of religion, and it is here that the weaknesses of this psychology become most apparent. Even as Maslow here retains a dichotomy of abstract and concrete that accords concreteness to the abstractions of "empirical" science and abstractness to those things that are most immediate, such as religious, mystical, and peak experiences, love, poetry, and play, so he retains a dichotomy between "supernatural" and "natural" that may accord with his antipathy to "old-fashioned religion" but not with his openness to wonder. At the same time, Maslow, who was personally chary of taking "psychedelic" drugs, claimed that such drugs "could be used to produce a peak-experience, with core-religious revelation, in non-peakers." This turns "religious experience" into the effect of a chemical cause rather than a reality in which a person participates!

Maslow sees "most fundamental religious or transcendent experience as a totally private and personal one that can hardly be shared (except with other 'peakers')." Indeed, he has no inkling of what I call "the dialogue of touchstones" ("It is as if two encapsulated privacies were trying to communicate with each other across the chasm between them"). Yet he sets forth peak-experience as the new perennial philosophy: "The very beginning, the intrinsic core, the essence, the universal nucleus of every known high religion (unless Confucianism is also called a religion) has been the private, lonely, personal illumination, revelation, or ecstasy of some acutely sensitive prophet or seer. . . . These 'revelations' or mystical illuminations can be subsumed under the head of the 'peak-experiences.' " "This private religious experience is shared by all the great world religions including the atheistic ones like Buddhism, Taoism, Humanism or Confucianism."[11] It seems to be a temptation that few modern thinkers can resist—to put forward their own central discoveries as the core of all the world's religions: Jung's archetypes, Fromm's humanistic religion, Huxley's unitive knowledge, Bergon's *élan vital*, Coomaraswamy's dragon and dragon-slayer, Campbell's hero journey, and Maslow's peak-experience, to name only a few! Even when they know something about the world's religions, they do not hesitate to ignore all the phenomena that do not fit their personal perception and with it the very fact that in spelling out an "essence" of all religions in one formula or another, they necessarily lose it.

Jung, who denies all true transcendence, claims for the archetypes of the collective unconscious the qualities of Rudolf Otto's *mysterium tremendum*, one of which, at least, we can certainly accord him—that of numinous awe. Maslow claims for peak-experiences:

> practically everything that Rudolf Otto defines as characteristic of the religious experience—the holy; the sacred; creature feeling; humility; gratitude and oblation; thanksgiving; awe before the *mysterium tremendum*; the sense of the divine, the ineffable; the sense of littleness before mystery; the quality of exaltedness and sublimity; the awareness of limits and even of powerlessness; the impulse to surrender and to kneel.[12]

Maslow, like Jung, has some justification in that he sees the "peaker" as experiencing such emotions as wonder, awe, reverence, humility, surrender, and even worship before the greatness of the experience, as well as a tremendous concentration such as the mystics report. Yet the key to Otto lies in the creature feeling that arises before the encounter with an irrational and totally other transcendence, which is precisely what Maslow rejects!

Still relying on his outworn dichotomy, Maslow holds that what remains of disagreement is only "the concept of supernatural beings or of supernatural laws." The God of the Hebrew Bible is not "supernatural" any more than this God is "natural." The "miracle" of the parting of the Red Sea, as Buber, for example, expounds it in his *Moses*, is not the setting aside of the laws of nature but an event of wonder that shines through nature without displacing it. Maslow, in any case, sees "sophisticated theologians and sophisticated scientists" as coming closer in their conception of the universe as a unified, integrated, and meaningful organism.[13]

It is to Maslow's credit that his openness to the ideas of other people and his sensitivity to the dangers his own conceptions gave rise to in many people led him to put forward some powerful cautionary statements in the 1970 Preface to the new edition of *Religious, Values, and Peak-Experiences*:

> Out of the joy and wonder of his ecstasies and peak-experiences he may be tempted to *seek* them, *ad hoc*, and to value them exclusively, as the only or at least the highest goods of life, giving up other criteria of right and wrong. Focused on these wonderful subjective experiences, he may run the danger of turning away from the world and from other people in his search for triggers to peak-experiences, *any* triggers. . . . In a word, he may become not only selfish but also evil. My impression, from the history of mysticism, is that this trend can sometimes wind up in meanness, nastiness, loss of compassion, and even in the extreme of sadism.[14]

Another danger Maslow points to is the need to escalate the triggers, to *force* the issue by striving, hunting, and fighting for them. What is more, spontaneity can become confused with impulsivity and acting out, the sudden insight can become all and the patient and disciplined working through devalued. " 'Turning on' is scheduled, promised, advertised, sold, hustled into being." The peak-experiencer can easily lose the great lesson "that the sacred is *in* the ordinary, that it is to be found in one's daily life, in one's neighbors, friends, and family, in one's backyard, and that travel may be a *flight* from confronting the sacred." Speaking positively Maslow asserts that "self-actualizing people, our best experiencers, are also our most compassionate, our great improvers and reformers of society, our most *effective* fighters against injustice, inequality, slavery, cruelty, exploitation." The reason that the best helpers are the most fully human persons, says Maslow, is that basic human needs can be fulfilled *only* by and through other human beings, i.e., society. The need for community (belongingness, contact, groupness) is itself a basic need.[15]

Consonant with these qualifications, Maslow now puts forward a "plateau-experience" as the mature expression of what he formerly sought for only in peak-experiences:

This is serene and calm, rather than a poignantly emotional, climactic, autonomic response to the miraculous, the awesome, the sacralized, the Unitive, the B-values. So far as I can now tell, the high plateau-experience *always* has a noetic and cognitive element, which is not always true for peak-experiences, which can be purely and exclusively emotion. It is far more voluntary than peak-experiences are.[16]

Peak-experiences may offer transient glimpses, but plateau-experience tends to be a lifelong effort, "not to be confused with the Thursday-evening turn-on that many youngsters think of as *the* path to transcendence." In fact, it should not be confused with any single experience but requires a lifetime of spiritual discipline, study, and commitment.[17]

I am struck by how close what Maslow says in his Preface is to what I wrote at the very end of this era in 1974 in my discussion of encounter groups in *The Hidden Human Image*. Our deep and perhaps violent emotional breakthroughs reveal something hidden in the depths of our souls, I wrote there, but they can also mislead us into seeing the emotions that are thus brought to light as the *only* reality and into seeing "the breakthrough as complete in itself, instead of seeing it as a little light lighting up a long, dark road up a mountain and down into a canyon—a road which you have to walk in your everyday life before this 'breakthrough' can be made lasting and meaningful."[18]

Chapter 8

RELIGION AS THE SEARCH FOR MEANING: VIKTOR FRANKL'S LOGOTHERAPY

IN OUR CHRONOLOGICAL SURVEY of psychologies of religion, Viktor Frankl's logotherapy is not only the most recent but also the most satisfying in terms of our original concern with the *meeting* of psychology and religion. Frankl recognizes that contemporary psychologists and their followers often seek to make a religion out of psychology. He is clear about the separation between religion and psychotherapy, and at the same time he does not shirk from confronting those realms where psychotherapy necessarily touches on what have traditionally been religious concerns. He was a pioneer in criticizing potentialism and self-actualization as goals in themselves. Potentialism is just the beginning. One must then decide which of a thousand possibilities must be actualized and the rest left unused. He came to his views through an experience that has particularly marked, nay branded, our century—that of the Holocaust. This gives Frankl's thinking an especially contemporary relevance. Finally, by emphasizing meaning, dialogue, and the unique, Frankl shows himself the most open to religion and religious reality in their own terms.

In his famous book *Man's Search for Meaning*, originally entitled *From Death-Camp to Existentialism*, Frankl distinguishes logotherapy "from psychoanalysis insofar as it considers man a being whose main concern consists in fulfilling a meaning, rather than in the mere gratification and satisfaction of drives and instincts, or in merely reconciling the conflicting claims of id, ego and superego, or in the mere adaptation and adjustment to society and environment." "Psychoanalysis," says Frankl, "destroys the unified whole that the human person is, and then has the task of reconstructing the whole person out of the pieces."[1]

There are three possibilities of meaning in Frankl's philosophy: That which comes from active achievement, that which comes from passive enjoyment, and that which comes when neither of the first two are possible. Meaning comes from *what we give* to life, from *what we take* from the world, and from the *stand we take* toward "the tragic triad of human existence"—pain, guilt, and death.[2] Even in the face of totally unavoidable suffering and death, it is possible to find meaning in the attitude that one takes toward it. This leads Frankl to declare that meaning is always possible for the human being—in any and all circumstances. He recognizes, to be sure, that most of the inmates in the camp did not find such meaning. But he holds that the fact that it was possible for any has universal human significance:

> The way in which a man accepts his fate and all the suffering it entails, the way in which he takes up his cross, gives him ample opportunity— even under the most difficult circumstances—to add a deeper meaning to his life. It may remain brave, dignified and unselfish. Or in the bitter fight for self-preservation he may forget his human dignity and become no more than an animal. Here lies the chance for a man either to make use of or to forget the opportunities of attaining the moral values that a difficult situation may afford him. And this decides whether he is worthy of his sufferings or not.[3]

In the next paragraph Frankl recognizes "that only a few people are capable of reaching such high moral standards," that only a few of the prisoners "kept their full inner liberty." Yet he concludes this same paragraph with the statement "Everywhere man is confronted . . . with the chance of achieving something through his own suffering." In another place Frankl asserts that in appealing to the capacity for deci-

sion and freedom of attitude, psychotherapy must assert not only man's
will to meaning but also the freedom of man's will.[4]

Inner liberty and freedom of will, however, are not just philosophical
matters. They are also a question of the resources that one has at any
given time. Very few prisoners could tide themselves over their suffer-
ings, as Frankl did, through imagining themselves lecturing about them
in Vienna after the war. Very few had the inner resources to become the
moral heroes that Frankl wants to point to as a possibility for everyone.
What is disturbing about Frankl's position, in fact, is that it seems to be a
sort of "hero journey" with not very much compassion for those whose
lack of confirmation in their past lives left them unequipped for such a
journey.

I had two friends who like myself became conscientious objectors
during the Second World War. Both, like me, were from Oklahoma, and
both were sent to the same prison when the Oklahoma draft boards
refused to recognize their position, as they regularly did. One was
regarded by the fellow prisoners as a saint; the other experienced prison
as a hell and almost suffered a nervous breakdown. Yet both before and
after prison were men of great personal integrity and character. Frankl's
naive assertion of total inner liberty may be contrasted with
Kierkegaard's recognition that we can never judge another person because we cannot know how much of his or her action is the result of
suffering and how much of temptation—how much was compelled and
how much had freedom of choice.[5] In the writings of Elie Wiesel and
Primo Levi, both of whom were also survivors of the Holocaust, there is
much more concern for those who did *not* survive, or those who became
Musselmaenner—walking dead. In a rare note that he does not sound
elsewhere, Frankl declares in *Man's Search for Meaning*, "The best of us
did not survive."

What we learned and taught other despairing men, writes Frankl, is
that what matters is not what we expect from life but rather what life
expects from us. Meaning is not found by asking about the meaning of
life but by answering the daily and hourly questions that life puts to us,
taking responsibility to find the right answers, to fulfill the tasks, which
differ from person to person and from moment to moment. Therefore,
the meaning of life is never vague and general, but real, concrete, and
unique.[6] Every person's life is unique in the universe, says Frankl in *The*

Doctor and the Soul. Therefore, "meaning must be specific and personal, a meaning which can be realized by this one person alone." Frankl ties this recognition in with existentialism, which he calls "the summoning philosophy." Existential analysis and logotherapy must "show how the life of every man has a unique goal to which only one single course leads."[7]

Along with the unique meanings of unique situations Frankl posits meanings shared by human beings across society and throughout history, meanings that refer to the human condition and that give rise to values. In fact, Frankl defines values as "meaning universals which crystallize in the typical situations society or even humanity has to face." For both the meanings of unique situations and of typical ones true responsibility depends upon conscience—"the intuitive capacity of man to find out the meaning of a situation." Such conscience is creative, often contradicting the accepted values of society. "Conscience not only refers to transcendence; it originates in transcendence," writes Frankl in *The Unconscious God.*[8]

The result of Frankl's locating meaning in the situations that summon us and call us out is that meaning, for him, cannot be invented by the self, as in Sartre, or even discovered in self-actualization and self-realization, as in Maslow and Rogers. It must rather be a product of our openness to the demand of otherness, of what transcends us. Maslow also refers to this as a cleavage between what I am and what I ought to be. Man transcends himself not only toward the world but toward an *ought*, which Frankl calls the noetic, or spiritual dimension of human existence and the true existential act.[9] Such transcending is possible even in the face of suffering and dying, as we have seen. Like Alfred North Whitehead, Frankl sees what has happened as saved and delivered into the past. Therefore, life's transitoriness and the fact of death cannot make our existence meaningless. In the 1984 Postscript that Frankl added to *Man's Search for Meaning*, Frankl characterizes his view as a "tragic optimism," asserting that at its best human potential "always allows for: (1) turning suffering into a human achievement and accomplishment; (2) deriving from guilt the opportunity to change oneself for the better; and (3) deriving from life's transitoriness an incentive to take responsible action."[10]

Frankl extends uniqueness from the individual person to the relation between person and person. Love, in particular, he sees as grasping and affirming the unique essence of another person. "Only to the extent to which an I is lovingly directed toward a Thou—only to this extent is the ego also capable of integrating the id, of integrating the sexuality into the personality." Such love is of lasting value and reality beyond ephemeral sexual attraction and erotic passion.

> The spiritual act by which the person comprehends the spiritual core of another outlasts itself; to the degree that the content of that act is valid, it is valid once and for all. Thus true love as a spiritual relationship to the other person's being, as the beholding of another peculiar essence, is exempt from the transitoriness which marks the merely temporary states of physical sexuality or psychological eroticism. Love is more than an emotional condition; love is an intentional act. What it intends is the essence of the other person.[11]

Frankl is not only concerned with existentialism, but also with what I call the existentialism of dialogue, or the I-Thou relationship. At the same time in his insistence that man transcends himself not only to another person in love but also toward meaning, Frankl adds a third dimension to dialogue, which he calls logos. Instead of the dialogical therapist's "healing through meeting," Frankl puts forward "healing through meaning." Ludwig Binswanger's *Daseinanalyse* (which is based in large part on Buber's philosophy of dialogue) has freed man from his ontological deafness, says Frankl. Logotherapy goes beyond this to free man from his ontological blindness. In language that the German existentialist philosopher Martin Heidegger might have used, Frankl speaks of having "to make the meaning of being shine forth." "More and more the I-Thou relation can be regarded as the heart of the matter." Yet the dialogue between I and Thou "defeats itself unless I and Thou transcend themselves to refer to a meaning outside themselves."[12] Like some existentialists of dialogue, Frankl holds that there must be a third-personal object that is the subject of the dialogue between I and Thou. Yet unlike them Frankl turns this object from the content of the dialogue into a separate and transcendent objective dimension above the meeting between person and person.

Even if the personal quality of encounter is preserved, the I-Thou relation should not be regarded as a closed system. . . . From the viewpoint of the one who speaks, language is expression; from that of the person to whom the speaker addresses himself, language is appeal; and from the viewpoint of the subject matter of which one speaks, language is presentation. It is the third aspect . . . that is overlooked whenever one forgets that the therapeutic relationship is not yet exhaustively characterized by the concept of encounter between two subjects but hinges on the object with which one subject is confronting the other. . . . there is a meaning waiting to be fulfilled by him [the patient]. Therefore, the therapeutic relationship is opened, as it were, onto a world. The world, however, is to be considered assignment and challenge.[13]

In *The Unheard Cry for Meaning*, his most recent book, Frankl demonstrates the pitfalls of the dimensional terms in which he customarily thinks. He cannot imagine that the "logos" is included in the dialogue itself, as Buber explicitly says, but instead sees himself as adding an extra dimension that transcends the dialogue toward some transcendent "meaning":

Buber . . . not only discovered the central place that encounter occupies in the life of the human spirit but also defined this life as basically a dialogue between an I and a Thou. However, it is my contention that no true dialogue is possible unless the dimension of the logos has been entered. *I would say a dialogue without the logos, lacking the direction of an intentional referent, is really a mutual monologue, merely mutual self-expression.* . . . True encounter is a mode of coexistence that is open to the logos, allowing the partners to transcend themselves toward the logos, and even promoting such mutual self-transcendence.[14]

I italicized the sentence in the above quotation because it shows how easily Frankl falls into a caricature of what he does not understand in depth. In the next paragraph, to be sure, he distinguishes between the "impersonal logos" of meaning and the "personal logos" of love, reserving "meaning fulfillment" for the former and not the latter. A few pages later he makes a critique of encounter groups with which I could not agree more. "Pseudo-encounter . . . *is based on a 'dialogue without logos'* . . . It is only a platform of mutual self-expression."[15] Such encounter, in fact, is not dialogue at all. It is mutual monologue. But this is exactly how Frankl characterizes Buber's dialogue in the italicized sentence from the quotation above when it is not illuminated by Frankl's discovery of meaning! Frankl does not speak of going beyond self-actualization to dialogue, as I would, but "to that sphere of human existence where [man] chooses what he will do and what he will be in the midst of an objective world of meaning and values."[16]

If Frankl had read Buber with any care, he could not have imagined that Buber's dialogue left out either challenge, demand, address, or transcendence. What Buber says of the logos in *The Knowledge of Man* shows that for him, in contrast to Frankl, neither word nor meaning can be separated from dialogue and made into a separate dimension.

[The] concept of logos cannot be understood otherwise than from the primal establishment of the wedding between meaning and speech. . . . Each soul does, of course, have its logos deep in itself, but the logos does not attain to its fullness in us but rather between us; for it means the eternal chance for speech to become true between men.[17]

It is in his understanding of religion and the spiritual and the place of the therapist in this realm that Frankl makes his most significant contribution to psychology of religion. The spiritual dimension, to Frankl, is that which makes us human. Therefore, our search for meaning, so far from being pathological, is the surest sign of being truly human, and the frustration of this search is spiritual distress, not mental disease. Frankl points beyond reason and the intellect to an existential act that is basic trust in Being. "Faith in the ultimate meaning is preceded by trust in an ultimate being, by trust in God."[18]

In *The Doctor and the Soul* Frankl defines religion and the religious "as experiencing the ultimate 'Thou.' " "For the religious person also God is always transcendent—but also always intended . . . , forever silent—but also forever invoked . . . the inexpressible—but is always addressed."[19] On the other hand, Frankl loses the paradoxical tension that sees God as absolute and yet becoming a person in relation to us when he writes:

The "living" God has been a "hidden" God all along. You must not expect him to answer your call. . . . If God exists, however, he is infinite, and you wait for an echo in vain. The fact that no answer comes back to you is proof that your call has reached the addressee, the infinite.[20]

As we have already seen from Frankl's critique of Jung's collective unconscious, Frankl posits a spiritual unconscious in addition to the instinctual unconscious of Freud and Jung. Spiritual phenomena may be unconscious or conscious, but the spiritual basis of human existence and the center of the human person in his very depth is unconscious. "In its origin the human spirit is unconscious spirit." Therefore, therapy must be aimed at what is called in logotherapy "de-reflection"—giving back to the patient the trust in the unconscious. By the same token, Frankl rejects any attempt to trace the self back to drives and instincts. "The self has the function of repressing and sublimating the drives and instincts but can itself never be derived from them."[21]

The corollary of this spiritual unconscious is unconscious religious-ness, which Frankl defines as "a latent relation to transcendence inher-ent in man . . . a relationship between the immanent self and a transcendent thou"—a "transcendent unconscious" that is part and parcel of the spiritual unconscious. Frankl's "unconscious God" does not mean that God is unconscious to himself but rather that our relation to God may be unconscious. This does not mean that we carry God along in the form of an innate archetype but rather in religious forms that wait to be assimilated by us in an existential way, i.e., to be made our own. We have got beyond Freud's "future of an illusion," claims Frankl, to the recognition of the apparent timelessness and ever-presence of that reality that man's intrinsic religiousness has revealed itself to be. "It is the task of logotherapy to re-mind the patient of his unconscious religiousness—that is to say, to let it enter his conscious mind again."[22]

Frankl denies in the strongest possible terms that this means that the logotherapist is a covert minister, priest, or rabbi who imposes reli-giousness on the patient. Genuine religion is not only existential but spontaneous. It must unfold in its own time. One cannot be pushed to it by a psychiatrist. A psychiatrist could, to be sure, take the place of a priest and offer consolation on the grounds of a common faith. Frankl even sees this as the psychiatrist's religious duty where a priest is not available. However, "the psychiatrist is never entitled to such a religious approach qua psychiatrist, but only as a religious person. Furthermore, only a psychiatrist who is himself a religious person is justified in bringing religion into psychotherapy."

In *The Doctor and the Soul*, Frankl expresses himself still more cautiously. Psychotherapy can produce the spiritual anchor that religion provides as an unintended side effect, but that is not the aim or intention of the therapist, who must always beware of forcing his philosophy upon the patient. The aim of logotherapy is medical ministry, but this is not intended as a substitute for religion. Medical ministry deals increasingly with those existential and spiritual problems that psychotherapy can never entirely escape. "As soon as logotherapy ventures upon a 'psychotherapy in spiritual terms,' it touches upon questions of values and enters into a borderland of medicine." But this can never mean taking over the patient's responsibility or anticipating decisions or imposing them upon the patient. The logotherapist's task is to make it possible for the patient to reach decisions, to endow the patient with the capacity for deciding.[23]

What puzzles me most about Frankl's position is his assertion that it is *always* possible to find meaning. This gives meaning a universal status that divorces it from the very existential and unique situations that Frankl claims give rise to it. There is no room left for the absurd or for what I call "the Dialogue with the Absurd." Existential trust and existential grace must go together. A meaning that can be simply asserted as always there to be had is neither. Frankl is fond of quoting Nietzsche's saying that any *how* can be borne where there is a *why*. Primo Levi in his *Survival in Auschwitz* tells of how one day as an inmate in this death camp he reached out his hand for an icicle outside the window to slake his unbearable thirst. A guard came by just then and knocked the icicle down so that Levi could not get it. "Why?" the anguished Levi cried out. "Hier ist kein Warum."—"Here there is no Why," the guard responded. It is precisely this confrontation with meaninglessness that one finds in every page of Elie Wiesel and Primo Levi and that I find missing in Frankl. This is, as I have suggested, part of that focus on the hero and the saint that makes him give his attention to the few who were able to preserve their 'inner liberty' and find meaning in suffering. From this Frankl turned his search for meaning not only into an approach to therapy but also into a philosophical dogma. Otherwise he would not be able to assert that meaning is always possible in every situation. Job's question has no place in Frankl's world nor the way in which Job contended even in the midst of his trust.

The passages in which Frankl speaks of the uniqueness of meaning far outweigh those where he speaks of its objectivity. Yet by divorcing meaning from the lived dialogue itself and making of it an extra, transcendent dimension, Frankl leaves us with the question of just where he derives the meaning that he posits—that noetic or noological realm that he calls the impersonal logos. Despite the fact that a chapter in one of his books is entitled "The Meaning of Meaning" Frankl does not really answer this question. We cannot know whether he assumes a Platonic realm of objective knowledge, truth, and value or a Heideggerian philosophy of creating meaning through letting it shine forth from being. What we can say is that he has divorced meaning from the very concreteness that he claims to ground it in and lifted it to a pseudo-objectivity that fatally flaws his psychology of religion and undermines his emphasis on uniqueness.

Our complaint is not that Frankl has failed to define meaning intellectually or prove it logically. As he himself would say, it is beyond both reason and logic and can only be pointed to. It is rather that he has removed meaning to a "higher sphere" that is anything but existential. This does not invalidate his great contribution to our understanding of the *meeting* between religion and psychology, but it qualifies its value and with it that positing of spirituality and unconscious religiousness that at times he sees as the meeting with the Thou and at other times as separate from it. Because he does not really see dialogue or the "between" as an ontological reality, Frankl has reduced dialogue to the simple act of one person speaking to another and has no understanding of the dialogue with the eternal Thou that arises when we answer the address and respond to the claim of situations, including, above all, our meeting with our fellow human beings.[24]

Part Three

ISSUES IN THE MEETING
BETWEEN RELIGION AND
PSYCHOLOGY

Chapter 9

THE LIMITS OF THE PSYCHE AS TOUCHSTONES OF REALITY

IN CHAPTER 4 on religion and psychology we defined psychology of religion as the discipline that deals with religious materials in psychological categories. Strictly speaking, this is not wholly true of any of the psychologies of religion that we have discussed in Part Two. Even Freud, who comes nearest to fitting the definition, proceeds from what he himself calls "metapsychological" considerations and bases much of his view of religion on his own ideas of myth, totem and taboo, the origin of monotheism, and the like. Jung, in contrast, to Freud, is open to a vast panorama of religious material that he takes seriously and does not try to reduce or explain away. On the other hand, as we have seen, he *does* convert it to "the religion of pure psychic immanence."

Erich Fromm is by no means so open to all religious phenomena as Jung. In fact, in perhaps unfair criticism of Jung, Fromm says that the welcoming of all unconscious material as religious would make even insanity religious! Fromm is open, as we have seen, to what he calls "humanistic religion" while he recognizes but disparages "authoritarian religion" as something that certainly exists but does so at the expense of man's realizing his own powers. One basis for this is the pragmatism that Fromm takes over from the American philosopher and psychologist William James. Religion is true if it "works," if it has real results, something that sets both James and Fromm apart from the religious people of all ages who were not aiming at the by-products of religion but at the relation with the divine itself, as I write in my critique of James in *To Deny Our Nothingness*:

> The saints, mystics, converts, and fundamentalists whom James studied [in *Varieties of Religious Experience*] all wholeheartedly believed in a God Who was something more than their own unconscious, and this belief transformed and energized their lives. James and his readers, on the other hand, wish to partake of the good results by acting *as if* they, too, believed. Such a "belief" can never be wholehearted, since one part of one knows that one is acting *as if*. One does not act spontaneously for the sake of what one believes, but with calculation in hopes of attaining *élan vital*, peace of mind, or "successful living." Precisely through this double-mindedness, the by-products of the truly religious life (not all of which are happy ones) are absent. . . . One may respect the witness of the religious man, but "a will to believe" is a contradiction in itself. It is autosuggestion, hypocrisy, or magic, but it is not religious reality.[1]

As I have written in my critique of the American Jewish Reconstructionist philosopher Mordecai Kaplan, there is no religion "as if":

> William James to the contrary, one cannot will to believe *just in order to attain beneficial results*. Either there *is* meaning in life that can be discovered in our meeting with reality, or there is not. There is no meaning "As If."[2]

Fromm, unlike James, is very critical of the results, welcoming only the religion that promotes the fulfillment of man's productivity and rejecting that which thwarts it. Even so, we must recognize that Fromm's touchstone of reality is not religion itself but its psychological effects. On the other hand, this is not, as Fromm would recognize himself, a value-free criteria. On the contrary, it rests on a hidden set of values that Fromm undoubtedly derived from his Judaism and his affinity to the other manifestations of what he calls humanistic religion.

Abraham Maslow is very close to Fromm in proceeding from a naturalistic view that still includes human wholeness and human freedom. Fromm is open to certain types of mysticism. Maslow is still more so. Both, as we have seen, are like Jung, Bergson, and Huxley in offering us a "perennial philosophy" that tells us the core and essence of all religion. That core is determined in each case not by a phenomenological study of the religions or even of great mysticisms but by a scattered knowledge of religions coupled with whatever the given thinker has decided is central to his thought and to his saving message to the world. We would have no reason to object if they contented themselves with sharing with us their touchstones of reality. It is only when they proclaim that their unique touchstone is the essence of all religion or all mysticism that we must object. Is this psychologizing religion? Yes, but then we must recognize that their psychologies, in turn, rest on philosophical bases and assumptions, and that those bases and assumptions ultimately rest upon touchstones of reality.

What then are we to say about Viktor Frankl? Of all those we have considered, Frankl's psychology of religion is least open to the criticism that he has simply dealt with religion in psychological categories. What is more, he has been very open and honest in showing us the origins of his philosophy and psychology of meaning in his experiences in the death camps. He is concerned with each person's unique meaning discovered for his or herself in unique situations—hence with their touchstones of reality. He has provided us with meaningful critiques of Freud's "future of an illusion" and Jung's archetypal or collective unconscious. What is more, he has made one of the earliest and best critiques of that philosophy of self-actualization and self-realization that has permeated humanistic psychology.

Our criticism of Frankl, ironically, is that he has not spelled out what he means by meaning and, in so doing, has and has not imposed his psychology on his view of religion! We have criticized his turning his personal experience in the camps into what is tantamount to a universal dogma of meaning that applies to any and all situations and leaves no room for that meaninglessness and absurdity that was the very hallmark of the Holocaust, or, as it is better called, the *Shoah*. In line with his own valuation of existentialism as the summoning philosophy, we can recognize the therapeutic value of appealing to people's resources and will so that they do not settle down either into fatalism, cynicism, determinism, self-pity, or generalities about the meaning of life or what they expect to get out of life.

Frankl does not seem to recognize, however, the implied moral judgment on those who have not been sufficiently confirmed to have the resources to retain their full inner liberty. This is not a question of either/or. We can only applaud Frankl's recognition, like the existentialists in general, that there is not only what we meet but the attitude we bring to that meeting, and in that sense we are freer than we might think. As we have seen, even our personal response is not and can never be one of total freedom. It depends upon inner resources that are not ours to command at will.

What comes to the free person from without is only the precondition for his or her action, it does not determine its nature. This is just as true of those social and psychological conditioning influences that he or she has internalized in the past as of immediate external events. To the former as to the latter, he or she responds freely from the depths as a whole and conscious person. The unfree individual, on the other hand, is so defined by public opinion, social status, or neurosis that he or she does not "respond" spontaneously and openly to what meets him or her but only "reacts." He or she does not see others as real persons, unique and of value in themselves, but in terms of their status, their usefulness, or their similarity to other individuals with whom he or she has had relationships in the past. We must bear in mind, however, that no one is a purely free person or purely unfree individual, pure responder or pure reactor. We are all a mixture at every moment. The important question in the admixture is which dominates.

One other critique we have made of Frankl is his tendency to think in terms of dimensions, such as the physical, the psychic, and the spiritual. It has always puzzled me how Frankl qua logotherapist can help his patients find meaning while Frankl qua neuropsychiatrist—by his own admission—prescribes electric shock treatments and lobotomies! As Leslie H. Farber said at a public meeting of the Washington School of Psychiatry in 1955 in criticism of Joseph Fletcher's advocacy of lobotomy, there is a moral choice involved even in psychosis. Lobotomy is an attempt to do violence to such choice, and so, I suspect, is electric shock.

In our discussion of Frankl, we commended him for his recognition that for many people today psychology itself is a religion. This is because for many people psychology has become *the* modern touchstone of reality in the way that religion was for people in the Middle Ages. To assess this phenomenon we need to be aware of the difference between a touchstone of reality as the result of the events and meetings of our lives and one that we have taken over passively from the cultural tenor of the age. Recognizing this important difference helps us to examine the limits of the psyche as touchstone of reality. This is a question that those who make psychology a religion are not likely to be even aware of. Our concern with the limits of the psyche as touchstones of reality does not imply, of course, that it is illegitimate for a psychologist to express his or her views on religion.

Religion has much to learn from psychology because religion has so often fallen into a false prating in the higher spheres quite opposite to its real motives underneath. Religion cannot blink when psychology tells us about the depth and complexities, the problematic and irrational aspects of man, nor about the task, which I believe is an essentially religious one, of bringing the whole of oneself—and not some conscious, willed part alone—into one's life relationships. But psychology also has something to learn from religion. A great deal more has been written about the psychology *of* religion than has been written about psychology *and* religion.[3] As long as we think in terms of psychology *of* religion, then psychology is given license to dispose of whatever in religion falls, or seems to fall, within its jurisdiction. Whatever does not is conveniently referred to some other discipline. But as soon as we think in terms of psychology *and* religion, then a meeting is envisaged on equal terms between two essentially different realities: a body of knowledge within the structure of a science and a body of tradition, ritual, history, and experience accessible in parts to many sciences but as a whole to none. To envisage this meeting is to raise a question that is almost by definition never raised within the field of psychology *of* religion, namely, the limits of the psyche as a touchstone of reality. "Psyche" here is used in the most general sense possible—mind and soul, conscious and unconscious, thought, feeling, intuition, and sensation.

Today the psychological in the sense of objective analysis and the psychic in the sense of subjective experience are confusedly intermingled. Yet this confused intermingling has taken shape in the popular mind not only as a single phenomenon but as *the* modern touchstone of reality in the way theology was for the Middle Ages, physics for the Newtonian age and the age of Enlightenment, and evolution for the mid-nineteenth to mid-twentieth centuries. Here I am using the phrase "touchstone of reality" in a derivative, objectified, and cultural sense rather than in an existential sense: as a product of some direct encounter or contact with an otherness that transcends our own subjectivity even when we respond to it from that ground.

> A coloration that we take on from the culture or *Zeitgeist* but have not made our own is not a touchstone: it is only fool's gold. A touchstone cannot be passively received. It must be won by contending, by wrestling until dawn and not letting the nameless messenger go until he has blessed us by giving us a new name. Touchstones only come when we have fought our way through to where we are open to something really other than our accustomed set of values and our accustomed ways of looking at the world.[4]

These two senses of "touchstones of reality" are often quite distinct but seldom entirely so since we live in a culture and our contracts with any reality whatever are refracted through that culture—including language, concepts, worldviews, ways of seeing, thinking, and experiencing, attitudes, and expectations.

But if there is no contact with reality that is wholly separate from culture, there *is* culture, which is far, far removed from any direct contact with reality. In this latter case our "touchstones" become both obstacle to and substitute for any immediacy of apprehension or reapprehension of the reality known in mutual contact. The limits of the psyche as touchstone of reality is a problem for this very reason. For those who take the psychological or the psyche on faith as ultimate reality, the question of touchstones of reality in the more immediate and concrete sense in which they derive from concrete encounters or events can hardly arise.

Once when I was teaching the biblical Prophets in a class at Sarah Lawrence College, I was startled by a freshman who insisted that Isaiah was a paranoiac. "How can you call him a paranoiac?" I asked. "A paranoiac is one who lives in a sealed-off world of his own whereas Isaiah was more aware of the realities of history than any man of his time." "Well then," the freshman replied, "he was an educated paranoiac!" While few of us would express ourselves with such frankness and naiveté, most of us are really on her side, even if we are not aware of it. If any of us had Isaiah's vision in the Temple, we would be more likely to consult a psychiatrist than to exclaim, "Holy! Holy! Holy!" Though we are far beyond Freud's dogmatic and simply negative approach to religion, popular Freudianism still dominates our thoughts and provides our most tenacious cultural "touchstone of reality." The search for linked causes, the distrust of motives, one's own and others, the distrust of the conscious, the conceptual, and the "merely verbal," the loss of trust in the immediacy of our feelings, intuitions, and insights, the loss of trust in our own good faith and that of others, enclose us round in a well-nigh hermetically sealed psychic ecology. Even in the age of the "group explosion," the search for joy, sense relaxation, non-verbal feelings, and gut-level hostility led many of us to new and more deadly forms of psychological self-preoccupation, and planned "spontaneity" made a mockery of the grace of true immediacy.

If the psyche is not given to us as an object that we can analyze, dissect, or even interpret according to the universal hermeneutic of myths, folklore, and fairy tales, neither is it given to us as sheer immediacy. Not only is it never accessible to us from without or in abstraction from a living person in relationship with other persons and with nature, but we never experience it directly minus an attitude toward it, a personal stance which already constitutes an interpretation of it.

The psychologizing of reality can be directly traced to the psychologizing of our understanding of experience, which now is something that happens *within* us rather than *between* us and the world. It means by the same token the abdication of our responsibility before the situations, events, and meetings of our existence, for we see "experience" as happening to us, or as "a happening," and we become the passive enjoyers, users, and observers of our turned-on lives. To face the fact that we cannot grasp the psyche either as an object or in sheer immediacy is to come face to face with a whole host of basic problems, no one of which can be located simply within "psychology" minus the wholeness of reality. If the "I" is not merely the passive servant of three masters, as Freud saw it, or the "persona," or social role, as Jung saw it, then what is its relation to the psyche? To speak, as Jung does, of an integration of the self that takes place in the unconscious with or without the consent of the "I" and without the active relationship to and valuing of what is not the self, to speak of an individuation that discovers personal uniqueness through a combination of one's archetypal destiny and the limitations of one's environment, to speak of individuation without personal uniqueness or that direction of meaningful personal existence that I have called the image of the human is, to my mind, a contradiction in terms.

An equally grave problem is the relationship of the psyche to consciousness. Consciousness is not the sum total of reality, nor is Freud's goal of making the unconscious conscious an adequate aim for either therapy or personal or social fulfillment. The world in which we live is more than consciousness, and our existence itself is more than consciousness. An alteration of consciousness, even in the form of an intercourse between the archetypal depths and the personal unconscious and conscious, can never be the sum and substance of concrete existence.

Another problem that arises from the tendency to take the psyche as touchstone of reality is that of time. The fleeting moment, the full present, the flow of present to past, and the anticipation of the future carry within them an undeniable fact of existence to which the psyche itself can never bear adequate witness. The psyche, indeed, is the very seat of illusion in much of the literature of mankind. Nothing suggests the unreal and illusory quality of life more poignantly then to compare it to a dream, an image, a tale that is told.

The psyche, to be sure, has its revelations to make to us in anger, hate, rage, in love and mystic ecstasy. Yet we cannot follow Huxley in identifying the interpretation—the mystical philosophy or metaphysics—with the experience itself. Nor can we follow the "basic encounter" cults in absolutizing individual feeling as the one incontrovertible authority on where you are. Even Abraham Heschel's awareness of the ineffable, which includes far more than the psyche alone, cannot be identified with the *insights* that derive from this awareness. The attempt to identify the psyche and truth—never more boldly made than by Jung in his universals of meaning originating in the psychic depths—must always shipwreck on the fact that truth means a relationship to *existence*. It can never be restricted to one aspect of existence—the inner— to which all the outer must *de facto* if not *de jure* be subordinated. Like the nineteenth-century theory of social harmony arising from *laissez faire* in which each follows his individual interests, this necessitates a magical assumption of one universal that guides each of us separately in such a way that all is somehow for the best for all. Either truth is reduced to the psychic and becomes mere tautology or the psychic is elevated to Truth and becomes a false hypostatizing.

None of this is to deny the overwhelming experience that we all have at some time or other of a revelation that comes to us through the psyche, whether it be dreams, intuitions, or the liberation and expression of emotions so deeply suppressed that we did not even suspect their existence. But this is revelation precisely because the psyche is thus brought into the fullness of human existence and interhuman coexistence, not because the truth already exists as such "down there" in the psychic depths or "in there" in the hidden recesses of our being.

Chapter 10

PSYCHOLOGISM AND
THE CULT OF EXPERIENCE

IF WE FOLLOW THROUGH on the insights that led us to recognize the limits of the psyche as touchstone of reality, we encounter two other interesting, contemporary, and related issues that arise from the meeting of psychology and religion: psychologism and the contemporary cult of experience. Psychologism is the tendency to convert the events that take place between us to intrapsychic happenings. The contemporary cult of experience is an extension of this same tendency.

One of the most common forms of that psychologism that reduces the events that take place between people to what happens inside them is the modern tendency to explain away both actions and conscious motives on the basis of hidden and often unconscious motivation. Motives that in the past might have been taken at their face value—humility, love, friendship—must now be looked at more carefully. For, as Dostoevsky saw even before Freud, they may, in fact, mask resentment, hatred, or hostility. When we think of the humility of St. Francis, we may also see the masochistic Marmeladov allowing his wife to drag him by the beard, or Dostoevsky's "Eternal Husband" who, after ministering to the sick friend who has taken his wife, tries to kill him in his sleep.

For Nietzsche, too, people dissemble without knowing it, unaware of the ignoble lust that conceals itself behind the noble ideal. Zarathustra labels as "Tarantulas" those socialist and humanitarian "preachers of *equality*" whose demand for "justice" masks a secret desire for revenge. The person "who will never defend himself" is the person of *ressentiment* who "swalloweth down poisonous spittle and bad looks, the all-too-patient one, the all-endurer." The chaste are those who seek in chastity the satisfaction that has been denied them elsewhere.

And how nicely can doggish lust beg for a piece of spirit, when a piece of flesh is denied! . . .
Ye have too cruel eyes, and ye look wantonly towards the sufferers. Hath not your lust just disguised itself and taken the name of fellow suffering?[1]

Friendship, similarly, is often merely an attempt to overleap envy, and the love of one's neighbor nothing but the bad love of oneself.

Ye call in a witness when ye want to speak well of yourselves; and when ye have misled him to think well of you, ye also think well of yourselves . . .
The one goeth to his neighbor because he seeketh himself, and the other because he would fain lose himself.[2]

That modern psychoanalysis has attempted to find a rational pattern behind these hidden motivations that Dostoevsky and Nietzsche have unmasked in no way reduces the problematic nature of the mistrust that impels such unmasking and of the bad faith—with others and with oneself—that is unmasked. Both the bad faith and the mistrust mean essentially the fragmentation of the self. Modern Man knows his alienation nowhere so intensely as in the alienation from oneself that results from this inner division and conflict. In the modern age it is no longer possible to accept any person, not even oneself, at "face value." Yet it is equally impossible simply to explain away the reality of a person by reducing that person to the psychologically determined being pictured by one or another school of psychoanalysis. What confronts us again and again in others and in ourselves, in the characters of our literature and in the authors who create them, is the bewildering intermixture of personal freedom and psychological compulsion; and the specific form that this intermixture takes differs with each person and with each unique situation.

To what extent can religious experience be explained by psychological categories? When depth psychology burst upon the world, it became fashionable to look for hidden motives in everything and not least of all in religion. In so far as any given experience is psychopathological, then it may indeed be explained by psychological categories even though it may have the holiest of religious coverings. What is more, even non-pathological religious experience has an intrapsychic accompaniment that may properly be the province of psychology. But "experience" itself is a questionable category, as we shall see, since it tends to remove everything that is "experienced" into the self.

It is one thing to speak of specific pathology, moreover. It is quite another to attempt to unmask all religious motives as pathological or psychological—something no psychologist can properly do. If we begin with general mistrust, like Nietzsche, or with a theory of the origin of all religion in psychological need, like Freud, then we shall be tempted to *deduce* the motives of others from our general antipathy to religion. But this can never be legitimately done; for we have no right to go from a generalization about motives or psychological complexes to the particular unique person before us.

Twenty years after my own confirmation, I returned to a liberal temple as the leader of a post-confirmation discussion group. One Sunday when the rabbi was called away, he asked me to take over his confirmation class. Informed that each student was reading in preparation for his or her confirmation, I asked each in turn what subject she was studying. One girl said she was studying theology and explained that according to the book she was reading this was really a matter of psychology—what psychological needs cause an individual to believe one religious concept or another. Another girl said that she was studying man and explained that, according to the Bible, man was created in the image of God.

"But if theology is really psychology," I queried, "does that not mean that God was created in the image of man?" Since no one was disturbed by this, I put on the blackboard two propositions, "God is created in the image of man" and "Man was created in the image of God," and went round the room to find in which each individual really believed. I discovered that without a single exception this class believed that God is created in the image of man and that religion is really a matter of psychological needs.

An even more insidious relativization of values than the pragmatic inversion that defines them functionally rather than intrinsically is the psychologism that pervades every aspect of our culture. Psychologism is not psychology or psychoanalysis. It is the subjectivist reduction that leads us to turn events that take place between ourselves and the world into psychic happenings within ourselves. To psychologism, religion is either the projection of our wishes and illusions onto the cold and empty sky (Freud) or it is a purely psychic phenomena—the integration of the self in the depths of the collective unconscious (Jung)—or it is, in its good form, a humanism in which God is merely a symbol of the potentialities of man and religion a means to the end of realizing those potentialities (Fromm). Moral values by the same token are defined in pragmatic psychological terms, the good being that which contributes to the mature and integrated personality, vice being that which destroys it (Fromm, *Man for Himself*). When applied by the logical positivists and the linguistic analysts, who do not use the tools of depth psychology, this psychologism results in the "death of God by a thousand qualifications." God dies through semantics, or rather he does not even need to die. It is only the word 'God' that has to die, and it is dead already since it has no real referent aside from subjective feeling. Any sort of immediacy in relationship to God is reduced to an inner feeling in the same way that any value statement is reduced to: "This is the way I feel. I wish you would feel this way, too." Thus if I say anything about religious reality, I am making an unjustified inference from a feeling that is real in itself but has no referent or content beyond itself. The linguistic analyst and his theological fellow travelers chop off the "inference" and leave us with our subjective feeling—now neither numinous nor momentous.

Psychologism is a habit of mind. It is the tendency to divide the reality that is given to us into two parts—one of which is an outer world into which we fit ourselves and the other of which is an inner psyche into which we fit the world. This is an understandable division. Much of our lives is lived in terms of it. But the wholeness that is possible for us as human beings can never be found by regarding the outer as a mere reflection of the inner, but only by overcoming the division itself. The real person—and by "person" I do not mean Jung's "persona," the mask, or social role—has to live with that inner brought into relation to the outer. If we have "vocation," a term that Jung also uses, it is because we are called, and that call cannot come to us only from within. Even if the call comes in mystic ecstasy or in a dream, we do not have the right to say that it is simply *in* us. We do not actually exist divided into "inner" and "outer" except for certain useful purposes. In reality we are a whole in every moment in streaming interaction with everybody and everything.

By robbing us of these simple contacts with what is not ourselves and the touchstones that emerge from them, psychologism robs life of its finest reality. This is a reality that we cannot sustain and maintain, to be sure, a reality that does not relieve us of the task of working with and on ourselves when we are brought back to ourselves. Nonetheless, the possibility is there of finding real life—of revealing the hidden human image—not by leaving our inwardness behind but by bringing it with us as a whole in our response to whatever comes. This is not a question of "inner" versus "outer." We need all our inwardness, for it is an integral part of our wholeness as persons. Our wholeness is not a state of being but a presence, an event, a happening that comes into being again and again in our contact and response.

At the end of a one-day seminar that I led, I suggested that the people present break up into small groups, one of which I joined as a participant-observer. In that small group there were two people, a woman and a man, who had the same complaint—that they continually observed themselves in all that they were doing and therefore never did anything freely, spontaneously, with their whole being. "My problem is that I am really a very good psychological analyst, and I know it," said the woman. "I bring it to all of my relations in life," she added, "and therefore I never feel anything that catches me up." She brought to my mind Virginia Woolf confessing with shame in her diary that she could never meet a friend without thinking, "How can I use her in my novels?" The man leading the small group asked her, "Is there any place where you do, in fact, come out of this?" "Yes," she answered, "if I go to a ballet, or if I get angry." Here at least—caught up by beauty or taken over by anger—she forgot herself and broke out of the vicious circle!

Even this hope seemed denied to the man in question. After my talk to the group as a whole, he had asked me, "Isn't the most important thing to discover your conflicts, your defensiveness, and work on that?" "Yes," I replied, "that is true. Yet you may never get beyond that." He had been with enough groups, he continued, to become aware that he was a defensive person. His problem, he realized, was that he did not hear things as they were said and respond to them spontaneously but heard them only in reference to his own feeling of being vulnerable. He wanted to get out of this by focusing on the fact that he was defensive. But this was equally self-preoccupation. The story he told our small group—of his one and only encounter, in which he got everyone so angry that they stripped him naked and threw him into the hall!—was told so matter-of-factly and impersonally that even this sharing could not break him out of the circle. He was wrapped up in his image of himself.

The corollary of psychologism is the emphasis upon "experience." Once a perfectly good word, "experience" has gotten turned inside out. You go abroad and find yourself in conflict again and again between looking at a beautiful scene and taking a picture of it. We are more interested in *possessing* the experience than in going out to meet the really unique moment that faces us. People now talk about sex experience, drug experience, and religious experience in exactly the same terms. They are all means of *having* an experience. Experience is now something inside you, not something that seizes and transforms you. It is an individual "trip" rather than a relationship into which you enter or an event that catches you up. This enables you to remain, in the most gripping of experiences, partly an observer—a "drip-dry tourist." If it is a "bad trip," you can always find someone to tell you how to get a better one. In other words, the emphasis on experience can reach the point where experience itself is empty of what it formerly was: going out from yourself to what is not yourself. Earlier, the experiencer was like the hero of a picaresque novel, a David Copperfield who set out into the world. Today the "experiencer" is like the reader of such a novel or the viewer of a TV movie. He stays home, and the experiences are injected into him like vaccine.

An article I read some years ago comparing the teachings of a Hasidic rabbi and Alan Watts' *The Joyous Cosmology* concluded by conceding that the rabbi was more serious about his mysticism. But he had spent years getting there, whereas we can attain the same thing just by taking a pill. So naturally it is all a cosmic joke for us. While the rabbi remains stuck at the level he reached, we can move along to higher levels by means of still another pill. Religion becomes like a good shot of whiskey or a good drug or any other means to "self-realization," to be judged or set aside in terms of whether it produces the desired effect. The drug cult, the whiskey cult, the TV cult, the movie cult, the sport cult, the sex cult, the sensory awareness cult, and the "basic encounter" cult are all so many means of planning "spontaneous" happenings, and the "religious" cult is often the same.

It was popular a few years ago to imagine that taking LSD produces a religious experience. To seek to "have" an experience is already to risk not having it; for the more we focus on it as a goal, the more we are in danger of removing it into ourselves, of psychologizing it. The word *psychologism* is in no sense an attack either on psychology or psychotherapy when these observe their proper limits. It is an attack on the tendency to make the reality of our relationship to what is not ourselves—persons and cats, sunsets and trees—into what is essentially *within* ourselves.

The very notion of *having* experience, whether it be psychedelic, mystical, sexual, travel, or adventure, robs us of what experience once meant—something that can catch us up, take us outside ourselves, and bring us into relationship with the surprising, the unique, the other. Secondly, it robs us of spontaneity; for one part of us will always be planning the experience, observing it as it is taking place, checking it out to see whether it is working. One may have a religious response—the response of the whole person in the situation—to anything: pain, sickness, death, suicide. But one does not have it automatically, and one does not have it as an "experience."

In one sense, human experience includes everything in a person's life, inner and outer, conscious and unconscious, waking reality, fantasy, or dream. In another, it may be limited to what is singled out from among the stream of happenings, that which has an impact and stands out for itself. When we say, "I had an experience," we mean just that: something surfaces from the general flux as an event in itself and does so precisely because it impinges on us in some way, whether through the feelings it arouses—pleasure, pain, joy, misery—or through the significance we attach to it, or through the awe or wonder that it evokes. Although we certainly are not consciously aware of all the experiences that happen to us, we can, nonetheless, say that experience is that which we become aware of.

But today, as we have seen, experience is often thought of as essentially an internal matter. If one speaks of drug experiences, "the Jimi Hendrix experience," sex or love experiences, or even religious experience, one means primarily the experience of being "turned on." "I saw you last night and got that old feeling." If the song concludes, "That old feeling is still in my heart," that is as it should be; for, essentially, it is the feeling *within* me that I am concerned with, not what is *between* me and you. The feeling may be so expansive that it seems to include us both, as in the song "Marie Elena": "A love like mine is great enough for two. To share this love is really all I ask of you." But a love that demands so little, and so much, is the love of one's own feelings that "Marie Elena" arouses and occasions, not a love *between* Marie Elena and me. If "altered states of consciousness" is substituted for love, the situation is in no way changed. My concern with the reality that I meet is at best incidental. Either it and the meeting with it are the mere occasions for my elevations and ecstasies or these altered states of consciousness are held to be the higher reality itself. Consciousness, and in particular "higher consciousness," has become for many the new, self-evident touchstone of reality.

A look at dreams may further illustrate our problem. Dreams are regarded by Freudians and Jungians alike as "within," the pure raw material of the unconscious. Yet if we look at dreams more closely, we shall see that this cannot possibly be the case. Researchers tell us that we "dream" all the time. But when I tell you that I had a dream last night, I am not referring to some activity that can be picked up through appropriate electrodes placed in my brain and connected with an encephalograph, but to a series of events that I remember precisely because their impact on me enabled me to lift them out of the general flow. In this sense, dreams are exactly the same as any other experience. We "have" the dream through remembering it and, perhaps in addition, writing it down and/or recounting it to others. But in that remembering, writing, and recounting, three other things are taking place. First, we cut the dream loose from the aura of less well-remembered "dream events" as well as from emotions and sensations that cling to it but cannot be communicated. By the same token, we give the dream a form, a *Gestalt*, that enables us to contemplate it as a whole in itself. Second, we transfer the dream from the peculiar logic of our sleeping world to the very different logic of our waking consciousness and, in so doing, shape and elaborate it. We also elaborate it through our own first thoughts and feelings about it *and*, equally importantly, through our anticipations of whom we might tell it to. If we tell it to our therapist, we are likely to find ourselves highlighting those aspects that fit his or her school of psychology, whether Freudian, Jungian, Adlerian, Gestalt, or whatever. Third, and most important of all, having set the dream over against us, thus having isolated, shaped, and elaborated and given it form as an independent opposite, we enter into dialogue with it. From now on, it becomes one of the realities that addresses us in the world, just as surely and as concretely as any so-called external happening.

From this illustration it should be clear that we cannot understand human experience either as merely external or internal or even as a sum of the two, with some part of each experience the one and some part the other. Experience in the truest sense is itself an event of the "between." It is our meeting with whatever accosts us in the situation in which we find ourselves, dragon, damsel, or dream. One of the things that makes it difficult to understand this, as we have said, is our habit of regarding experience as something that takes place inside ourselves. Another is the pseudo-objectification that arises from our identifying experience with experiential and experiential with science. The so-called empirical sciences do, indeed, have a foundation in our experience. Yet they become sciences precisely by abstracting from the concrete uniqueness of the experienced event and turning what is thus abstracted into data that can be set into relation to other data through placing them into categories of class, condition, cause, or field of operation and interaction.

If there are difficulties that attend any phenomenology of human experience, there are still greater difficulties that attend a phenomenology of religious experience. When William James wrote his great classic, *The Varieties of Religious Experience*, he presented with admirable openness a whole range of "religious experiences" from mysticism and drugs to saintliness and conversion. Though his conclusion was pragmatic ("Religion is real because it has real effects"), it was not yet subjective in the way that religious experience has since tended to become. Today a religious experience is less something that seizes one on one's way than it is an experience that one "has," often by willfully setting out to have it. This is so much the case that I am often inclined to jettison the term *religious experience* entirely in favor of *religious reality* or *religious event* or any other term that might help liberate us from the bondage of the new subjectivism.

Another, older problem in the phenomenology of religious experience arises from the tendency to regard religion as a special experience to be set alongside sensory experience, aesthetic experience, sexual experience, or the like. If we do that, we give up once and for all the claim that religion has to do with human wholeness in favor of seeing religion as one special sphere of life, perhaps that of mystic ecstasy, higher consciousness, fervent devotion, contemplation, trance, or even, as some would hold today, schizophrenia! Religion then becomes relegated to special times and places—Easter Sunday and Yom Kippur, the church or synagogue. As the "upper story" of our lives, it then usually has less claim on our total response than an absorbing piece of theater or symphony orchestra concert, or even a very good dinner or an engrossing game of football. It becomes, indeed, with all its prescribed creeds and rituals, downright tedious and boring.

On the other hand, if we seek to make religion equal to the sum total of human experience, we have either robbed religion of its reality entirely or we have reduced it to John Dewey's common faith, a vague idealism superimposed upon experience as the "religious" dimension of everyday life. For the whole to be greater than the sum of its parts, that whole must have a wholeness that is integral to it. It must come together into a whole the way the various notes of a composition come together, when performed, to become a piano concerto or a string quartet. If religion is a way that we walk, then the whole of human life is included in it. Yet that life comes to wholeness not addictively or by abstraction but only in the upsurging of events in which all the moments of the past are caught up into the present and given new reality by it. Such an event could be an hour of prayer at a time of great need—when we are facing death or are facing the death of loved ones. Or it could be a moment of breathtaking awe before a waterfall or in the midst of a raging storm at sea. Or it could be an action in which we gather together all the past meanings of our life in one great hour of devotion or sacrifice. In all cases, it is an event in which we attain selflessness not by giving up the self, as the ascetics suggest that we do, but by the totality of our response. In such a totality we are taken out of ourselves, called out by something to which we respond so fully and spontaneously that our self is neither our aim nor our concern but only the self-understood and self-evident ground of our responding.

Experience is, in one sense, itself a product of meeting. It is also the springboard and base for future meetings. We go out from our present experience to meet the new that befalls us. We bring our experience with us into what we meet. We meet that experience itself in our reflections on it and our concern with it—as in holding in our mind a dream or a personal exchange that has touched our heart, not analyzing it but letting it speak to us and letting ourselves answer this address. *Religion* is often treated as being the external forms that seem to the observer to make up religion—ritual, organization, creed—and experience is often seen as the subjective aspect of our existence—our feelings, our consciousness, or even our unique participation in an event common to ourselves and others.

The psyche as the touchstone of reality, psychologism, and the cult of experience are all aspects of what Martin Buber called the psychologizing of the world. By the psychologizing of the world Buber meant that inclusion of the world in the soul that goes so far that the essential basic relation from which our life receives its meaning is damaged: the facing of I and world in which the real happens. If we regard more deeply what we call psychic phenomena, we find that all of them, and their connections, have arisen dynamically only out of the relationship between the I and the other and are comprehensible only through this relationship. In so far as the soul is comprehended exclusively as I, however, it is comprehended in amputation, in abstraction, not in its *whole* existence. "Psychologizing of the world" thus means an attempt of the soul to completely detach itself from its basic character of relationship.[3]

The essence of genuine dialogue lies in the fact that "each of the participants really has in mind the other or others in their present and particular being and turns to them with the intention of establishing a living mutual relation between himself and them." The basic movement of the life of "monologue," in contrast, is not turning away from the other but "reflexion" (*Rückbiegung*) in the physiological origin of the term—bending back on oneself. "Reflexion" is not egotism but the withdrawal from accepting the other person in his particularity in favor of letting him exist *only as one's own experience*, only as a part of oneself. Through this withdrawal "the essence of all reality begins to disintegrate." The erotic is almost throughout only differentiated self-enjoyment, Buber declared, and what is elementally perceived is what takes place in one's own soul. Even the attempts at the spiritual and religious life are soaked through with the same poison—the poison of the human spirit bent back upon itself and deluding itself that spirit occurs in man.[4]

The therapist deals with the patient as an individual yet his sickness is a sickness of the "between."

The sicknesses of the soul are sicknesses of relationship. They can only be treated completely if I transcend the realm of the patient and add to it the world as well. If the doctor possessed superhuman power, he would have to try to heal the relationship itself, to heal in the "between."[5]

Thus in psychotherapy itself Buber was aware of the need to burst the bounds of psychologism, which refers all events and meaning back to the psyche, and to reach the ground of "healing through meeting"—a healing *in* and *of* the "between."

Chapter 11

INTERPRETATIONS OF MYTH:
MARTIN BUBER, MIRCEA ELIADE,
T.S. ELIOT, JOSEPH CAMPBELL

MYTH, AT FIRST GLANCE, is not at all contemporary, but the cult of myth is thoroughly contemporary and is first cousin to psychologism and the cult of experience in its tendency to convert myth not only into universal gnosis but also into a reality that is to be found *within* our psyches, rather than, as with archaic human beings, in community, nature, and the world. Although the subject of myth is far more complex and many-sided than that of experience, for myth too as for experience the main choice that we are presented with today is between a psychological approach and a dialogical one. It is in plumbing that choice that we shall best understand the issue of myth that arises in the meeting between religion and psychology. To understand this choice, however, and the contemporary psychologizing and universalizing of myth we must first explore briefly the subject of myth in itself.

The most concrete and dramatic form of the religious symbol is the myth. Or perhaps it would be more accurate to say that one of the first

144

abstractions from myth is the symbol. C.G. Jung and Ananda K. Coom-araswamy tend to see the myth as an embodiment in different forms and cultures of a perennial reality, the psychological process whereby integration of the personality is achieved and the divine Self realized within the personal unconscious or the spiritual process whereby the one becomes the many and the many returns unto the one. Ernst Cassirer's understanding of myth, in contrast, leaves room for the concrete, particular events and the dialogue with it; and his distinction between *discursive* and *mythical thinking* offers us an important insight into the place of myth in the dialogue of touchstones that constitutes much of religious tradition.

Discursive thinking denotes what has already been noticed. It classifies into groups and synthesizes parts into a whole. It does not contemplate a particular case but instead gives it a fixed intellectual meaning and definite character by linking it with other cases into a general framework of knowledge. The particular is never important in itself but only in terms of its relation to this framework. An even, grey light illumines the whole series of linked happenings. Mythical thinking, in contrast, is not concerned with relating data but with a sudden intuition, an immediate experience in which it comes to rest. It is like a strong white light that focuses on a single event in such a way that everything else is left in darkness. "The immediate content . . . so fills his consciousness that nothing else can exist beside and apart from it." This content "is not merely viewed and contemplated, but overcomes a man in sheer immediacy."[1] For all this, there is a telltale residue of German philosophical idealism in Cassirer that leads him to see the historical fact as meaningful only as a member of a course of events or a teleological nexus and not in its particularity and uniqueness, as one would suppose from the rest of his thought on myth.

Henri Frankfort's treatment of myth builds on that of Cassirer but is more dialogical than is Cassirer's. Making use of Buber's distinction between the I-Thou and I-It relations, in itself quite close to Cassirer's contrast between mythical and discursive thinking, Frankfort identifies myth with the dynamically reciprocal I-Thou relationship in which every faculty of the human being is involved. He recognizes, moreover, the unique and unpredictable character of the Thou—"a presence known only insofar as it reveals itself."

"Thou" is not contemplated with intellectual detachment; it is experienced as life confronting life. . . . The whole man confronts a living "Thou" in nature; and the whole man—emotional and imaginative as well as intellectual—gives expression to the experience.

Frankfort recognizes that myth arises not only in connection with humanity's relation to nature, the cosmos, and the change of season, but also in our relation to a transcendent God in the course of history. But when he speaks of the will of God, the chosen people, and the Kingdom of God as "myths," he tends to remove from history the concreteness that is of its very essence.

The doctrine of a single, unconditioned, transcendent God . . . postulated a metaphysical significance for history and for man's actions. . . . In transcending the Near Eastern myths of immanent godhead, they [the Hebrews] created . . . the new myth of the will of God. It remained for the Greeks, with their peculiar *intellectual* courage, to discover a form of speculative thought in which myth was entirely overcome.[2]

It appears that, even for Frankfort, myth is primarily important as a form of thought rather than as an embodiment of concrete events.

We must turn to Martin Buber for a thoroughly dialogical and consistently concrete understanding of myth. Although in his early thinking Buber also saw myth as a particular manifestation of a universal mystical reality, by 1907 he already distinguished between the *pure myth* in which there is variety without differentiation and the *legend* in which the subject is divided and God and the hero or saint stand opposed to one another as I and Thou. In 1921 Buber elaborated this concept into a distinction between myth, saga, and legend. *Myth* is the expression of a world in which the divine and the human live next to and in one another; *saga* is the expression of a world in which they are not longer intertwined and man already begins to sense with a shudder what is over against him; *legend* expresses a world in which the separation is completed, but now a dialogue and interchange takes place from sphere to sphere and it is of this that the myth tells. True history must include just that concreteness and uniqueness that Cassirer attributes to mythical thinking; for real history contains at its core the memory of the concrete and particular meeting between I and Thou. "I hold myth to be indispensable," writes Buber, "but I do not hold it to be central. . . . Myth must verify itself in man and not man in myth. What is wrong is not the mythicization of reality that brings the inexpressible to speech, but the gnosticizing of myth that tears it out of the ground of history and biography in which it took root." Buber refuses the alternatives of factual history or universal and timeless myth and proclaims the history that gives rise to myth, the myth that remembers history:

> What is preserved for us here is to be regarded not as the "historization" of a myth or a cult drama, nor is it to be explained as the transposition of something originally beyond time into historical time: a great history-faith does not come into the world through interpretation of the extra-historical as historical, but by receiving an occurrence experienced as a "wonder," that is as an event which cannot be grasped except as an act of God.[3]

The *saga* is the direct and unique expression of the reporter's knowledge of an event. Rather, this knowledge is itself a legendary one, representing (through the organic work of mythicizing memory) the believed-in action of God in dialogue with a person or people. It is not fantasy that is active here but memory—that believing memory of the souls and generations of early times that arises without arbitrary action from the impulse of an extra-ordinary event. Even the myth that seems most fantastic of all is created around the kernel of the organically shaping memory.

> Here history cannot be dissevered from the historical wonder; but the experience which has been transmitted to us, the experience of event as wonder, is itself great history and must be understood out of the element of history. . . . Here, unlike the concept familiar in the science of religion, myth is nothing other than the report by ardent enthusiasts of that which has befallen them.[4]

This same combination of history, event, and wonder recurs in Buber's mature retelling of Hasidic tales in which he reconstructed the pure event in the form of the legendary anecdote.

> They are called anecdotes because each of them communicates an event complete in itself, and legendary because at the base of them lies the

stammering of inspired witnesses who witnessed to what befell them, to what they comprehended as well as to what was incomprehensible to them; for the legitimately inspired has an honest memory that can nonetheless outstrip all imagination.[5]

This approach to events does not dismiss the comparative aspects of the history of religion, but leaves room for uniqueness. "Irrespective of the importance of the typological view of phenomena in the history of the spirit, the latter, just because it is history, also contains the atypical, the unique in the most precise sense." This concern with uniqueness is a natural corollary of the bond between the Absolute and the concrete, the particular. From this standpoint, legend, myth, and tale point us back to the concrete, unique event from which they took their rise. The mythical element may also, of course, become so strong that the kernel of historical memory tends to be obscured. Then, where event and memory cease to rule, myth replaces them by a timeless image.

Some myths contain within themselves the nexus of a historical event experienced by a group or by an individual; many have lost their historical character and contain only the symbolic expression of a universal experience of man. Even in the latter case, countless concrete meetings of I and Thou have attained symbolic expression in the relatively abstract form. The universality and profundity of these myths lie in the fact that they are products of actual human experience and tell us something about the structure of human reality that nothing else can. The myth of the Garden of Eden is universal, not as a timeless truth arising from somewhere beyond concrete human existence, but rather as something that happens anew to every human being.

"The point of mythology," writes Harry M. Buck in an article on the subject, "is that man does not act objectively toward the world; he encounters it and participates in it. Myth is not merely a story told, but a reality lived, a sanction for a way of life and a pattern for worship." The type of myth that Buck has in mind is what we have called universal—one in which the universality grows out of the existential:

> The myth is not meaningful or true because it contains elements of history, but because it places certain events—whether or not items of chronological history—into a scheme which possesses an existential character. That scheme is an expression of man's view of himself.[6]

The first criterion for a religious myth, according to Buck, is its involvement with metahistorical time. In this he follows Mircea Eliade, who succeeded his and my teacher Joachim Wach to the chair of History of Religion at the University of Chicago. Like Eliade, Buck sees the myth as paradigmatic, "an expression of a classical archetype and itself the archetype for future thought and action." Though this emphasis on archetypes has a Jungian slant that Eliade shares, for Eliade and Buck the importance of true myth is that it points us back to the primordial time that Eliade calls *in illo tempore*. From this perspective "the Passover is not a true myth, because it does have a point of origin in historical time and not *in illo tempore*; but it fulfills many of the same functions as a myth." The Passover, indeed, is what Buber calls a *saga*, the product of the organically shaping memory that is still faithful to a kernel of historical event.

In *Cosmos and History* Mircea Eliade sets in opposition the archetypal, cyclical approach to time of archaic man, which in the last analysis nullifies history and with it any uniqueness of event, with the historical, linear approach of modern man that he sees as abandoning us in the end to the terror of history. Archaic humanity defended itself with all the weapons at its disposal against that very novelty and irreversibility that make up the essence of historical time. The archaic, or "primitive," human being, like the mystic and the religious person in general, lives in a continual present in which he relives and repeats the gestures of another and, through this repetition, lives always in an atemporal present:

> What is of chief importance to us in these archaic systems is the abolition of concrete time, and hence their antihistorical intent. This refusal to preserve the memory of the past, even of the immediate past, seems to us to betoken . . . archaic man's refusal to accept himself as a historical being, . . . the will to devaluate time.[7]

In biblical Judaism, and hence in Judaism, Christianity, and Islam, there is affirmed for the first time "the idea that historical events have a value in themselves, insofar as they are determined by the will of God":

> Without finally renouncing the traditional concept of archetypes and repetitions, Israel attempts to "save" historical events by regarding them

as active presences of Yahweh. . . . History no longer appears as a cycle that repeats itself *ad infinitum*, as the primitive peoples represented it. . . . Directly ordered by the will of Yahweh, history appears as a series of theophanies, negative or positive, each of which has its intrinsic value.[8]

Having set forth this contrast, Eliade advances numerous arguments against the historical view of time and in favor of the antihistorical, archaic view, which is also his own: The great majority of Jews and Christians have not accepted the historical view anyway; even the élite who accepted it looked forward to its abrogation in a Messianic age that places *illud tempore* at the end of time instead of the beginning; in the myth of the eternal return even history is taken up into archetypal time; even the three great history religions—the Iranian, Judaic, and Christian—"affirm that history will finally cease *in illo tempore*," thus reviving the ancient doctrine of the periodic regeneration of history; Marxism implies the overcoming of history in the "true" history that follows it, whereas various doctrines of historical immanentism, such as Nietzsche's and Heidegger's, have no relief to offer in the face of the terror of history. Eliade also contrasts the doctrines of progress and historical linearism of the modern world with the recrudescence of cyclical views of time in Spengler, Toynbee, and Sorokin and the longing for the return to the "golden age" in Joyce and T.S. Eliot.

Eliade, to be sure, sees Christianity as transcending, once for all, the old themes of eternal repetition and other archaic approaches to time by revealing the importance of the religious experience of faith, the value of the human personality, and the uniqueness of the fact of the Incarnation. Nonetheless, and by the same token, he sees Christianity as the religion of "fallen man"; for history and progress are both, in his view, a fall, "both implying the final abandonment of the paradise of archetypes and repetition." Lest we think this is simply a detached academic exposition, we must note Eliade's judgment on modern history. Though historical man might reproach archaic man with having sacrificed creativity through remaining imprisoned within the mythical horizon of archetypes and repetition, archaic man (speaking through Eliade) sees modern man as without defenses against the terror of history and, so far from being able to *make* history, as totally compelled and controlled by it:

For history either makes itself . . . or it tends to be made by an increasingly smaller number of men who not only prohibit the mass of their contemporaries from directly or indirectly intervening in the history they are making . . . , but in addition have at their disposal means sufficient to force each individual to endure, for his own part, the consequences of this history, that is, to live immediately and continuously in dread of history. Modern man's boasted freedom to make history is illusory for nearly the whole of the human race.[9]

In contrast to this sorry fate of modern "historical" man, archaic man "can be proud of his mode of existence which allows him to be free and to create. He is free to be no longer what he was, free to annul his own history through periodic abolition of time and collective regeneration." Christianity stands somewhere in between, because its new category of faith, which sees all things possible to man as well as God, emancipates man from any kind of natural "law" and constitutes the only new formula for man's collaboration with the creation since the traditional horizon of archetype and repetition was transcended.

It is only by presupposing the existence of God that he conquers, on the one hand, freedom (which grants him autonomy) in a universe governed by laws or, in other words, the "inauguration" of a mode of being that is new and unique in the universe and, on the other hand, the certainty that historical tragedies have a transhistorical meaning, even if that meaning is not always visible for humanity in its present condition. Any other situation of modern man leads, in the end, to despair. It is a despair provoked not by his own human existentiality, but by his presence in a historical universe in which almost the whole of mankind lives prey to a continual terror (even if not always conscious of it).[10]

In the light of this situation, Christianity as the "religion of the 'fallen man,' " is, at most, the best of a very bad bargain!

Because of Eliade's eminence, because of his growing influence, because of the vast array of facts from the historical and archaic religions that he marshalls in support of his point of view, and because, on the face of it, his point of view seems the opposite of the approach that I am here taking toward history and myth, I must make some response to the thesis that he has so compellingly set forth.

One must distinguish, to begin with, between the validity of Eliade's thesis as the description of many archaic and not-so-archaic religious doctrines and as the overall point of view to which he wishes to elevate it. As he himself recognizes, what is in question here is a matter of interpretation, i.e., each set of facts may be interpreted from the standpoint of the other:

> The crucial difference between the man of the archaic civilizations and modern, historical man lies in the increasing value the latter gives to historical events, that is, to the "novelties" that, for traditional man, represented either meaningless conjunctures or infractions of norms (hence "faults," "sins," and so on) and that, as such, required to be expelled (abolished) periodically. The man who adopts the historical viewpoint would be justified in regarding the traditional conception of archetypes and repetition as an aberrant reidentification of history (that is, of "freedom" and "novelty") with nature (in which everything repeats itself). For, as modern man can observe, archetypes themselves constitute a "history" insofar as they are made up of gestures, acts, and decrees that, although supposed to have been manifested *in illo tempore*, were nevertheless manifested, that is, came to birth in time, "took place," like any other historical event.[11]

This recognition that archetypes are themselves born of historical events in no way invalidates those religions and myths that do rest upon an archetypal point of view in which all history is removed to sacred space and sacred time. But it does invalidate any general claim that *all* religious myth must be of this nature, and it supports what we have earlier observed concerning the historical and/or existential kernel even of universal myths.

The second response that we can make is that Eliade nowhere discusses faith as existential trust but sees it basically as a worldview that posits the existence of God and deduces from this the transhistorical meaning of history. Coupled with this is the fact that he regards historical and linear time only from the "apocalyptic" standpoint and not at all from the "prophetic":

> Since the days of Isaiah, a series of military defeats and political collapses had been anxiously awaited as an ineluctable syndrome of the Messianic *illud tempus* that was to regenerate the world.[12]

Actually, the Hebrew prophets sought God to "know" Him, to be in direct contact with Him, and not in order to hear future things. Even their predictions of the future were for the sake of the present, that the people might turn again to the way of God. They are distinguished from the apocalyptic ones, as from the seers and diviners of other religions, by the fact that they did not wish to peep into an already certain and immutable future but were concerned only with the full grasping of the present, both actual and potential. Their prophecy was altogether bound up with the situation of the historical hour and with God's direct speaking in it. They recognized the importance of man's decision in determining the future and therefore rejected any attempts to treat the future as if it were simply a fixed past that had not yet unfolded. Their attitude corresponds to the basic biblical view that man is set in real freedom in order that he may enter the dialogue with God and through this dialogue take part in the redemption of the world. The time of the true prophet is not *illud tempore* but the experienced hour and its possibility. That of the apocalyptic writer is an inevitable future in which history is overcome. The prophetic approach to history "promises a consummation of creation," the apocalyptic "its abrogation and supersession by another world completely different in nature."[13]

Eliade's understanding of biblical Judaism and Christianity is essentially apocalyptic, not prophetic, which is not surprising considering that his own view of the "terror of history" is essentially an apocalyptic one. Furthermore, though he recognizes a difference between the archaic and antihistorical religions and the historical ones, in the end he takes the antihistorical as the normative approach to all religions. He offers us as the objective conclusions of the historian of religion what is, in fact, the passionate choice of a "live forced option," in William James' phrase. Nowhere is this clearer than in his discussion of "the East," by which he apparently means Hinduism and early Buddhism:

The East unanimously rejects the idea of the ontological irreducibility of the existent, even though it too sets out from a sort of "existentialism" (i.e., from acknowledging suffering as the situation of any possible cosmic condition). Only, the East does not accept the destiny of the human being as final and irreducible. Oriental techniques attempt above all to annul or transcend the human condition. In this respect, it is justifiable to speak not only of freedom (in the positive sense) or deliverance (in the negative sense) but actually of creation; for what is involved is creating a new man and creating him on a suprahuman plane, a man-god, such as the imagination of historical man has never dreamed it possible to create.[14]

If we recognize this passionate statement for what it is—a touchstone of reality representative of Eliade's own view—and not as the necessary conclusion of the phenomenological study of the history of religions, we can make it a part of our own dialogue with the touchstones of others. Then, too, we can avoid the equal and opposite error of imposing a biblical view of history on non-history religions. In the face of this, what general statements can we make about myths? First, the one we have already made—that some myths do, in fact, have a historical kernel and other, universal ones, an existential kernel, one that is repeated over and over in the history of the human race. Second, that there are, indeed, myths that have come loose from both the historical and the existential kernels that gave rise to them. This latter type of myth, in its regular recurrence, gives rise to the perennial philosophies and theories of archetypes. But even here, "myth must verify itself in man and not in myth." The archetypes too have a human base and arise out of the loam of earthly, human existence. This in no way denies the archetypes, but it roots them in the lived concrete rather than in some Platonic universal or some mystical sphere floating above time and history. In this sense, we may echo Buber's words: "What is wrong is not the mythicization of reality which brings the inexpressible to speech, but the gnosticizing of myth which tears it out of the ground of history and biography in which it took root." What is inexpressible is that betweenness that lies at the heart of the life of dialogue. Myth is the pure form of the meeting. It points us back to the immediacy as no concepts could.

What we have said of legend and myth can also shed light on the relation between religion and literature. Some of the world's great literature, such as the Book of Genesis and the tragedies of Sophocles, is built upon myth. But even when it is not, literature in its very particularity is often far closer to religious reality than are the dogmas of theology or the abstractions of metaphysics. Literature retains much of the concreteness of persons and their interrelationships while at the same time enabling us to enter into a sufficiently close relationship with these persons so that they can speak to us as bearers of the human—as exemplifications of what it does and can mean to be a human being. It is for this reason that I claim in my book *To Deny Our Nothingness* that literature is the real homeland of the human image.

This does not mean a representational image, of course. Rather it means the characters of literature seen in the interactions through which they make manifest their basic life attitudes, their life-stances, and through which they acquire their own touchstones of reality—and become touchstones of reality for us, the readers.

This is exactly the opposite of that approach to religion and literature that seeks to extract religious symbols from the context of the literature and interpret them as if the literature were simply an allegory waiting for us to puzzle out its hidden meanings. If we approach literature looking for illustrations of a given philosophy or theology, we destroy the concreteness of our encounter with the literature and make it subservient to already fixed patterns of thought. To this attempt at finding meaning in symbols outside of the dynamic and dramatic event in which the symbol occurs I have given the name *symbolmongering*. When Queequeg's coffin-lifebuoy surfaces at the end of Melville's *Moby Dick*, it can be easily taken as a resurrection symbol, just as in Dostoevsky's novel *Crime and Punishment* there is a whole symbolism of Lazarus risen from the dead. Yet we dare not go from the symbol to the meaning of the novel unless that symbol has become dramatically real in the novel itself, as it has not in either book.

What is true of the universalizing of symbols is also true of the universalizing of myth. Both lie at the heart of the *mismeeting* between literature and religion. The collector's urge of modern man leads him to seek a universal myth in the myths of all peoples, whether it be that of the flood, of creation, or of the dragon and the dragon-slayer. These myths were the human being's first way of thinking—dramatic events rather than discursive reasoning. We try instead to derive a secondary meaning by identifying resemblances among myths. We extract a perennial myth and feel we are very close to the heart of reality when in fact we are freezing on the doorstep! Seldom if ever does a myth catch us up, as it did ancient man, so that for that moment all that is real and important is the heightened reality of the mythic event. Many thinkers today tend to see particular literary works as endlessly reproducing universal themes. In so doing they lose the very heart of religion, literature, and myth. They find the meaning of literature in the static symbol or concept and not in the concrete unique event and its dramatic, dynamic unfolding in time.

An excellent example of the way in which our contemporaries use myth is T.S. Eliot's famous poem *The Waste Land*. The central theme of *The Waste Land* is the absence of water, the sterility of the land. Building on the ancient associations of water and life, Eliot creates a modern myth in which fertility cults, the hanged and drowned gods of ancient religions, and the Tarot cards all work together to establish a universal statement with particular application to the inauthenticity of modern man. In this way, Eliot reenergizes the ancient myths and at the same time gives a depth dimension of his statement about the modern waste land.

The waste land is the land on which the curse has come, as we are told from the ancient Grail stories in which the court of the Fisher King is hidden from the view of mankind when the virgins of the shrine are raped. The cause of the curse, then, is violation, the rape that produces sterility. In the fertility cults, the relationship between human sex and the fertility of nature was basic. But what Eliot is talking about here is the sterility of modern life; this sterility grows out of the modern violation of sex, the rape of lust without love.

In "Death by Water," the next to the last section of *The Waste Land*, the way to a new life is indicated through the death of the self, the death of lust and craving that overcomes sterility and leads to a rebirth in spirit. This coming to life is magnificently portrayed in the final section, "What the Thunder Said," in which the thunder comes at last bringing rain. The garden of Gethsemane and the Crucifixion are coupled with the death of the fertility god to create a common expectation of resurrection. The breakdown of our civilization is coupled with the coming of a new theophany. The meaning of this breakthrough from sterile into fertile existence is couched in Sanskrit terms—*datta, dayadhvam, damyata*: give, sympathize, control. Only sympathy, Eliot implies, can begin to overcome the isolation of modern man. And with it control, discipline, direction, bringing oneself into the focus of a single intent.

The force of this poetic myth is the suggestion of its universality. Yet if we look at it more carefully, we see that it is not, in fact, universal. Not only is it Eliot's own personal synthesis, rather than the myth of a people, but also it is a myth of and for modern man, a sophisticated mosaic with eight pages of footnotes in five languages. The assent that it claims is not that of immediate experience and response, but of the interrelationships of meaning suggested by multifarious allusions and ironic contrasts. Hence, it is the exact opposite of what myth has always been to those among whom it has arisen—an immediate, dramatic presentation of a unique event. It belongs, rather, to that modern approach that substitutes the secondary meaning derived from the similarity of myths in different times and places for the direct meaning of the myth taken by itself that was available to ancient man. This approach asks us to accept a rich sense of everything having significant relation to everything else in place of any immediate insight into any particular event or reality. The modern myth that is created in this way is a confession of the absence of meaning: In the end, it betrays its own nihilism.

The central paradox in Eliot's waste-land myth is that the myth itself, the evocation of history and tradition, and the depiction of modern civilization all depend for their force on a sense of community, of common destiny and common suffering. Yet the solution offered is one that leads the individual off to his own private purgation, to set his own lands in order, leaving the universal statement with only a negative meaning. In "What the Thunder Said," the breaking through of rain seems a primeval, universal event, just as all the previous sections have seemed. Yet at the end of the poem, no rain has fallen, the plain is still arid, the waste land is as sterile as before, and only the "I" of the story has experienced any transformation. There has been no general rebirth, only an individual one. We are still in the waste-land world. I can seek some meaningful life for myself, but our civilization itself is decadent and crumbling.

The same thing can be said of Jung's use of myth. The myths that he evokes are communal myths. Yet the uses he puts these myths to in his psychology are all individual ones, connected with the individuation, or integration, of the isolated individual, who rediscovers the myth in the archetypal depths of the collective unconscious via the route of the personal unconscious. Among Jung's disciples, many like Erich Neumann and Karl Kerényi have dealt with myths and others, like Marie

Louise von Franz, with their first or second cousin, the fairy tale. But it is Joseph Campbell who has given us the richest understanding of folklore and myth the world over and their relevance for contemporary man. Through his television interviews with Bill Moyers, Joseph Campbell has achieved posthumous fame, and his books are now widely read throughout America.

Joseph Campbell is a great comparative mythologist, perhaps the very greatest. Campbell uses myth not only to see metaphysics in terms of psychology but also, as he explicitly points out, psychology in terms of metaphysics. ("The unconscious=the metaphysical realm.") Nonetheless, the total effect is that of the psychologizing of myth if we use "psychologizing" in the broader sense of finding myth in the depths of the soul rather than in the reality of communal life where Campbell himself recognizes that it originated. In *The Hero with a Thousand Faces* he several times suggests an equation of myth with psychology even in the narrower sense:

> The doctor is the modern master of the mythological realm, the knower of all the secret ways and words of potency. His role is precisely that of the Wise Old Man of the myths and fairy tales whose words assist the hero through the trials and terrors of the weird adventure.[15]
>
> In the office of the modern psychoanalyst, the stages of the hero-adventure come to light again in the dreams and hallucinations of the patient. Depth beyond depth of self-ignorance is fathomed, with the analyst in the role of the helper, the initiatory priest. And always after the first thrills of getting under way, the adventure develops into a journey of darkness, horror, disgust, and phantasmagoric fears.[16]

Campbell by no means equates dream and myth. On the contrary, dreams are still marred by the eccentricity of the individual whereas myths carry the stamp of the universal and the general:

> Dream is the personalized myth, myth the depersonalized dream; both myth and dream are symbolic in the same general way of the dynamics of the psyche. But in the dream the forms are quirked by the peculiar troubles of the dreamer, whereas in myth the problems and solutions shown are directly valid for all mankind.[17]

It soon becomes clear, indeed, that Campbell's psychologizing of myth is primarily not in Freud's sense but that of Jung's, namely not a reduction of the myth to instinctual drives but a location of both meaning and "the spiritual" in the unconscious. Myths "link the unconscious to the fields of practical action, not irrationally, in the manner of a neurotic projection, but in such fashion as to permit a mature and sobering, practical comprehension of the fact-world to play back, as a stern control, into the realms of infantile wish and fear." Mythological figures are not only symptoms of the unconscious "but also controlled and intended statements of certain spiritual principles, which have remained as constant throughout the course of the human history as the form and nervous structure of the human physique itself." The meaning of the biblical image of the Fall, to Campbell, is nothing other than the lapse of superconsciousness into the state of unconsciousness.[18]

There can be no doubt that for Campbell, as for Jung and for James Hillman, the world is, in John Keats' phrase, "a vale of soul-making." God "is but a convenient means to wake the sleeping princess, the soul." "Wherever the hero may wander, whatever he may do, he is ever in the presence of his own essence." "The modern hero-deed must be that of questing to bring to light again the lost Atlantis of the co-ordinated soul."[19]

Campbell, to be sure, identifies his psychologizing of myth with the ancient Hindu teaching of *tat twam asi*—"That art Thou." The way of exile brings the hero to the Self in all. Questions of selfishness and altruism disappear in the hero's reborn identity with the whole meaning of the universe. Both the hero and the world are of one essence so the hero "is free to wander as that essence in the world. . . . There is no separateness." Yet this seeming universality, as Campbell himself recognizes, is the only possibility left to the modern hero who is cut off from the group, who does not know toward what he is propelled, and who experiences the cut in the lines of communication between the conscious and the unconscious zones of the human psyche.[20]

In a later part of the book Campbell points to the resemblance of the ancient mythological doctrine of the dynamics of the psyche to the teachings of the modern Freudian school, with its life-wish and death-wish. Here, however, he makes an important distinction between the aims of the traditional and modern teachings that brings the "hero journey" into line with Hindu and Buddhist teaching:

> Psychoanalysis is a technique to cure excessively suffering individuals of the unconsciously misdirected desires and hostilities that weave around them their private webs of unreal terrors and ambivalent attractions; the patient released from these finds himself able to participate with comparative satisfaction in the more realistic fears, hostilities, erotic and religious practices, business enterprises, wars, pastimes, and household tasks offered to him by his particular culture. But for the one who has deliberately undertaken the difficult and dangerous journey beyond the village compound, these interests, too, are to be regarded as based on error. Therefore the aim of the religious teaching is not to cure the individual back again to the general delusion, but to detach him from delusion altogether; and this not by readjusting the desire (*eros*) and hostility (*thanatos*)—for that would only originate a new context of delusion—but by *extinguishing* the impulses to the very root . . .[21]

The goal of myth, according to Campbell, is to dispel life ignorance (the Hindu *maya*) by effecting a reconciliation of individual consciousness and universal will. This in turn is done "through a realization of the true relationship of the passing phenomena of time to the imperishable life that lives and dies in all." The hero dies to his personal ego and arises again established in the Self (a term that Campbell sometimes seems to use in the Hindu sense of the term as identical with Brahman and sometimes in Jung's sense of individuation). The hero does not fear the destruction of permanence by change but rather permits the moment to come to pass. He does this through giving up the particular and the unique in favor of the general and the universal.[22]

Thus Campbell puts forward that substitution of the universal and perennial for the unique that we have already pointed to as the very heart of the cult of myth of our age:

> Looking back at what had promised to be our own unique, unpredictable, and dangerous adventure, all we find in the end is such a series of standard metamorphoses as men and women have undergone in every quarter of the world, in all recorded centuries, and under ever odd disguise of civilization.[23]

Campbell sets up a dichotomy between outer fact and inner psychological truth. The exodus from Egypt of which the Hebrew Bible tells and the Resurrection of Christ that is reported in the New Testament are now in question as historical facts. Yet they can be saved for us if we understand them "as merely imagined episodes projected onto history." "Such universally cherished figures of the mythic imagination must represent facts of the mind." Thus the inner/outer split that we have already seen as characteristic of psychologism is carried through by Campbell into the psychologization of myth. The true meaning of the myth of the Fall is that our knowledge of good and evil has "pitched us away from our own center" and from that eternal life that is already ours "since the enclosed garden [of Eden] is within us." History, event, and the unique are all destroyed in favor of the internal universal: "Nor does it matter from the standpoint of a comparative study of symbolic forms whether Christ or the Buddha ever actually lived and performed the miracles associated with their teachings."[24]

Another even more startling implication of Campbell's psychologizing of myth is that "good and evil" are relegated to the merely external whereas "eternal life," in true Nietzschean fashion, is "beyond good and evil"! This Nietzschean note becomes explicit in Campbell's book *The Power of Myth*. In Nietzsche's *Thus Spake Zarathustra*, Zarathustra contrasts the camel of "Thou shalt" with the lion of "I will." Campbell, in conversation with Bill Moyers, states that we must return to the Eden before the Fall so that the child learns to shed every "Thou shalt" that "inhibits his self-fulfillment":

> For the camel, the "thou shalt" is a must, a civilizing force. It converts the human animal into a civilized human being. But the period of youth is the period of self-discovery and transformation into a lion. The rules are now to be used at will for life, not submitted to as compelling "thou shalts."[25]

We shall not be mistaken if we discern here an alarming relativism and amoralism that jettisons all social and even interhuman concern. (We cannot make the world a better place, says Campbell. We must leave as it is.) Jesus says that we should love our enemies for they too are children of God on whom the rain falls as it does on us. The Hasidic master Rabbi Yehiel Mikhal of Zlotchov in a tale that Buber gives the title "Love for Enemies" adjured his sons to pray for their enemies that all may be well with them because "more than all prayers, this is, indeed, the service of God."[26] Joseph Campbell, in quintessential psychologism, said to Bill Moyers, "Love thine enemies because they are the instruments of your destiny."[27]

Like Jung, Campbell proclaims the new religion of pure psychic immanence in which even an historical event of the magnitude of the Holocaust can be reduced to a psychological problem:

> The ultimate divine mystery is there [in the Orient] found immanent within each. It is not "out there" somewhere. It is within you. And no one has ever been cut off. The only difficulty is, however, that some folk simply don't know how to look within. The fault is no one's, if not one's own. Nor is the problem one of an original Fall of the "first man," many thousand years ago, and of exile and atonement. The problem is psychological. And it *can* be solved.[28]

Campbell's enigmatic saying "Follow your bliss" became a catchword throughout America as a result of his television interviews with Bill Moyers. It has little resemblance to that Hindu *ananda* from which it is taken; for that, along with *sat* (being) and *chit* (knowledge), is a characterization of the non-dual Absolute Brahman and not of any individual self. "If you follow your bliss," writes Campbell, "you put yourself on a kind of track that has been there all the while, waiting for you, and the life that you ought to be living is the one you are living. Wherever you are—if you are following your bliss, you are enjoying that refreshment, that life within you, all the time." "Go where your body and soul want to go. When you have the feeling, then stay with it, and don't let anyone throw you off." If you follow your bliss and are not afraid, "doors will open where you didn't know they were going to be." You live the potentiality of your incarnation by following your bliss: "There's something inside you that knows when you're in the center, that knows when you're on the beam or off the beam."[29]

Whatever else "Follow your bliss" may mean, Campbell's emphasis on inner feeling as the touchstone of reality to the virtual exclusion of the interhuman and the social is the final apex of his psychologism and his psychologizing of myth. "You begin to meet people who are in the field of your bliss, and they open the doors to you."[30] Or, as Campbell put it before, they are instruments of your destiny. Like Jung in his preoccupation with one's own "individuation," Campbell encourages us to regard others as functions of our becoming and to expect others to regard us in the same way. Thus with Campbell even more than with T.S. Eliot, "You must set your own lands in order" is the only answer we can give to the modern waste-land world, and myth, from being a communal concern of mankind, becomes the province of the deepest psychological inwardness.

Part Four

THERAPEUTIC IMPLICATIONS OF THE MEETING BETWEEN RELIGION AND PSYCHOLOGY

Chapter 12

HEALING THROUGH MEETING:
DIALOGICAL PSYCHOTHERAPY

EXISTENTIAL AND RELATIONAL TRUST stand at the heart of the life of
dialogue: "All real living is meeting." By the same token they stand at
the heart of healing through meeting. From our perspective, the meeting
between psychology and religion is most fruitful in dialogical psychotherapy, or "healing through meeting," for it is this approach to therapy
that takes most seriously otherness and the "between" without ignoring
the depths of psychic inwardness. It avoids the dangers we have pointed
to of psychologism and the psychologizing of the World and yet it takes
fully seriously the sicknesses of the soul in its relation to itself, others,
community, and the world.

To understand what is meant by healing through meeting, we must
first look briefly at what Martin Buber has to say about the relation of the
dialogical to the psychological and about the role of mutual confirmation and "making present" in becoming a self.

In human life together, it is the fact that we set the other at a distance
and make the other independent that enables us to enter into relation, as
an individual self, with those like ourselves. Through this "interhuman"
relation we confirm each other, becoming a self with the other. The

inmost growth of the self is not induced by one's relation to oneself but by the confirmation in which one person knows him- or herself to be "made present" in his or her uniqueness by the other. Self-realization and self-actualization are not the *goal* but the *by-product*. The goal is completing distance by relation, and relation here means cooperation, genuine dialogue, and mutual confirmation.

Buber distinguishes the "interhuman" from the "social" in general and, by the same token, from the "interpersonal." The "social" includes the I-It relation as well as the I-Thou: Many interpersonal relations are really characterized by one person's treating the other as an object to be known and used. Most interpersonal relations are a mixture of I-Thou and I-It and some are almost purely I-It. Buber calls the unfolding of the sphere of the between the "dialogical." The psychological, that which happens within the soul of each, is only the secret accompaniment of the dialogue. This distinction between the dialogical and the psychological constitutes a radical attack on the psychologism of our age that tends to remove the events that happen between persons into feelings or occurrences within the psyche. It also makes manifest the fundamental ambiguity of those modern psychologists, like Carl Rogers and Erich Fromm, who affirm the dialogue between person and person, but who are unclear about whether this dialogue is of value in itself or is merely a function of the individual's self-realization. By pointing to dialogue as the intrinsic value and self-realization as only the corollary and by-product, Buber also separates himself from those existential analysts and psychotherapists like Ludwig Binswanger and Rollo May who tend to make the I-Thou relationship just another dimension of the self, along with one's relation to oneself and to one's environment.

It is the privilege of the human being, through the hidden action of our being, to be able to impose an insurmountable limit to our objectification. Only as a partner can a person be perceived as an existing wholeness. To become aware of a person means to perceive his or her wholeness as person defined by spirit: to perceive the dynamic center that stamps on all his or her utterances, actions, and attitudes the recognizable sign of uniqueness. Such an awareness is impossible if, and so long as, the other is, for me, the detached object of my observation; for he or she will not thus yield his or her wholeness and its center. It is possible only when the person becomes present for me.

Mutual confirmation is essential to becoming a self—a person who realizes his or her own uniqueness precisely through relations to selves whose distance is completed by his or her own distance from them. True confirmation means that I confirm my partner as this existing being even while I oppose him or her. I legitimize my partner over against me as the one with whom I have to do in real dialogue. This mutual confirmation is most fully realized in what Buber calls "making present," an event that happens partially wherever persons come together, but in its essential structure only rarely. Making the other present means to "imagine the real," to imagine quite concretely what another person is wishing, feeling, perceiving, and thinking. This "inclusion," as Buber calls it, is not empathy but a bold swinging into the other that demands the intensest action of one's being to make the other present in their wholeness, unity, and uniqueness. One can do this only as a partner, standing in a common situation with the other, and even then one's address to the other may remain unanswered and the dialogue may die in seed.

HEALING THROUGH MEETING

I have taken the phrase "healing through meeting" from the title Martin Buber gave the posthumous book by the Swiss analytical psychologist Hans Trüb (*Heilung aus der Begegnung*). All therapy relies to a greater or lesser extent on the meeting between therapist and client and, in group and family therapy, the meeting among the clients. But only a few theories have singled out the meeting—the sphere of the "between"— as the central, as opposed to the ancillary, source of healing. As long as there has been society, something that can be recognized as healing through meeting has taken place. The parent, the teacher, the nurse, the shaman, the medicine man—anyone who lays hands on another or helps another—is involved in healing through meeting.

From the very beginning of formal psychoanalysis, healing through meeting was already built into the system as an indispensable means to the end of overcoming fixation and repression. Even if the therapeutic situation was modified by Freud's asking the patient to lie on the couch rather than to face him, it was still a meeting—in contrast to those operant conditioning and psychopharmacological forms of psychology and psychotherapy that entail little or no actual contact between psychologist and client. Freudian theory, to be sure, sees the ego as the servant of three masters—the superego, the id, and the environment—but nowhere does Freud place the meeting between self and self at its center, except in theories of transference and countertransference. "Freud fought against his humanistic personal urges through his scientism," writes Ivan Boszormenyi-Nagy, "and he abhorred Ferenczi's relational emphasis on therapeutic methods."[1]

Yet we cannot imagine Freud working year after year with people and dealing with them only as objects. When we turn to Carl Jung, who is even more preoccupied with the intrapsychic than Freud, it is startling to realize the extent to which his *therapy* is centered on the dimension of meeting, or dialogue. In *The Undiscovered Self*, Jung says, "All over the world, it is being recognized today that what is being treated is not a symptom, but a patient." The more the doctor schematizes, the more the patient quite rightly resists. The patient demands to be dealt with in his or her uniqueness, not just as part of a problem, and to do this the therapist must engage and risk himself or herself as a person.[2] "The dream of half a century has run its course," says Viktor Frankl, "the dream in which what was held of value was a mechanics of the psyche and a technology of psychotherapy." In the place of this interpretation of psychic life on the basis of mechanisms and this therapy of psychic disorders with the help of techniques, Frankl puts forward healing through meeting as the true center of psychotherapy:

> Provided that one does not shudder at that so fashionable word, one can aptly speak of human meeting (*Begegnung*) as the actual agent in the modes of acting in psychoanalytic treatment. The so-called transference is also probably only a vehicle of such human meeting. . . . *Within the framework of psychotherapy, the methodology and technique applied at any given time is least effective of all: rather it is the human relationship between physician and patient which is determining.*[3]

One of the most important issues the approach of healing through meeting addresses is the extent to which healing proceeds from a specific healer—priest, sorcerer, shaman, or therapist—and the extent to which healing takes place in the "between"—in the relationship between therapist and client, among the members of a group or family, or even within a community. When it is the latter, is there a special role, nonetheless, for the therapist as facilitator, midwife, enabler, or partner in dialogue? We must also ask whether such healing takes place through an existential grace (a term I coined in *Touchstones of Reality*), which cannot be planned and counted on, however much it can be helped along. To what extent does healing through meeting imply that meeting must also be the *goal* as well as the means to that goal? And to what extent are we talking about a two-sided event that is not susceptible to techniques in the sense of willing and manipulating in order to bring about a certain result?

Another important problem that healing through meeting encounters is that of the limits of responsibility of the helper. To what extent do therapists have an ego involvement such that they feel themselves a success if the patient is healed and a failure is he or she is not? Therapists open to the new vistas of healing through meeting will feel that more is demanded of them than their professional methods and their professional role provide. The "abyss calls to abyss," or self to self, as Buber wrote in his preface, "Healing Through Meeting," to Trüb's book; the technical superiority of the therapist is not required, but rather his or her actual self. In *Power and Innocence* (1972), Rollo May writes of a black woman patient who felt so powerless and so cut off from her own anger that May had to become angry for her. But he added, "I did not do this just as a technique. I really became angry." Only through his personal involvement was the woman able to gain access to her anger.[4]

What is crucial is not the skill of the therapist, but rather what takes place *between* the therapist and the client *and* between the client and other people. The one *between* cannot totally make up for or take the place of the other. No amount of therapy can be of decisive help if a person is too enmeshed in a family, community, or culture in which the seedlings of healing are constantly choked off and the attempts to restore personal wholeness are thwarted by the destructive elements of the system. If this fact underlines the importance of supplementing one-to-one therapy with family therapy and even intergenerational (three or more generations) family therapy, such as Ivan Boszormenyi-Nagy practices and advocates, it also underlines the importance of creating that climate of trust, that confirmation of otherness, in which healing through meeting can flourish on every level. That there are tragic limitations to such healing is obvious, but it is not equally obvious that we should accept the present state of "community" as a given and restrict ourselves to the intrapsychic or to the intrafamilial.

Insanity, writes Ferdinand Ebner, is the end product of "I-solitude" and the absence of the Thou—the complete closeness of the I to the Thou. It is a spiritual condition in which neither the word nor love can reach the individual. The irrationality of insane persons lies in the fact that they talk past other persons and are unable to speak to a concrete Thou. The world has become for them the projection of their I, not just theoretically, as in idealism, but practically, and for this reason they can only speak to a fictitious Thou.[5] This type of psychosis is explained by Martin Buber in somewhat more poetic terms in *I and Thou*. "If a man does not represent the *a priori* of relation in his living with the world," writes Buber, "if he does not work out and realize the inborn *Thou* on what meets it, then it strikes inwards." As a result, confrontation of what is over against one takes place in oneself, and this means self-contradiction—the horror of an inner double. "Here is the verge of life, flight of an unfulfilled life to the senseless semblance of fulfillment, and its groping in a maze and losing itself ever more profoundly."[6]

For the therapist, the distinction between arbitrary and true will rests on a quite real and concrete experiencing of the client's side of the relationship. Only if the therapist discovers the "otherness" of the client will he or she discover his or her own real limits and what is needed to help the client. He or she must see the position of the other in that person's concrete actuality, yet not lose sight of his or her own. Only this will remove the danger that the will to heal will degenerate into arbitrariness. This type of help stands in sharp contrast to the doctor and the psychotherapist who give others technical aid without entering into relationships with them. Help without mutuality is presumptuousness, writes Buber; it is an attempt to practice magic.

> As soon as the helper is touched by the desire, in however subtle a form, to dominate or enjoy his patient, or to treat the latter's wish to be dominated or enjoyed by him as other than a wrong condition needing to be cured, the danger of falsification arises, beside which all quackery appears peripheral.[7]

In therapy, will and decision within dialogue are decisive. Therapy should not proceed from the investigation of individual psychological complications, but rather from the whole person; for it is only the understanding of wholeness as wholeness that can lead to the real transformation and healing of the person and of that person's relationships with others. None of the phenomena of the soul is to be placed in the center of observation as if all the rest were derived from it. The person ought not to be treated as an object of investigation and encouraged to see himself as an "it." He should be summoned "to set himself to rights," says Buber, to bring his inner being to unity so that he may respond to the address of being that faces him. Such response means the transformation of the urges, of the "alien thoughts," or fantasy. We must not reject the abundance of this fantasy, but rather transform it in our imaginative faculty and turn it into actuality. "We must convert the element that seeks to take possession of us into the substance of real life."

THE UNCONSCIOUS AND DREAMS

Martin Buber has suggested that the unconscious may really be the ground of personal wholeness before its elaboration into the physical and the psychic. Freud, he holds, and after him, Jung, have made the simple logical error of assuming that the unconscious is psychic since they wished to deny that it was physical. They did not, Buber holds, see this third alternative and with it the possibility of bursting the grounds of psychologism by recognizing that the division of inner and outer that applies to the psyche and the physical need not apply to the unconscious. There might be, as a result, direct meeting and direct communication between one unconscious and another. The unconscious, by this reading, is our being itself in its wholeness. Out of it the physical and the psychical evolve again and again and at every moment. Therefore, the exploration of psychology is not of the unconscious itself but rather of the phenomena that have been dissociated from it. The radical mistake that Freud made was to think that he could posit a region of the mind as unconscious and at the same time deal with it as if its "contents" were simply repressed conscious material that could be brought back, without any essential change, into the conscious. Dissociation is the process in which the unconscious "lump" manifests itself in inner and outer perceptions and may be, in fact, the origin of our whole sense of inner and outer.

Freud, holding that the unconscious must be simply psychical, places the unconscious *within* the person, and so do most of the schools that have come after Freud. (At some point both Freud and Jung spoke of the meeting between one unconscious and another. The Jungian therapist Marvin Spiegelman has stressed the creation of a third reality *between* one unconscious and another as an important transference phenomenon.[8])

As a result, *the basis of human reality itself comes to be seen as psychical rather than interhuman, and the relations between person and person are psychologized*. Freud held that the therapist can induce the patient to bring out into the open the materials that he had repressed into the unconscious. Buber, in contrast, holds that we do not have a deep freeze that keeps fragments that can be raised as they were. The dissociation into physical and psychic phenomena means a radical change of the substance. The therapist helps in this process and has an influence on it. This means that the responsibility of the therapist is greater than has usually been supposed. Buber calls for a more "musical," floating relationship of therapist to patient; for *the deciding reality is the therapist, not the methods*. Although no therapist can do without a typology, at a certain moment the therapist throws away as much of his typology as he can and accepts the unforeseeable happening in which the unique person of the patient stands before the unique person of the therapist. The usual therapist imposes himself on his patient without being aware of it. What is necessary is the conscious liberation of the patient from this unconscious imposition and from the general ideas of the therapist's school of psychology. "It is much easier to impose oneself on the patient," says Buber, "than it is to use the whole force of one's soul to leave the patient to himself and not to touch him. *The real master responds to uniqueness.*"[9]

Buber sees the dominating importance of repression as arising from the disintegration of the organic community from within so that mistrust becomes life's basic note: "Agreement between one's own and the other's desire ceases, and the dulled wishes creep hopelessly into the recesses of the soul. . . . Now there is no longer a human wholeness with the force and the courage to manifest itself. . . . *The divorce between spirit and instinct is here*, as often, *the consequence of the divorce between man and man.*"[10]

Hans Trüb, similarly, sees the unconscious as precisely the personal element that is lost in the course of development. Repression, instead of being a basic aspect of human nature or an inescapable manifestation of civilization and its discontents, becomes the early denial of meeting, and its overcoming means the reestablishment of meeting, the breakthrough to dialogue:

> The unconscious touched by us has and takes its origin from that absolute "no" of the rejected meeting behind whose mighty barrier a person's psychic necessity for true meeting with the world secretly dams itself up, falls back upon itself, and thus, as it were, coagulates into the "unconscious." [11]

In the relatively whole person, the unconscious would have a direct impact, not only on the conscious life, but also on others, precisely because it represents the wholeness of the person. In the relatively divided person, on the contrary, the unconscious itself has suffered a cleavage so that not only are there repressed materials that cannot come up into consciousness but what does come up does not represent the wholeness of the person but only one of the fragments. As the unconscious of the relatively whole person is the very ground of meeting and an integral part of the interhuman, the unconscious of the relatively divided person is the product of the absence or denial of meeting. From this we can infer that the overcoming of the split between the repressed unconscious and the conscious of the divided person depends on healing through meeting, including such confirmation as the therapist can summon from the relationship with the client to counterbalance the "absolute no" of the meeting rejected or withheld in childhood.

Healing through meeting means the concrete unfolding in therapy of the "ontology of the between." That means, among other things, the discovery of the implications of our understanding of the unconscious for the dream-work that the client carries out in dialogue with the therapist. Martin Buber questions whether we know or *have* dreams at all. What we possess, rather, is the work of the shaping memory that tells us of the dreamer's relation to the "dream," but nothing of the dream in itself. The dreamer, so long as he is dreaming, has no share in the common world and nothing, therefore, to which we can have access. Dreams are the residues of our waking dialogues. Not only is there no real meeting with otherness in our dreams, but even the traces of otherness are greatly diminished. This does not mean, as Jung and Fritz Perls hold, that every person in the dream is really ourselves. But we cannot speak of dream relations as if they were identical with relations to persons in waking life. What we can say is that having set the dream over against us, thus isolated, shaped, elaborated, and given form as an independent opposite, we enter into dialogue with it. From now on it becomes one of the realities that addresses us in the world, just as surely and as concretely as any so-called external happening. From this it follows that the therapist cannot know what method of dream interpretation he will use beforehand but must place himself in the hands of the patient and, practicing what Buber calls "obedient listening," letting himself be guided by what the patient brings him.[12]

CONFIRMATION

If we can confirm ourselves, it is only because we have been confirmed by others, and if others can confirm us, it is only because we can accept being confirmed by them. We need to be confirmed in our uniqueness, yet we need to be confirmed by others who are different from us. This is not a paradox so long as genuine interhumanness stands at the center of human existence; for our very existence as selves originates in and perseveres through the interhuman. But other persons, including our parents, are not always willing to confirm us in our uniqueness. We cannot become ourselves without other people who call us to realize our created uniqueness in response to our life tasks. Many of us, unfortunately, have experienced "confirmation" of a very different nature, confirmation with strings attached. Many of us are, in effect, offered a contract that reads: "We will confirm you only if you will conform to our model of the good child, the good churchgoer, the good student, the good citizen, the good soldier."

Once we have bought that bargain, and most of us buy it more or less, we are placed in an impossible double bind. We know somewhere in our heart of hearts that it is not we who are being confirmed but rather the role that we are acting to please significant others. Yet if we try to rebel against and break out of this pseudo confirmation, the other half of the contract goes into effect; for we have internalized the proposition that if we do not "behave," we *cannot* be confirmed because we are not lovable.[13]

Now we are able to see why "inclusion," or "imagining the real," lies at the heart of confirmation. Inclusion, as we have seen, is bipolar— swinging over to the other while remaining on one's own ground. No one can confirm us through *empathy* in the strict sense of the term—because they do not give of themselves thereby—or through *identification*— because they miss us in our uniqueness and filter through only what is like themselves. They can confirm us only if they bring themselves in their uniqueness into dialogue with us in ours and confirm us while holding in tension the "overagainstness," and, if necessary, even the opposition and conflict that comes out of this unique relationship between two unique persons. Only inclusion, or imagining the real, really grasps the other in his or her otherness and brings that other into relationship to oneself.

If confirmation is central to human and interhuman existence, then it follows that disconfirmation, especially in the earliest stages of life, must be a major factor in psychopathology. Instead of finding the genesis of neurosis and psychosis in frustrated gratification of drives, à la Freud, we shall find it more basically and more frequently in disconfirming situations in the family that impair the child's basic trust. "One can hypothetically assume that if the parent is prematurely lost as a component of the child's identity delineating ground," writes Ivan Boszormenyi-Nagy, "a fixated bottomless craving for trust becomes his permanent character trait."[14] Nagy's hypothesis is confirmed at length by the theories and clinical practice of Heinz Kohut, Harold Searles, Ronald Laing, Helm Stierlin, and Carl Rogers.[15]

If disconfirmation or the absence of confirmation lies at the root of much psychopathology, then confirmation lies at the core of healing through meeting. Healing through meeting is that therapy that goes beyond the repair work that helps a soul that is diffused and poor in structure to collect and order itself to the essential task—the regeneration of an atrophied personal center. This means the healing not just of a certain part of the patient but also of the very roots of the patient's being. Without the existential trust of one whole person to another, there will be no realization on the part of the patient of the need to give up into the hands of the therapist what is repressed. Without such trust even masters of method cannot effect existential healing.

To confirm the other is only possible within the relationship itself, insofar as the other can communicate his or her self to you and you can experience both the other's and your own side of the relationship. Real confirmation cares enough about the other person to wrestle with and for him—confirming him even while opposing him, contending within the dialogue.[16] In the first stage of therapy, as Hans Trüb suggests, the person who comes before the therapist is one who has been disconfirmed by the world, one who needs a confidant who will understand through imagining the real. Part of the sickness of this person lies in the fact that, because of this nonconfirmation, he or she has withdrawn from active dialogue with family, friends, and community. At some point, therefore, the therapist must enter a second stage in which he helps the client resume the interrupted dialogue with the community by placing on the client the demand of the community.

Without that second stage—not replacing but combined with the first—there can be no real healing. The same is true of the approach to existential guilt. It is not enough for the therapist to help call people to account in terms of their self-betrayal or even their guilt toward their family. It must, at the same time, be a calling back into the dialogue with the community. Both stages must probably be there at every moment, but the right proportion between the two at any one time is a matter of real listening and of the "grace" that allows one to discover what is called for in each situation through openness and response. There are persons who could be severely injured by a premature placing upon them of the demand of the community, just as there are persons who could be severely injured if the therapist never reached that stage. True confirmation is an event that happens *between* the therapist and patient, one that helps the patient go back into the world to give and receive confirmation in the mutual interaction with others.

ACCEPTANCE AND CONFIRMATION

The American psychologist Carl R. Rogers uses Buber's phrase "confirming the other," accepting the person not as something fixed and finished, but as a process of becoming. Through this acceptance, Rogers says, "I am doing what I can to confirm or make real his potentialities." If, on the contrary, writes Rogers, one sees the relationship as only an opportunity to reinforce certain types of words or opinions in the other, as Verplanck, Lindsley, and B.F. Skinner do in their therapy of operant conditioning, then one confirms him or her as a basically mechanical, manipulatable object and then tends to act in ways that support this hypothesis. Only a relationship that "reinforces" *all* that one is, "the person that he is with all his existent potentialities" Rogers concludes, is one that, to use Buber's terms, *confirms* him "as a living person, capable of creative inner development."[17]

Rogers, however, tended to equate acceptance and confirmation, while Buber said no, I have to distinguish between the two. I begin with acceptance, but then sometimes to confirm this person I have to wrestle with, against, and for him or her. Although one part of you has direction, the other part of you is an aimless whirl. I have to help you in taking a direction rather than just remaining with the aimless whirl.

In the course of his 1957 seminars at the Washington School of Psychiatry, Martin Buber threw out some hints concerning confirmation in therapy and its relation to healing through meeting. The therapist's openness and willingness to receive whatever comes is necessary in order that the patient may trust existentially, Buber said. A certain very important kind of healing—existential healing—takes place through meeting rather than through insight and analysis. This means the healing not just of a certain part of the patient, but also of the very roots of the patient's being. The existential trust of one whole person in another has a particular representation in the domain of healing. So long as it is not there, the patient will not be able to disclose what is repressed to the therapist. Without such trust, even masters of method cannot effect existential healing.

The existential trust between therapist and patient that makes the relationship a healing one in the fullest sense of that term implies confirmation, but of a very special sort. Everything is changed in real meeting. Confirmation can be misunderstood as *static*. I meet another—I accept and confirm the other as he or she now is. But confirming a person *as he* or *she is* is only the first step. Confirmation does not mean that I take the person's appearance at this moment as representative of the person I want to confirm. I must take the other person in his or her dynamic existence and specific potentiality. In the present lies hidden what can *become*.

This potentiality, this sense of the person's unique direction, can make itself felt to me within our relationship, and it is that I most want to confirm, said Buber. In therapy, this personal direction becomes perceptible to the therapist in a very special way. In a person's worst illness, the highest potentiality of this person may be manifesting itself in negative form. The therapist can directly influence the development of those potentialities. Healing does not mean bringing up the old, but rather shaping the new: It is not confirming the negative, but rather counterbalancing with the positive.[18]

Buber's insistence that confirmation is not static, but rather is a confirmation of the potentialities hidden in the worst illness of the patient, touches on the issue that arose in a dialogue between Buber and Rogers concerning the difference between *accepting* and *confirming*. True acceptance, Rogers holds, means acceptance of this person's potentialities as well as what the person is at the moment. If we were not able to recognize the person's potentiality, Rogers says, it is a real question whether we could accept him or her. If I am accepted exactly as I am, he adds, I cannot help but change. When there is no longer any need for defensive barriers, the forward-moving processes of life take over. Rogers holds that we tend to be split between our "should" part in the mind and a feeling part in the stomach. We don't accept ourselves, so if the therapist accepts us we can somehow overcome that split. If we overcome it we will become the person(s) we are meant to be. In his stress on an unqualified acceptance of the person being helped, Rogers says that if the therapist is willing for the other person to *be what he is*— to possess the feelings he possesses, to hold the attitudes he holds—it will help him to realize what is deepest in the individual, that is, the very aspect that can most be trusted to be constructive or to tend toward socialization or toward the development of better interpersonal relationships. Human nature, for Rogers, is something that can be trusted because the motivation toward the positive or constructive already exists in the individual and will come forward if we can release what is most basic in the individual. What is deepest in the individual can be released and trusted to unfold in socially constructive ways.[19]

Buber replied that he was not so sure about that; for what Rogers saw as most to be trusted, Buber saw as least to be trusted. This does not mean that Buber saw man as evil while Rogers saw man as good, but that Buber saw man as polar. It is precisely Rogers's assumption that the processes of life will always be forward-moving that Buber questions:

> What you say may be trusted, I would say this stands in polar relation to what can be least trusted in this man. . . . When I grasp him more broadly and more deeply than before, I see his whole polarity and then I see how the worst in him and the best in him are dependent on one another, attached to one another.

This doctrine of polarity leads inevitably to Buber's distinction between acceptance and confirmation; for confirmation means wrestling with the other against his or her self in order to strengthen the one pole and diminish the power of the other:

> I may be able to help him just by helping him to change the relation between the poles. Not just by choice, but by a certain strength that he gives to the one pole in relation to the other. The poles being qualitatively very alike to one another. There is not as we generally think in the soul of a man good and evil opposed. There is again and again in different manners a polarity, and the poles are not good and evil, but rather *yes* and *no*, rather acceptance and refusal. And we can strengthen, or we can help him strengthen, the one positive pole. And perhaps we can even strengthen the force of direction in him because this polarity is very often directionless. It is a chaotic state. We could bring a cosmic note into it. We can help put order, put a shape into this. Because I think the good, what we may call the good, is always only direction. Not a substance.[20]

Rogers speaks of acceptance as a warm regard for the other and a respect for the other as a person of unconditional worth, and that means an acceptance of and regard for a person's attitudes of the moment, no matter how much they may contradict other attitudes he or she has held in the past. In response to my question as moderator as to whether he would not distinguish confirmation from acceptance of this sort, Buber said:

Every true existential relationship between two persons begins with acceptance. . . . I take you just as you are. . . . But it is not yet what I mean by confirming the other. Because accepting, this is just accepting how he is in this moment, in this actuality of his. Confirming means first of all, accepting the whole potentiality of the other and even making a decisive difference in his potentiality, and of course we can be mistaken again and again in this, but it's just a chance between human beings. . . . And now I not only accept the other as he is, but I confirm him, in myself, and then in him in relation to this potentiality that is meant by him and it can now be developed, it can evolve, it can answer the reality of life. . . . Let's take, for example, man and a woman, man and wife. He says, not expressly, but just by his whole relation to her, "I accept you as you are." But this does *not* mean, "I don't want you to change." Rather it says, "Just by my accepting love, I discover in you what you are meant to become." . . . it may be that it grows and grows with the years of common life.[21]

Rogers, in his reply, recognizes that we could not accept the individual as is because often he or she is in pretty sad shape, if it were not for the fact that we also in some sense realize and recognize the individual's potentiality. But he went on to stress the acceptance as that which makes for the realization of potentiality: "Acceptance of the most complete sort, acceptance of this person as he is, is the strongest factor making for change that I know."[22] To this Buber replied:

There are cases when I must help him against himself. He wants my help against himself. . . . The first thing of all is that he trusts me. . . . What he wants is a being not only whom he can trust as a man trusts another, but a being that gives him now the certitude that "there *is* a soil, there *is* an existence. . . . The world *can* be redeemed. I can be redeemed because there is this trust." And if this is reached, now I can help this man even in his struggle against himself. And this I can do only if I distinguish between accepting and confirming.[23]

Rogers says, in effect, "I will come to you and I will be concerned about you, I'll have unconditional positive regard for you, I'll have empathic understanding of you, but I can only do so if I do it authentically as the person I am." That is what Rogers calls congruence. But confirmation, as distinct from congruence, has to do with the other person. People do not just naturally develop so that all I have to do is accept them—in this I agree with Buber. They are in a struggle themselves about their own direction. While I cannot impose on them what their direction should be, I can help them in their struggle.

I don't confirm you by being a blank slate or blank check. I can confirm you only by being the person I am. You'll never be confirmed by me by simply putting myself aside and being nothing but a mirror reflection you. Confirming the other may mean that I *don't* confirm him in some things, precisely because he's not taking a direction. It's not just that he is wrestling with himself; I am wrestling with him. There's an added factor here that is not what one calls being empathic. It's not just that I'm watching him wrestle with himself, but I am also entering into the wrestling. It means I wrestle with you, not just that I provide a ground for your wrestling, even though I may not impose myself on you, and say, "I know better than you." It's only insofar as you share with me and we struggle together that I glimpse the person you are called to become.[24]

EMPATHY AND INCLUSION

In contrast to both empathy and identification, inclusion means a bold imaginative swinging "with the intensest stirring of one's being" into the life of the other so that one can, to some extent, concretely imagine what the other person is thinking, willing, and feeling and so that one adds something of one's own will to what is thus apprehended. As such, it is the very opposite of the abstraction to which the psychologist Kenneth Clark relegates empathic concern for others. It means, on the contrary, grasping them in their uniqueness and concreteness. As such, too, it presupposes a philosophical anthropology in which we become human in our interaction with other persons, not secondarily, but primarily and ontologically.

A person finds himself as person through going out to meet the other, through responding to the address of the other. He does not lose his center, his personal core, in an amorphous meeting with the other. If he sees through the eyes of the other and experiences the other's side, he does not cease to experience the relationship from his own side. We do not experience the other through empathy or analogy. We do not know his anger because of our anger; for he may be angry in an entirely different way from us. But we *can* glimpse something of his side of the relationship. That is because a real person does not remain shut in himself or use his relations with others merely as a means to his own self-realization.

Inclusion, or "imagining the real," does not mean at any point that one gives up the ground of one's own concreteness, ceases to see through one's own eyes, or loses one's own "touchstone of reality." In this respect, it is the complete opposite of empathy in the narrower and stricter sense of the term in which we discussed it above. It is striking that in his later formulations of "empathic understanding" Rogers has stressed this very point. Roger said to Buber in describing his own therapy: "I am able to sense with a good deal of clarity the way his experience seems to him, really viewing it from within him, and yet without losing my own personhood or separateness in that." Rogers stresses accurately seeing into the client's private world *as if* it were his own without ever losing that *as if* quality. This, too, is very close to Buber's definition of "inclusion" as the bipolar experiencing of the other side of the relationship without leaving one's own ground. The therapist runs the risk of being changed by the client, but never loses his or her own separateness or identity in the process.

Those who are used to using "empathy" in the customary larger, looser way may well ask what practical difference is made by the fine distinctions between empathy in the stricter sense, identification, and inclusion. A first answer would be that empathy (in the narrower sense) and identification are both very limited means of understanding, within therapy and without, and for the same reason: Both rely on only one side of the relationship. Empathy attempts to get over to the other while leaving oneself; identification tries to tune in to the other through focusing on oneself. Neither can grasp the uniqueness of the other person, the uniqueness of oneself, and the uniqueness of the relationship.

A second, deeper answer is that neither empathy, in the strict sense, nor identification can really confirm another person, since true confirmation means precisely that I confirm *you* in your uniqueness and that I do it from the ground of my uniqueness as a really other person. Only inclusion, or imagining the real, can confirm another; for only it really grasps the other in his or her otherness and brings that other into relationship to oneself.

Leslie Farber provides us with an excellent example of this relationship between inclusion and confirmation—not from the realm of therapy, but rather from that of the relationship between man and woman:

> Equally important, perhaps more important [than the attraction of sexuality] in real man/woman talk, is the exciting possibility of receiving and offering a range of perception and sensibility whose otherness can be uniquely and surprisingly illuminating. . . . So long as equality and honesty prevail, and so long as each person tries to imagine the other's reality without dishonoring his own, the manner or mood of such talk can be various: humorous, serious, philosophical, concrete, abstract, gossipy, and so on. Employing Martin Buber's terminology, and at the same time shifting its focus from friendship between people of the same sex, I would maintain that such talk contains the supreme potentiality of confirming the other, not only as a particular human being, but as a particular man or woman, and, of course, of being confirmed in the same way.[25]

Our distinction among inclusion, identification, and empathy may also illuminate another very loosely used term—"intuition." Often the word intuition is used in a way very similar to empathy in the narrow sense of the term, or identification. The French philosopher Henri Bergson goes even further and suggests that there is an absolute intuition through which one can make oneself identical with the *élan vital*, or *durée*, of other persons and beings in their particularity. In his Introduction to the Hebrew edition of Bergson's works, Martin Buber offers a definition of intuition that does not make this claim of absoluteness and that, by the same token, distinguishes intuition from both empathy and identification and links it to imagining the real:

> Intuition, through vision, binds us as persons with the world which is over against us, binds us to it without being able to make us one with it, through a vision that cannot be absolute. This vision is a limited one, like all our perceptions, our universal-human ones and our personal ones. Yet it affords us a glimpse in unspeakable intimacy into hidden depths.[26]

Intuition as imagining the real is the very stuff of "betweenness" because it is, in the first instance, the stuff of immediacy that only later becomes something we may ruminate over and think about. The therapist with years of experience and with the knowledge of the many case histories that are reported in the literature will naturally think of resemblances when a client tells him something. But if he is a good therapist, he must discover the right movement back and forth between his patient as the unique person he is and the categories and cases that come to his, the therapist's, mind. He cannot know by scientific method *when* a particular example from case histories, his earlier clients, or even his own experience applies. This is where true intuition—imagining the real or inclusion—comes in. That is what some people mean when they describe psychotherapy as an art, or what I would call a grace of allowing oneself to be led.

Some people seem to possess this grace more than others. There are people who are gifted with an unusual degree of inclusive intuition who do not have any degrees in psychiatry or psychology. And there are other people who somehow seem obtuse. These latter either do not pick up cues or do not allow themselves to be aware of what they do pick up. That may be because they come to therapy with a certain mind-set, perhaps that of their school of therapy or just their own ways of thinking. But it may also be because it makes them anxious. We communicate to each other all the time far beyond our words—by our gestures, our actions, our silence, the set of our head. And we pick up far more than we know from others. Often, however, we do not allow ourselves to be aware of what we are picking up because it carries a double meaning or because the nonverbal communication contradicts the verbal, which we want to believe!

Buber's statement about the interpretation of dreams at the seminars of the Washington School of Psychiatry in 1957 is a good example of the contrast. There are two sorts of relation to dreams, he suggested. One is the scientific one that wants to interpret the dream according to the tenets of a particular school of psychoanalysis or psychotherapy. The other is a musical, free-floating relationship that relates to each dream as one might interpret a poem—in its own terms and not in the way in which one would interpret the dreams (or novels, plays, and poems) of another.

There is no system for being intuitive in this broader and more concrete sense of imagining the real, other than what I have called the courage to address and the courage to respond—existential trust. On the other hand, there is one sort of intuition I profoundly distrust. This is the "intuition" that can reach right into the heart of the person and say, "This is what makes that person tick." This intuition sets itself up even against the other's own responses. It does not see the relationship through the eyes of the other or imagine the real. Rather it reaches into the person and discovers a brilliant, but partial, truth that imprisons that person in a still more sophisticated category or label than the ones that are already besieging him or her. This intuition is dangerous and destructive to human relationships, and it is one that is all too often used by therapists, gurus, teachers, ministers, and friends. Knowing through mutual contact I *would* trust as opposed to the "intuition" that turns the other into an object.

THE PROBLEMATIC OF MUTUALITY

As soon as healing through meeting is made the focus of therapy, the question inevitably arises as to how much mutuality is possible and desirable between therapist and patient. This is a question that begins on the far side of the terminology of transference and countertransference. In its original usage by Freud, transference implies the projection by the patient upon the analyst and countertransference implies the projection by the analyst upon the patient. Whether one regards countertransference negatively, as Freud did, or positively, as Jung did, it is still largely an intrapsychic matter, even as is transference. The problematic of mutuality, in contrast, has to do with the real interhuman relationship between therapist and patient and with the extent to which that relationship can be fully mutual.

In friendship and love, imagining the real, or "inclusion," is mutual. In the helping relationships, however, it is necessarily one-sided. The patient cannot experience equally well the relationship from the side of the therapist or the pupil from the side of the teacher without destroying or fundamentally altering the relationship. This does not mean that the therapist is reduced to treating the patient as an object, an It. The one-sided inclusion of therapy is still an I-Thou relationship founded on mutuality, trust, and partnership in a common situation, and it is only in this relationship that real healing can take place. If the psychotherapist is content to "analyze" the patient,

> i.e., to bring to light unknown factors from his microcosm, and to set to some conscious work in life the energies which have been transformed by such an emergence, then he may be successful in some repair work. At best he may help a soul which is diffused and poor in structure to collect and order itself to some extent. But the real matter, the regeneration of an atrophied personal center, will not be achieved. This can only be done by one who grasps the buried latent unity of the suffering soul with the great glance of the doctor: and this can only be attained in the person-to-person attitude of a partner, not by the consideration and examination of an object.[27]

A common situation, however, does not mean one that each enters from the same or even a similar position. In psychotherapy the difference in position is not only that of personal stance but also of role and function, a difference determined by the very difference of purpose that led each to enter the relationship. If the goal is a common one—the healing of the patient—the relationship to that goal differs radically as between therapist and patient, and the healing that takes place depends as much upon the therapist's recognition of that difference as upon the mutuality of meeting and trust.

The amount of mutuality possible and desirable in therapy depends not only upon the stage of the relationship, but also upon the unique relationship between this particular therapist and client and upon the style and strength of the therapist. Therapists often testify to bringing their feelings into the therapeutic encounter to a greater or lesser degree, and many testify to themselves being healed through that encounter or at the very least growing in creativity and wisdom. None of this changes the basic fact that the therapist's expression of emotion is always made in the service of the therapy and never in the service of the healing of the therapist or of mere self-indulgence on the part of the therapist. If the eventual result of an "ideal type" of therapy is mutual friendship, that friendship is definitely not any longer a healing and helping relationship, but rather just what Buber describes it as—one of concrete and mutual inclusion, mutual dependency, and mutual concern.

The healing relationship must always be understood in terms of the quite concrete situation and life-reality of those participating in it. It is not always necessary or even helpful to label the client by such terms as "schizophrenic," "neurotic," "obsessive-compulsive," "borderline psychotic," or any of the other categories of the DSM Manual. But it is necessary to recognize that in the healing partnership one person feels a need or lack that leads him or her to come to the other for help and that the other is a therapist or counselor who is ready to enter a relationship in order to help.

This excludes neither Erich Fromm's conviction that the therapist at the same time heals himself in some measure through his own response to the patient nor Carl Rogers's feeling of the equal worth and value of the patient (which leads Rogers, mistakenly in my opinion, to stress the *full* mutuality of the patient-therapist relationship). But it does preclude accepting the therapist's *feeling* of mutuality as equivalent to the actual existence of full mutuality in the situation *between* therapist and patient. The "scientific" impersonalism that characterized orthodox psycho-analysts (though not so much even by them, particularly Freud, as some imagine) is rightly rejected by many present-day therapists. But this should not lead us to a sentimental blurring of the essential distinction between therapy and other, less structured types of I-Thou relationships. In the latter, as Buber puts it, there are "no normative limitations of mutuality," but in the former, the very nature of the relationship makes full mutuality impossible.

Having stressed this limitation, we must also stress the fact that healing through meeting *does* imply mutuality between therapist and patient, that the therapist is called on to be present as a person as well as a smoothly functioning professional, that he is vulnerable and must take risks, that he is not only professionally *accountable*, but also personally *responsible*. The professionally oriented therapist tends to regard those of his patients who commit suicide as his personal failures and those who get better as his personal successes, as if the patient's actions were simply the effect of which the therapist is the cause. Healing through meeting suggests a very different approach.

This approach, to begin with, accepts the uniqueness of each relationship and does not imagine that what worked in one case will necessarily work in another. In the second place, it accepts the limitations that are discovered in that unique relationship—not theoretical limitations, but actual ones, though it is also willing on another occasion to try to test those limits and see how they can be pushed back. Above all, it accepts the reality of the *between* and recognizes that it is not entirely to the therapist's credit if the therapy goes well, or to his discredit if it does not.

Harry Stack Sullivan was deeply affected by a patient who almost committed suicide, and Martin Buber by a man who was in despair and did not oppose his own death. Sullivan concludes his narration of this event with the statement of how it affected his subsequent approach to the therapeutic relationship.

> The subsequent course of his mental disorder was uninterruptedly unfortunate and he has resided for years in a State hospital. I have not since then permitted a patient to enter upon the communication of a gravely disturbing experience unless I have plenty of time in which to validate his reassurance as to the effect of the communication on our further relations.[28]

Leslie Farber in his essay "Martin Buber and Psychotherapy" compares these two events and what Buber and Sullivan concluded from them. In his lengthy comment, Farber delineates the very contrast we have made above between the prideful "responsibility" of the "professional scientist" and the more modest and truly responsible acceptance of the reality of the "between":

> Each instance, touching in its confession of failure, speaks of "conversion": Buber is converted from the private, the rhapsodic, the mystical, into the world; Sullivan, on the other hand, shakes the claims and interruptions of the hospital world to move into a more private attention to his patient's existence which would allow for relation. While Buber convicts himself for his fragmentary response to his friend's despair, he resists arrogating to himself prideful responsibility for the other's fate: he could not necessarily save this young man; he could only have been "present in spirit" when his visitor sought confirmation and meaning from him.
>
> If we turn now to the instruction Sullivan derived from his tragedy, we find him perhaps more faithful to his science than to his humanity. On the one hand, psychiatry is indebted to him for his ideal, still unachieved, that the psychiatric hospital should exist primarily for the psychiatric patient. On the other hand, unlike Buber, Sullivan's devotion to the techniques of his science leads him to the immoderate claim that such desperate mo-

ments may be postponed until there is time to "validate" the "reassurance." Leaving aside the question whether "reassurance" can or should be "validated," I believe that with more modesty or less devotion, he might not have taken on the sole responsibility for his patient's fate.[29]

I do not think that any therapist could accept the suicide of a patient with equanimity and without searching for his own responsibility in the situation. Yet part of the realism and seriousness of what we are talking about is to recognize that the responsibility of whether the therapy works or not does not lie entirely on the therapist, any more than it rests entirely with the patient. In the final analysis, it is a matter of the "between."

Chapter 13

CONTEXTUAL THERAPY:
RESTORING RELATIONAL TRUST

IT IS IN ITS ENDEAVOR to restore relational trust that modern psychology, particularly in the "contextual therapy" of Ivan Boszormenyi-Nagy and Barbara R. Krasner, has its most fruitful meeting with religion. Boszormenyi-Nagy carries forward Erik Erikson's concept of "basic trust" from *Childhood and Society* by contrasting fixity of frozen role obligations with the atmosphere of basic trust existing in a family. Though Erikson coined the term as a psychological stage of individual psychosocial development, Boszormenyi-Nagy points out that it is predicated upon a relationship structure in which each individual as a separate entity can draw from and has to be accountable to a just human order—a concept that he draws from Martin Buber's philosophical anthropology. In such an order genuine accountability plays a stronger role than any other fixed obligation.[1] Boszormenyi-Nagy and Barbara R. Krasner trace the development of the concept of basic trust first through Erikson, then through Heinz Kohut's Self-Psychology with its hope for restoration of self through empathic therapeutic parenting, and finally to the contextual therapist's recognition that individual models of psychic restoration must be integrated with that supra-individual regulatory force that Buber termed the "justice of the human order."[2]

The *personalized human order* that relating partners form between them . . . constitutes relational justice and leads to interpersonal trust. Contextual theory and practice are based on the conviction that the prospect of trust among people is rooted in the degree of *interhuman justice* that exists between them.[3]

In Contextual Therapy, "the ethical dimension of trust between relating partners is the invisible thread of both individual freedom and interindividual balance." The relational world is so vitally needed by the person that self-serving progress toward "doing one's own thing" can only fragment it and do disservice to the self. The relating partners' shared need for trust bridges dialectically the apparent contradiction between self-interest and consideration of others. This "capacity to acquire and retain at least a few trustworthy relationships in the face of increasing dehumanization and alienation in the public world cannot be equated with either altruism or with guilt-laden compliance fueled by superego demands."[4]

Ideally what is learned and developed in the earliest phase of parent-child relationships is a capacity for mutual trust and loyalty commitments based on the laws of reciprocity and fairness, which depends in turn upon the parents having experienced trust in their own early relationships with their parents.[5] If the parents can give the gift of basic trust to the child, they themselves gain in return self-enhancing merit leading to a transgenerational chain of credits and debits.

A successive chain of maturely parenting generations, . . . is a result of consequences that establish trust . . . Born into a world that offers care and engenders trust, offspring are dynamically obliged to rebalance the benefits they received through offering more of the same to subsequent generations.[6]

Like Erikson, contextual therapy postulates a coalescence of constructive, vital forces between a child's inner need and readiness for trust development and a trustworthy environment through which the young are likely to grow into people capable of healthy relating:

They can risk and are beholden to offering their love and trust to others, they can discover the liberating aspects and effects of giving, and they can induce others to give in return. Or, if others fail to give in return, a healthy youngster can learn to recognize the loss and turn his relational needs in another direction.[7]

Boszormenyi-Nagy and Krasner carry this idea over even into loss by death. If the parent-child relationship fails to develop into a trustworthy dialogue of care, it is lost even though the parents are still alive. On the other hand, should the dialogue between parent and child exist, even physical death is not likely to interrupt its trustworthy impact. Instead of being the ultimate arbiter of dialogue, death "is a stage which seals out the chance for another intergenerational try at care."[8] The word "seals" brings to mind the passage from the Song of Songs, "Set me as a seal upon they heart, for love is stronger than death." Here is a marvelous, factual, and wholly concrete and realistic statement of what that means. Even in death, the relational dialogue continues.

Boszormenyi-Nagy and Krasner also call Buber's just order of human existence that regulates the relations between individuals "the context of residual trustworthiness." This is "a realm that plays a vital role in enabling self-sustaining trust," for that trust is regulated by the degree of justice that a person has met in his or her own human order. Partners in relationship try to broaden the base of the residual trustworthiness that they hold in common, earning constructive entitlement and helping reinvest in the quality of interpersonal relating. "Much of the desperate behavior of seemingly uncaring adolescents and young adults is rooted in an intrinsic need to test their world's residual trustworthiness." Even therapeutic work with psychotics relies on existing pockets of residual trustability, which are used but not created by the therapist and originate from our common humanity and the gain that each of us receives from due consideration of another person's needs.[9]

Conversely, a failure to develop trust in a just human order and residual trustworthiness have the severest possible effect on the individual's personal development and his or her capacity for relationships. "A generalized loss of equity of justice can jeopardize the creativity or even the survival of the group, and its members' chances for achieving basic trust will diminish to a dangerous point." This leads to that alienation from the resources and possibilities of one's present living context and that vindictive input that Boszormenyi-Nagy and Krasner call "destructive entitlement." "Lasting damage takes place when the young experience a massive loss of trust and conclude that theirs is an intrinsically exploitative and manipulative world."

Boszormenyi-Nagy and Krasner go so far, indeed, as to declare that having missed a caring, early environment, children can lose their option for ever gaining basic trust. The threat of severe mistrust between the parents can crush the autonomous growth of the young adult who has to leave home. Subtle forms of mistrust permeate peer relationships and marriage and carry over into split loyalties that bear ominous consequences for the next generation. As a result, countless intergenerational and interpersonal injuries and injustices arise, including relational stagnation and "pathological" regression (though even here the trustworthy language of relational fairness and devotion can penetrate the psychotic's "crazy talk"). Another specific example is that of adult sex with a child, the first casualty of which is the child's trust in the world in general.[10]

Contextual therapy utilizes Buber's concept of genuine dialogue to integrate individual theory—the psychological criteria of the need for trust—with relational theory—the ethical criteria of trustworthy relationship. "Contextual therapy focuses on *options for tapping trustworthy resources* in family relationships." It sees trustworthiness as the main resource of genuine dialogue and the glue of viable relationships. "The extent of actualized, responsibly caring reciprocity indicates the *degree of trustworthiness* in the relational context."[11]

Boszormenyi-Nagy sees the climate of trust that characterizes a social group as made up of the sum total of the subjective evaluations of the justness of each member's relational experience. "Such a climate is, in the long run, more significant in determining the quality of relationships with the group than any particular set of interactions."[12]

By their recognition that the areas of trustworthiness and mutuality of commitment offer people the most effective resources for hope, care, and fresh investments of good will and by their willingness to address justice issues, acknowledge them as valid, and structure room for them in the therapeutic domain, the contextual therapist offers his or her clients a reasonably safe forum for spontaneously examining justice issues. Contextual therapy assumes intergenerational dialogue with its will to mutual responsibility as an interhuman absolute, and it sees gaining trust as a more fundamental and pervasive therapeutic goal than elaborating the intricacies of matters like sexual identity formation, pleasure economy, and useful sublimation patterns.[13]

To help one's clients gain relational trust and trustworthiness the contextual therapist must, of course, be trustworthy him or herself and win the trust of the clients. A good technician can do his job whether or not he has a client's trust. Not so the contextual therapist who either earns a trustworthy position or has only a limited and short-lived effect. "A therapist offers responsibility, skill, care, and the willingness to open up controversial, painful, shameful, and trying issues, earning trustability in the process." Thus contextual therapy is based on the healing evoked through due concern. As Boszormenyi-Nagy and Krasner themselves state, it is "a refinement of 'healing through meeting.' "[14]

Contextual therapy cannot rely on transference and the curing of transference neurosis as a central key to therapy, as does traditional psychoanalysis, but must instead try to avoid transference in order to retain the trust of the client who otherwise would have to reject the therapist out of loyalty to the family of origin or the nuclear family. The contextual therapist, in fact, recognizes that winning and retaining the trust of the client and the healing through meeting that follow from it are neither simple nor easy:

> Without trust in the therapist . . . the family sees no reason to share painful and shameful information. [What is more,] the therapist may earn trust through his concern, experience, and sincerity, but he can still be defeated because his intervention is perceived by family members as lacking sensitivity to the stress of guilt generated by intrinsic disloyalty. Another issue of trust pertains to subgroups within the family. When the therapist is trusted by one, he then seems untrustable to another member or subgroup. . . . The therapist [in that case] should . . . initiate a new negotiation about reciprocal benefits and exchanges among the members. A final level of trust pertains to *cotherapy*. If there are two or more therapists involved, their trust of each other and their comparative trustability for the family are likely to be subjected to a strenuous test. They should watch for any sign of their team being split as if they were a good and a bad parent.[15]

"Multidirected partiality" has long been a central insight and concern of Ivan Boszormenyi-Nagy and with him of Barbara Krasner. It means that the therapist is able to practice what Buber calls inclusion, or imagining the real, first with one member of the family and then with another. Techniques fail to provide a basis for trust. "Only multidirected partiality can establish the kind of structure that provides the safety for exploring, identifying, mobilizing and earning residual trust."[16]

The therapist guides the family members to the place where fairness extends to every member of the family: One person's being heard or being held accountable makes it easier to hear others or to let oneself be called to account. Thus, the therapist helps them take the first steps toward engagement in a mutuality of trust and trustworthiness. "The lack of trustworthiness in one's relational world is the primary pathogenic condition of human life." The therapist can address this problem of eroding trust by eliciting every family member's own responsible review of his or her side of mutual entitlements and indebtedness. Trust resources among families are identified, elicited, mobilized, and used. Above all the family therapist looks for that atmosphere of trustworthiness and availability of basic trust that enables children to acquire the building material for the fundamental stage of personality development.[17]

Building trust makes possible the recognition and reworking of long-standing balances of unfairness in the legacies of parents, thus freeing them from defensive and retributive behavior and freeing their offspring from being overburdened by them and condemned to a similar fate. Building trust includes a respect for equitability on every member's own terms, an integrity of give-and-take in relationship, and a mutuality of consideration. Trust does not develop exclusively between client and therapist, as in much traditional therapy, but is rechanneled into strengthening relationships between family members. Through his multidirected trustbuilding efforts, the contextual therapist can help family members reveal one another's unacknowledged consideration and contributions and elicit responsible attitudes that may lead to a more genuine dialogue among them.[18]

A therapist can only achieve this therapeutic attitude if he or she has personal freedom, conviction, courage, knowledge and skills, a capacity for inclusion, and an ability to claim his or her own private existence.

As he stands for the positive element of each participant's contribution to a mature dialogue, he also takes a position against the negative forces, mainly the individual and shared resistances in all members. . . . The guiding principles of this comprehensive and intensive family therapy derive from the mastery of the therapist's own life-experiences, especially his own family relationships.[19]

Family therapists have to exemplify and *live* in trust and confidence in the frustrated and often hateful family atmosphere. Family therapists must be open and expose themselves, and they must let this affect their relationships to their own families. "It is our conviction that growth in our personal life is not only inseparable from growth in our professional experience, but that it is our greatest technical tool."[20]

There is a nonnegotiable correlation between the degree to which a therapist invests energy into the fairness of his own relationships and the degree to which he can be free to risk courage and invest trust into a more inclusive therapeutic concern.[21]

One cannot legislate relational trust nor can one make it the goal of planned social action. Yet there are things that we can do at every level to help bring it about. One of these is the recognition of its centrality for therapy, education, family life, community, and the fellowship that holds society together. Another is the movement to build climates of trust insofar as the situation, the structure, and our resources allow. Naturally a "climate of trust" too cannot be made into a specific goal without destroying the spontaneity and the "betweenness" that are essential to such a climate. Yet we can become more aware of what genuine listening and responding is; we can become more sensitive to the voices that are not ordinarily heard within the family, community, and society; and we can overcome that mistrust founded on hysteria that imagines that something dreadful will happen if we allow such voices to express points of view that may not accord with our own or even with the dominant structure of the group.

Chapter 14

NEUROTIC AND EXISTENTIAL
GUILT

NO ISSUE CAN BRING us closer to the heart of the meeting between psychology and religion than that of neurotic and existential guilt. One of the most important contours of all psychotherapy is the therapist's approach to guilt. Freud saw guilt as repressed from conscious awareness, and dreams as the royal road to guilt, as to the unconscious in general. Buber, although not denying the existence of repressed neurotic repressed guilt, went beyond Freud in positing the existence of an "existential guilt" attached to events that are accessible to the conscious mind, but that have lost their character of guilt because of our attitude toward them. The therapist must be ready to deal with that attitude in quite specific ways.

To Freud, guilt was the product of the introjection of the harsh superego. As such, it was identical with societal and parental taboos, at best, or the neurotic fixation of these processes, at worst. Although Freud did not imagine that one could overcome guilt entirely, he looked on it as something to be modulated, insofar as possible, in favor of what might allow the individual more happiness. Guilt to Freud, therefore, was a built-in part of the psychic and social system, but was inherently extrinsic as far as values go.

There is nothing paradoxical in all this. From the standpoint of healing through meeting, in contrast, guilt is doubly paradoxical. It is paradoxical, first, in that it necessarily implies the existence of a real, existential guilt, which, however, is usually confusedly intermingled with neurotic and/or merely social guilt. It is paradoxical, second, in that the predominance of neurotic guilt in our culture and the traumatized response to it on the part of many individuals makes it difficult to discuss real guilt without evoking the same reactions of acquiescence or rejection that are triggered by neurotic guilt.

The analyst, writes Buber in "Healing Through Meeting," must see the illness of the patient as an illness of his relations with the world. True guilt does not reside in the human person, but rather in his failure to respond to the legitimate claim and address of the world. Similarly, the repression of guilt and the neuroses that result from this repression are not merely psychological phenomena, but rather events between persons.[1]

The common order of the world that we build up through our common speech and the centrality of human existence as "We" are basic to Martin Buber's distinction in "Guilt and Guilt Feelings" between "groundless" neurotic guilt—a subjective feeling within a person, usually unconscious and repressed—and "existential" guilt—an ontic, interhuman reality in which the person dwells in the truest sense of the term.[2]

In "What Is Common to All" Buber unfolds the implications of Heraclitus' statement, "One should follow the common." Heraclitus found his fellow Ephesans to be present yet absent. Even in our dreams we contribute to building the world-order, but when we are awake we should not be like sleepwalkers. What we build together is more than the individual's consciousness, more than just each of us doing our thing by means of the other. Using the terms of Heraclitus, Buber calls that building together first the *logos*—the common speech-with-meaning— and then the *cosmos*—the world that humanity builds in concert over a thousand generations.[3]

From this common world comes the idea of the just human order that is central to the thought of Ivan Boszormenyi-Nagy. The just human order is nothing other than this world we build together. It is not a set of Platonic ideas or absolutes—Goodness, Beauty, Truth—but the concrete lived reality. We think of ourselves as within the world, but the world that we build together is within us. It is not just in our minds, and we do not establish it ourselves. Nonetheless, there is a very real sense in which this world is ours.

The simple moral that grows out of this is an anthropological one. Aldous Huxley suggests that we ought to take mescaline in order to have a holiday from everyday living. But the true name of all these chemical paradises, Buber points out in his critique of Huxley, is situationlessness:

> Man may master as he will his situation, to which his surroundings also belong; he may withstand it, he may alter it, he may, when it is necessary, exchange it for another; but the fugitive flight out of the claim of the situation into situationlessness is no legitimate affair of man. And the true name of all the paradises which man creates for himself by chemical or other means is situationlessness. They are situationless like the dream state and like schizophrenia because they are in their essence uncommunal, while every situation, even the situation of those who enter into solitude, is enclosed in the community of logos and cosmos.[4]

On this same basis Buber criticizes even the Vedanta's teaching that "I am you" or "That art Thou." The real beginning of human existence is meeting, and meeting means that I accept you as you are, not as one with myself but really other. We build this common foundation of human existence on the acceptance of otherness. That is why I call one of my books *The Confirmation of Otherness: In Family, Community, and Society*. The distinction between dialogue and monologue, the beginning of genuine dialogue, is when you are not just a part of my experience, but I accept you in your otherness, as a real, unique person in yourself. Carl Jung also includes all the others in his understanding of the self. But he includes them, Buber suggests, as "Its" and not as "Thous." He does not include them in their otherness and uniqueness but rather as psychic contents of the self.

This then is the common world that we build through speech-with-meaning. That we build it together does not mean that we have to conform. On the contrary, each of us where he or she is must stand our ground and make our unique contribution, even if like Jeremiah or Jesus or Socrates we have to do so at the cost of our lives. This is not a matter of the individual versus society; for we are all part of this common order together.

Given this understanding of the common order, it is also possible to understand how we injure it. We all stand, says Buber, in an objective world of relatedness, and this objective relatedness can then rise to an actual existential relation to other people. It is this existential relation that we can injure. "Man," Buber asserts in "Guilt and Guilt Feelings," "is the creature who can become guilty." The originators of primitive taboos did not invent guilt; they used it and manipulated it. To understand this, we must follow Buber in distinguishing between guilt feelings born of neurotic guilt and real, or existential, guilt. Existential guilt is guilt that you have taken on yourself as a person in a personal situation. Freud's guilt is repressed; you do not know it. But existential guilt you do know. Only you may no longer identify yourself with the person who committed the guilt.

Existential guilt, writes Buber, is "guilt that a person has taken on himself as a person and in a personal situation." Certainly there is purely social and even neurotic guilt derived from a set of mores and taboos imposed upon the individual by parents and society and incorporated into an internalized "superego." But there is also real guilt, guilt that has to do with one's actual stance in the world and the way in which one goes out from it to relate to other persons. Real guilt is neither subjective nor objective. It is dialogical—the inseparable corollary of one's personal responsibility, one's answerability for authenticating one's own existence, and by the same token, for responding to the partners of one's existence, the other persons with whom one lives. Where there is personal responsibility, there must also be the possibility of real guilt—for failing to respond, for responding inadequately or too late, or for responding without one's whole self.

Such guilt is neither inner nor outer. One is not answerable for it either to oneself alone or to society apart from oneself, but to that very bond between oneself and others through which one again and again discovers the direction through which one can authenticate one's existence. If a relation with another cannot be reduced to what goes on within each of the two persons, then the guilt one person has toward a partner in a relationship cannot be reduced to the subjective guilt he feels. "Existential guilt," writes Buber, "occurs when someone injures an order of the human world whose foundations he knows and recognizes [at some level of his being] as those of his own existence and of all common human existence." Hence, existential guilt transcends the realm of inner feelings and of the self's relation to itself. We can and do injure this order. No one can really say, "I have not done so." This is not a matter of original sin or of failing to repress libidinal urges. It is a matter of an actual violation.

The order of the human world that one injures is not an objective absolute, whether of Platonic ideas, society, or the church, hence something that we may see as purely external and alien to ourselves, however much we must submit ourselves to it. It is the sphere of the "interhuman" itself, precisely those We's that we have built in common in family, group, and community and to which our own existence belongs in the most literal sense of the term. Although we may not recognize what it means to injure an "order of the human world," everyone knows quite well how, through acts of omission or commission, attacking or withholding oneself, one may injure one's family, one's group of friends, one's community, one's colleagues, or one's fellow employees. The sphere of the interhuman and the guilt that arises in it cannot be identified with the taboos and restrictions of any particular culture and society. "The depth of the guilt feeling is not seldom connected with just that part of the guilt that cannot be ascribed to the taboo-offence, hence with the existential guilt."

Guilt is an essential factor in the person's relations to others: it performs the necessary function of leading one to desire to set these relations to right. It is actually here, in the real guilt of the person who has not responded to the legitimate claim and address of the world, that the possibility of transformation and healing lies. The therapist may lead the person who suffers from existential guilt to the place where that person can walk the road of illuminating that guilt, persevering in one's identification of oneself as the person who, no matter how different from what one once was, took on that guilt, and, insofar as one's situation makes possible, restoring and repairing "the order of being injured by one through the relation of an active devotion of the world."5

"Original guilt consists in remaining with oneself," writes Buber in criticism of the German existentialist philosopher Martin Heidegger. If the being before whom this hour places one is not met with the truth of one's whole life, then one is guilty. Primal guilt is not found in our relation to ourselves, but rather by becoming aware of the life in which we are essentially related to something other than ourselves.

By the same token, real guilt cannot be limited to the guilt that the existential psychoanalyst Medard Boss, following Heidegger, sees as arising from failing to fulfill one's indebtedness to Being through realizing one's potentialities:

> If you lock up potentialities you are guilty against (or *indebted to*) what is given you in your origin, in your "core." In this existential condition of being indebted and being guilty are founded all guilt feelings, in whatever thousand and one concrete forms and malformations they may appear in actuality.[6]

One's potential uniqueness may be given, but the direction in which one authenticates one's existence is not; one discovers it in constantly renewed decisions in response to the demand of concrete situations. When we are guilty, it is not because we have failed to realize our potentialities, which we cannot know in the abstract, but rather because we have failed to bring the resources we find available to us at a given moment into our response to a particular situation that calls us out. This means that we cannot be guilty *a priori* to any conception of the self, but only in relation to those moment-by-moment chances to authenticate ourselves that come to us in the concrete situation. Our potentialities cannot be divorced from the discovery of our personal direction, and this comes not in the meeting of a person with oneself, but rather with other persons. The order of existence that one injures is one's own order, as well as that of the others, because it is the foundation and the very meaning of one's existence as self.

The denial of "the depth of existential guilt beyond all mere violation of taboo" is what Freud sought to accomplish through relativizing guilt feelings genetically, writes Buber in "Guilt and Guilt Feelings." It is characteristic of that "advanced" generation for which "it now passes as proved . . . that no real guilt exists; only guilt-feeling and guilt convention." This denial amounts to a crisis not only in the life of modern man, but also of man as such, for "man is the being who is capable of becoming guilty and is capable of illuminating his guilt."

Buber puts forward three steps that can be taken toward overcoming existential guilt. The first is that I illuminate this guilt: I who am so different am nonetheless the person who did this. Perhaps I say, "I was just a boy," or "That was years ago." For all this, part of what it means to be a person is the recognition that I am still the one who became guilty. The word remorse is significant in this connection because it means regret for something that you cannot undo. Time is a torrent bearing us to our individual deaths, says Buber. We cannot say, "Play that over again." Secondly, we have to persevere in that illumination— not as an anguished self-torment but as a strong, broad light.

If we were only guilty in relation to ourselves, the process might stop there. But we are always also guilty in relation to others. Therefore, we must take the third step of repairing the injured order of existence, restoring the broken dialogue through an active devotion to the world. If we have injured it, only we can restore it. But we may not be able to find the person we injured: that person may be dead or the situation may be radically changed. Yet there are a thousand places where we can, in fact, restore the injured order of existence, not just the one in which we injured it.[7]

Ivan Boszormenyi-Nagy has built his therapy on the further reaches of Buber's philosophical anthropology—his understanding of the "essential We," the common world built by the common "speech-with-meaning" and the existential guilt that arises from the injury to this common world. According to Boszormenyi-Nagy, the patient cannot solve his problems with his family, as so many traditionally oriented psychoanalysts recommend, just by moving away from home and becoming independent or by bringing to consciousness his feelings of hatred for his parents. A mass escape from filial obligations through fear of responsibility can infuse all human relationships with unbearable chaos, Boszormenyi-Nagy says. The individual can become paralyzed by amorphous therapeutically inaccessible existential guilt. By the same token, "the true measure of human emotion is not the intensity of its affective or physiological concomitant, but the relevance of its interpersonal context." Boszormenyi-Nagy follows Buber in distinguishing between relationships that are merely functions of individual becoming, normalcy, adaptation, and perspective and relationships that are ontological in the sense that they have a reality, accountability, meaning, and value in themselves. This leads Boszormenyi-Nagy to forceful and repeated emphasis on Buber's distinction between *intrapsychic guilt feelings* and *interhuman existential guilt.*

The therapist who wants to liberate the patient from his concern for or guilt-laden loyalty to members of his family may succeed in removing certain manifestations of psychological guilt, but may at the same time increase the patient's existential guilt. Buber distinguished between guilt feelings and existential guilt. The latter obviously goes beyond psychology: It has to do with objective harm to the order and justice of the human world. If I really betrayed a friend or if my mother really feels that I damaged her through my existence, the reality of a disturbed order of the human world remains, whether I can get rid of certain guilt feelings or not. Such guilt becomes part of a systemic ledger of merits and can only be affected by action and existential rearrangement, if at all.[8]

However valuable its contribution to the understanding of man as a closed system, any psychodynamic theory that confines itself to the motivation of the individual can be potentially socially destructive in its failure to meet the demands of our age for being aware of and responding to the needs of others. What makes a family perspective on justice particularly essential is the fact that some persons will never face or even recognize the injustice they have inflicted upon others except through the penalty their children pay. The family therapist focuses on a specific existential dimension that is being avoided, denied, and eroded in our age: the accounts of the justice of the human world. The family therapist must act in terms of a transgenerational bookkeeping of merits, an invisible systemic ledger of justice that resides in the interpersonal fabric of human order or the "realm of the between."

The therapist must distinguish between the person-to-person exploitativeness of nongiving or nonreciprocal taking and the structural exploitation that originates from system characteristics that victimize both participants at the same time. An imbalance between two or more partners in relationships registers subjectively as exploitation by the other. Moreover, an individual can be "caught" in existential guilt through the actions of others as one inherits a place in the multigenerational network of obligations and becomes accountable in the chain of past traditions. The less one is aware of these obligations, the more one will be at the mercy of these invisible forces.[9]

Boszormenyi-Nagy sees the modern illusion of replacing rather than mitigating retributive justice with humanity as a great hypocrisy, which is a threat to the dynamic fiber of society itself. "Whereas an individual's *guilt feelings* can be understood without a consideration of the other members' feelings and reactions, the underlying existential guilt cannot." Therefore, the question of justice cannot be reduced to a matter of individual forgiveness or love, as so many imagine. What is more, "in not holding the innocent child accountable for the father's sins or the parents for their child's transgressions, we may overlook actual but hidden forces of complicity that reside in the family system."

The family therapist discovers that "past relational accounts which cannot be settled through self-reflecting analysis, transference resolution, and insight can actually be resolved through interpersonal initiative and corrective action, often in a three generational context." Personal exploitation is measurable only on a subjective scale that has been built into the person's sense of the meaning of his entire existence. The family therapist must deal with the subjective measure of exploitation of each member of the family system. "By opening up the door to rebalancing of merits through action, the process of therapy may reverse the accumulation and perpetuation of loaded, unsettled accounts which could otherwise prejudice the chances of future generations."[10]

Buber's and Boszormenyi-Nagy's concept of "the just order of the human world" is a dialogical one. However pathological it may be, the unique experience of each of the persons in the family is itself of value: It enters into the balance of merit and into the dialogical reality-testing—the "dialogue of touchstones." The scapegoater in the family can be looked upon as needing help and the scapegoat as a potential helper; for the former is taking an ever heavier load of guilt on himself and the latter is accumulating merit through being loaded on by others. Justice is, for Boszormenyi-Nagy, "a personal principle of equity of mutual give and take which guides the individual member of a social group in facing the ultimate consequences of his relationships with others."[11] The climate of trust that characterizes a social entity is the sum total of the subjective evaluations of the justice of each member's relational experiences within what Boszormenyi-Nagy calls the "revolving slate" of the historically formed merit ledger. The trustworthiness of relationships depends on earned relational merit.

We believe that the "interhuman" realm of justice of the human world is the foundation of the prospects of trust among people. . . . Attempts at denying or escaping from such accounting constitute a major dynamic of every relationship system. While such escape may be necessary temporarily for the person's autonomous explorations, it must be uncovered and faced if the social system is to remain productive of healthy growth.[12]

Insight alone—the confrontation with the merit ledger—is only the preface to the task of actively balancing relationships. In *The Knowledge of Man*, Martin Buber sees the overcoming of existential guilt as taking place through the three stages of illuminating that guilt, persevering in that illumination, and repairing the injured order of being by re-entering the dialogue with the world. In exact parallel, Boszormenyi-Nagy sees knowledge of the self and increased assertiveness as finding their place in the context of the accounts of fairness and justice in close relationships. No matter how vindictive a person may feel, the therapeutic goal must ultimately be focused on mutual clarification and reconstruction in order to provide the adult child and his parents with the opportunity to break the destructive chainlike patterns of relationship that may have continued for several generations.

The injustice of the parentification of children by their parents can only be redressed if one first goes back to the relationship of the parents to their family of origin and does something about constructive repayment of indebtedness there. Thus, as a therapeutic goal, by exonerating their parents, children extend to them an especially needed, primary form of inherent residual acknowledgment. The family therapist must help the children obtain release from their captive victimization. In order to accomplish this, however, it is first necessary that the adult's own unmet dependency needs and unresolved negative loyalty ties, based on unjust treatment and exploitation by their families of origin, be recognized and worked through—whenever possible with the families of origin themselves. In many cases, even the terminal illness of the grandparent offers the opportunity for repayment of obligations and subsequent emotional liberation of all three generations from guilt. "We believe that the major avenue toward interrupting the multigenerational chain of injustices goes via repairing relationships, and not through the dichotomy of either magnifying or denying the injury done to particular members."[13] One of the great opportunities of Boszormenyi-Nagy's three-generational approach lies in the possibility of rehabilitating the member's painful and shameful image of his parents through helping the member understand the burdens laid on his parents by their families of origin.

By opening up the door to rebalancing merits through action, the process of family therapy may reverse the accumulation and perpetuation of loaded, unsettled accounts that prejudice the chances of future generations. This applies even to the so-called "paranoid."

> If a human being has been too deeply hurt and exploited to be able to absorb his wounds, he is entitled to a therapeutic recognition of the reality of his wounds and to a serious examination of the others' willingness to repair the damage. Only through such a "concession by the world" will he be prepared to reflect on the possible injustice of his own actions to others. . . . The badly hurt paranoid person should be given an extra chance, at least to the extent that the unfair balance of his justice is recognized. Whereas the reality of each member's early exploitation is anchored in the family's multigenerational ledger, each individual family member's sense of suffered injustice becomes his life-long programming for "emotional distortions," a psychological reality.[14]

Justice, like trustworthiness, characterizes the emotional climate and the underlying existential ledger of a relationship system. Both concepts lie beyond the realm of individual psychology, and both lead to a reexamination and redefinition of the theories of projection, reality-testing, fixation, displacement, transference, change, ego strength, and autonomy. From the standpoint of the relationship system, paranoia, for example, may be a partly reality-based stage of mind. Although it may be an overreaction to this particular person, it still grows out of a real ethical imbalance of the past. This redefinition of traditional psychological terms also leads Boszormenyi-Nagy to insight into the application of his dynamic of justice to the larger society as a whole. The "generation gap" is not one of communication, but rather of justice, Boszormenyi-Nagy claims. "Retributory projection on all parent-like persons might be an important component of the hostility that exists between youth and the older generation in any culture." Healing through meeting goes over here in all explicitness to the "Caring Community" that confirms otherness. "The greatest cultural task of our age," writes Boszormenyi-Nagy, "might be the investigation of the role of relational, not merely economic justice, in contemporary society. And the greatest gap in our social science pertains to the denial of the psychological significance of retributive social dynamics."[15]

Buber's just order of human existence and the existential guilt that arises from injuring that order are central to *Invisible Loyalties: Reciprocity in Intergenerational Family Therapy*, as Boszormenyi-Nagy himself points out:

> Contextual therapists had to rely on a concept borrowed from Buber, "the justice of the human order," as a quasi-objective criterion of interpersonal fairness. . . . The objectivity of relational justice is not an independent entity. It really is a dialectical criterion derived from the simultaneous consideration of the balance between two (or more) relating persons' subjective, self-serving rights and entitlements.[16]

You may go to the other end of the world to escape your family and be paralyzed by interhuman existential guilt. *Invisible Loyalties* goes beyond ordinary psychology with its emphasis on the intrapsychic by bringing in the notion of the interpersonal fabric, the merit ledger that is passed on from generation to generation. Some people will never face or recognize the injuries that they have done to the common order except perhaps through their grandchildren. But even for those who do not face it there will be consequences:

> The party who fails to earn merit vis-à-vis his relational partners or lastingly ignores his factual accountability for damaging consequences to posterity may become depressed, insomniac, anorectic, addicted, ruined by success, sexually malfunctional, relationally stagnant, accident-prone, or psychosomatically ill. As a psychological consequence, conscious or unconscious feelings of guilt may or may not accompany the person's disentitlement, i.e., the accumulation of existential guilt on his or her side.[17]

Nagy points out that what Buber defined as the genuine "I-Thou dialogue" is implicit in the systemic notion of the ledger of merits and the balance of give-and-take. "Only through the dialectic of the genuine mutuality of needs . . . can we arrive at the concept of the ethical existential ledger, according to which no concerned relative can gain by the 'success' of exploitative mastery over the other members of the family."[18]

Like Buber, Boszormenyi-Nagy does not stop with insight but goes on to action. Insight alone cannot overcome existential guilt. There has to be "rejunction," an actual repairing of the injured order of the world. Rejunction in no way cancels out the necessary movement of the child toward autonomy:

> Rejunction should not be confused with a thrust toward clinging togetherness. On the contrary, anything that undermines the trustworthy credibility of individual integrity drives people away from each other. Exploitative clinging to one's children, for example, has to be examined in the light of multilateral interests. Reasonable steps have to be made toward the autonomous development of the child. The "permission" for individuation represents an important trust-generating or rejunctive measure.[19]

In *Between Give and Take* Boszormenyi-Nagy and Krasner say that "the fundamental premise of the dialogical process is that people can still hope to bridge the chasm that exists between them and their legacies without having to relinquish their personal integrity and their capacity to be fair."[20] They also speak at length of "entitlement" where through caring and concern for others you will become entitled yourself. Rejunction and entitlement are clearly their ways of repairing the injured order of existence, of overcoming existential guilt.

We tend to see guilt as something that others have imposed on us. William Blake writes in "The Garden of Love":

> *I went to the Garden of Love*
> *And saw what I never had seen:*
> *A chapel was built in the midst,*
> *Where I used to play on the green.*
> *And the gates of the chapel were shut*
> *And "Thou shalt not" writ over the door.*
> . . . .
> *And priests in black gowns*
> *Were walking their rounds*
> *And binding with briars*
> *My joys and desires.*

We get the feeling that guilt is something *they* have invented to prevent *us* from having a good time. But existential guilt is not that. It is the rupture of the dialogue that stands at the heart of human existence, and the restoration of the injured order is, in fact, a renewal of the dialogue. We renew it through trustworthiness, merited trust built in relationship, which Nagy calls the fundamental resource of family therapy. This rejunction is identical with repairing the injured order of existence:

> The goal of contextual therapy is re-junction, rejoining that which has come apart. That is 1) an acknowledgement of the principle of equitable multilaterality [For example, the therapist uses multidirected partiality to get every person to bring in his or her subjective accounts and their understandings of the others.], 2) an ethically definable process of re-engagement in living mutuality, and 3) a commitment to fair balances of give-and-take. In other words, family members explore their capacity for reworking stagnant imbalances in how each of them uses the other and in how they are available to each other. The courage they invest in the review and repair of inadvertent relational corruption and exploitation yields returns in therapeutic resources, the chief among them being: earned trustworthiness.[21]

One part of our contemporary crisis is the denial of real guilt. Another is the complex and confused intermingling of real and neurotic guilt even when real guilt is not denied. This makes it a very delicate and subtle matter for both therapist and client to sort out the strands and know which at any given instant is which. The clinical psychologist A. David Feinstein offers a helpful suggestion for the approach to this sorting out:

> Identifying whether a patient is suffering from a neurotic or existential guilt is complicated by the fact that the two often combine and interact. Existential guilt may begin to lift once its meaning has been grasped, but accompanying neurotic guilt may already have been engaged. For instance, enjoying favorable circumstances in a world where many are suffering invites existential guilt when you are in some fundamental way denying your calling in relation to the human community. If you were also programmed to decrease your sense of selfworth whenever you get the bigger piece of the pie, neurotic guilt will also be present. If both forms

are thus engaged, it can be therapeutically useful to separate the informative aspects of the existential guilt from the punishing qualities of neurotic guilt. . . . Once this has been recognized and changes are made but guilt persists, counseling that challenges such guilt becomes appropriate.[22]

After reading *Invisible Loyalties*, a highly competent family psychiatrist commented: "The whole aim of psychotherapy has been to get rid of guilt, and now Nagy wants to bring it back in!" This comment, I suspect, grows out of and illustrates all three paradoxes of guilt. It seems likely that this psychiatrist was not familiar with the notion of existential, or real, guilt, in the first place. Second, in his practice I am sure that he has been so occupied with the neurotic guilt that he encounters that even if he had encountered existential guilt he would be more concerned about the neurotic and would have difficulty in distinguishing the one from the other. Third, even if the first two suppositions were not true, his clients would undoubtedly be so hung up on neurotic guilt that he would hesitate to introduce any notion of real guilt for fear of triggering off unhealthy reactions on their part. For him, therefore, Boszormenyi-Nagy's position would not constitute an adequate answer to our question, "What can a therapist committed to healing through meeting do in the face of the paradoxes of guilt?"

I believe that here Hans Trüb can come to our aid. Trüb experienced a crisis as a therapist from his denial of *ethos* and with it real guilt in favor of a higher "spiritual" plane to which he wished to bring his patients. After his crisis, Trüb concluded that the acceptance of real guilt is the beginning of responsibility, and responsibility is what enables the person whose relationship with the community has been ruptured to reenter into dialogue with the community. But Trüb also recognized that this rejunction with the community, to use Nagy's phrase, has to take place in two stages: First, the therapist has to realize that the person before him is someone who has been rejected and disconfirmed by the community, someone who stands in need of the understanding and confirmation that a confidant and big brother or big sister can give. Only later, after the therapist has succeeded in giving the patient the confirmation he has been denied, does the therapist enter the second state and place upon the patient the demand of the community in order to help the patient renew the dialogue with the community that has been injured or destroyed.

Placing the demand of the community does not mean any moralizing from above. It means connecting the hour of therapy with real life so that the client can recognize in the therapist a really other person who himself has real ties to the community and stands within it. Trüb's two stages are remarkably parallel, indeed, to the comfort and demand that the Hebrew prophet brought to the community of Israel in order to bring it back into dialogue with God. One part of that message was the recognition of real guilt, but another was the promise and renewal of dialogue:

> For a brief moment I forsook you,
> but with great compassion I will gather you.
> In overflowing wrath for a moment
> I hid my face from you,
> but with everlasting love I will have compassion on you.
> . . .
> For the mountains may depart
> and the hills be removed,
> but my steadfast love shall not depart from you,
> and my covenant of peace shall not be removed,
> says the Lord, who has compassion on you.
>
> (Isaiah 54:7–10)

Trüb's two stages cannot be applied mechanically. Only out of the dialogue itself will the therapist know when to bring comfort and when to place demand and when, perhaps, a combination of the two. Some persons may be so injured that it is hardly possible to reach the second stage, in which the full reality of healing through meeting can take place. Here the therapist not only needs all the wisdom and tact he can summon, but also the courage to address and the courage to respond of existential trust. All these will only have meaning, moreover, if they take effect within the act of inclusion in which the therapist makes the patient present and, through a bold, imaginative swinging, experiences his side of the bipolar relationship.

Chapter 15

THE DIALOGUE OF TOUCHSTONES

MY METAPHOR OF "touchstones of reality" originally evolved, as we have seen, as an approach to religion. From there, however, it moved into an approach to education and communication, and finally, over the course of time, to psychotherapy. As such, "touchstones of reality" represents in itself a unique meeting between psychology and religion.

In speaking of "touchstones of reality," I imply no separate and prior definition of "reality." On the contrary, I presuppose that it is not possible to speak of reality directly. Therefore, I cannot answer the traditional philosopher who asks what I mean by "reality" by pointing to a set of Platonic ideas or to any metaphysical absolute. But neither can I go along with those in our age who will want to reduce my "touchstones" to one or another form of subjectivism—whether it be the cultural relativist who says that since customs differ from one place to another, there really are no values, there are simply the needs and interests of a particular group; or the behaviorist psychologist who wishes to reduce values to a collection of reactions or chemical formulations; or the Freudian psychoanalyst who wants to reduce values to the superego introjected from the father through the fear of punishment; or the Sartrian existentialist who claims that values do not exist and we must invent them; or the linguistic analyst who says, "It is all right for you to feel all these things about God and ethics and reality, but you should not make the false inference that your feeling refers to anything outside itself." In contrast to all of these "points of view," I offer no "reality" independent of "touchstones," but also no "touch" independent of contact with an otherness that transcends my own subjectivity even when I respond to it from that ground and know it only in my contact with it. What I am concerned with is glimpses of a way at once uniquely personal and, I believe, broadly human. These glimpses have come to me in a series of separate yet not unconnected events and meetings of my life—meetings with persons, with situations, with the characters of literature, the scriptures of religions, and the writers who have spoken to me through their thoughts. In the residues of these events and meetings, a way in the present and into the future has opened up for me. For these residues, I claim what cannot be claimed for any objective metaphysics or subjective inspiration. They are "touchstones of reality."

What is most needed by the bewildered man of today is not theological systems or linguistic analyses but "an opening way."[1] The way does not always move easily like a boat drifting down the stream. More often it is a path through a forest that at times leads through the densest thickets and at times opens onto glades of breathtaking beauty. Certainly my own way has known as many pitfalls and roadblocks as breakthroughs and illuminations. When we try to hold on to our touchstones, moreover, we often lose that impact of otherness that gave them their weight of reality. Pascal sewed the word "fire" into his coat to remind him of his hour of mystical ecstasy, and much in life and thought testifies to his faithfulness to that memory. But many of us are like the children in Maurice Maeterlinck's play, who find the bluebird and put it into a cage only to see it turn before their eyes into a blackbird. We retain our touchstones only by plowing them back into our lives.

Touchstones have a history. They live with us. More than that, they enter into other touchstones that we have along the road. They do not always enter easily. There is sometimes great conflict and deep confusion. Touchstones have a two-sidedness that is at the same time a form of immediacy. Nothing can be so deeply confusing as to have known that immediacy and then to find your touchstone shattered or no longer there, replaced by another or perhaps by none at all. Then you ask yourself,

"Was that a delusion? Was there anything real there?" What is left that I may be faithful to?"

A touchstone of reality is either present or it has ceased to exist. Insofar as it is renewed or is taken into another touchstone, it is present. Insofar as two touchstones clash, that is real, too. I cannot speak of a "progressive revelation" or unbroken evolution of touchstones. I can only witness to life as I and my contemporaries have known it: discontinuous and broken, walking over abysses, encountering the absurd, and finding, at the same time, moments of meaning, moments of trust. Walking on our path, we encounter something that lights up for us—an event perhaps, but it might also be the teaching of the Buddha if that speaks to our condition. We cannot rise above our culture, but neither are we hermetically sealed within it. A Greek tragedy or a Rig Veda may say something to us just as any contemporary happening may.

Along with its other connotations, the word "touchstone" suggests probing, testing, proving—but in an existential sense; that is, as something we take back with us into the new situation that we meet. It helps us relate to that new situation, but the situation also modifies the touchstone. On us is laid the task, as long as we live, of going on probing, proving, testing, authenticating—never resting content with any earlier formulation. However true our touchstone, it will cease to be true if we do not make it real again by testing it in each new situation. This testing is nothing more nor less than bringing our life-stance into the moment of present reality. In contrast to the scientist who is only interested in particulars insofar as they yield generalizations, we can derive valid insights from the unique situations in which we find ourselves without having to claim that they apply to all situations and test the limits of their validity. Sometimes we find that these insights do hold for a particular situation and sometimes that they do not or that they have to be modified. Yet that does not mean that they cannot be valid insights for other situations.

Touchstones of reality are like insights, except that they are closer to events. An insight arises from a concrete encounter, but we tend to remove it too quickly and completely to a plane of abstractions. Any existential truth remains true only insofar as it is again and again tested in the stream of living. We have no secure purchase on truth above this stream. If we are going to walk on the road from touchstone to touchstone, we will have to wrestle painfully with the problem of when it is right to move in the direction of insight and philosophical abstraction and when we must move back into the living waters. The simple formulae—the either-ors—will not help. I cannot, for example, be either for the "verbal" or for the "non-verbal" in the abstract. There is a time for words and a time for silence, and a time for words that have between them thick silence. Every form of intellectual, philosophical, theological, psychological, sociological, economic, or political "party line" that tells us in advance how we ought to regard a situation gets in between us and the possibility of a fresh, unique response.

As we move through life, our relation to the events of our past changes and with it our interpretation of their meaning. Sometimes these changing interpretations derive from new touchstones that we have acquired along the way. Sometimes it is the other way around: our new touchstones derive from our testing of the old ones and from our reinterpretation of the events of which they are the residue. This does not mean that we begin with raw experience and later add meaning or interpretation to it. We never have experience by itself. Our attitude toward experience is always present along with the experience itself, even at the moment we are having it. As we keep growing, however, our attitude changes—not only toward present experience but toward the experiences we have had in the past.

I claim for touchstones what I claim for touching. Even if it is only a partial contact, that contact itself is a reality and a form of direct knowing, however illusory the inferences from the contact may be. It is not just that we have the *experience* of touching. On the contrary, to touch is to go through *and beyond* subjective experiencing: If I touch, if we touch, then there is a communication that is neither merely objective nor merely subjective, nor both together. The very act of touching is already a transcending of the self in openness to the impact of something other than the self. When two people really touch each other as persons—whether physically or not—the touching is not merely a one-sided impact: It is a mutual revelation of life stances.

Real communication means that each of us has some real contact with the otherness of the other. But this is only possible if each of us has related to the other's touchstones in his or her unique way. We can only really listen if we are willing both to be open and to respond personally.

The real "dialogue of touchstones" means that we respond from where we are, that we bring ourselves into the dialogue. The other person needs to know that he is really coming up against us as persons with touchstones of our own. Although each of us has his or her own viewpoint, we are not completely alone. We are able to share what is uniquely our own and, each of us in his or her own way, bring it into a common reality.

True education is an education in the communication of touchstones. Touchstones of reality always include the component of our unique response to them. We think we communicate when we set ourselves aside as persons, agree on definitions, and meet on the high plane of abstractions. But this is really another form of subjectivism, since only a few people, if any, will agree with our terms and what we propose that they should mean, and even those who "agree" will do so from the ground of a different life stance. For the rest, most of what we call communication is simply misunderstanding and mismeeting—people using words in different ways and not even caring enough to ask the other person what he means by what he says.

We help one another along the road when we share our touchstones *and* the confusion that sometimes accompanies them. We evolve our touchstones in relation with one another; we witness to one another. We have an impact on one another through which we grow in our own touchstones. Growing in this way, we come to recognize that the "dialogue of touchstones" is itself a touchstone of reality.

When I wrote *Touchstones of Reality* I thought of the "dialogue of touchstones" as fully mutual. Shortly after its publication, while I was a visiting fellow at Carl Rogers' Center for the Study of the Person in La Jolla, California, I came to understand the possibility of the dialogue of touchstones as an approach to psychotherapy in which there would be both mutuality and a "normative limitation of mutuality."

I came to this insight through a simple incident, one which at first glance seems to have nothing to do with therapy but in fact represents the meeting of therapy and teaching. During the spring semester of 1972, when I was Visiting Distinguished Professor at San Diego State University, I taught a course in religion and literature. In the class of 30 students was a young man of 25 who described himself as always having been a loner and who demonstrated an astonishing capacity for alienating the other members of the class. After a moving discussion in which several persons shared the suffering over the death of a daughter by cancer, the sickness of a friend, or their own personal hurt, this young man said, "None of you has ever really suffered." Later he told me that he had been sent to a writing clinic where a philosopher had criticized a paper he wrote because it began with the sentence "We exist in order to survive." "Which should I accept," this student asked me, "this philosopher's view or my own?" It struck me that this was an impossible question, which admitted of no answer. If he gave up his sentence, he was submitting to authority and suppressing his own unique touchstones of reality. On the other hand, if he tried to speak as he was, he would not communicate at all. Either way he was condemned to isolation.

It struck me shortly afterward that this must be overwhelmingly and terrifyingly the case for the so-called psychotic, the schizophrenic, or the paranoid, who also live facing the impossible choice of retreating within and pretending to go along with socially approved ways of speaking and acting or of "expressing" themselves and alienating everyone else in so doing. If, as I felt, they too have their "touchstones of reality," such an impossible choice represents a sort of death for them. Carl Rogers shows a clear understanding of this impossible choice in his discussion of loneliness in his commentary on Ellen West:

> The other element in our loneliness is the lack of any relationship in which we communicate our real experiencing—and hence our real self—to another. When there is no relationship in which we are able to communicate both aspects of our divided self—our conscious facade and our deeper level of experiencing—then we feel the loneliness of not being in real touch with any other human being.[2]

In his discussion of the injection and concealment of meaning, Lyman Wynne speaks of a wife who surrendered her belief in her own ideas and took on those of her husband with the result that her own experience was invalidated. "Her consensual validation of his viewpoint was at the cost of her own belief system and her own integrity."[3] In *The Politics of Experience*, Ronald Laing extends this consensual *in*validation to the relationship between psychiatrist and patient in which the psychiatrist acts as if there were only *one* valid point of view, his own:

The psychiatrist's part . . . is taken as the very touchstone for our common-sense view of normality. The psychiatrist, as *ipso facto* sane, shows that the patient is out of contact with him. The fact that he is out of contact with the patient shows that there is something wrong with the patient, but not with the psychiatrist. . . .

Psychiatrists have paid little attention to the *experience* of the patient. Even in psychoanalysis there is an abiding tendency to suppose that the schizophrenic's experiences are somehow unreal or invalid; one can make sense out of them only by interpreting them; without truth-giving interpretations the patient is enmeshed in a world of delusions and self-deception.[4]

Laing quotes Bert Kaplan's introduction to his collection of self-reports on the experience of being psychotic:

The process of psychotherapy consists in large part of the patient's abandoning his false subjective perspectives for the therapist's objective ones. But the essence of this conception is that the psychiatrist understands what is going on, and the patient does not.[5]

When a person is put in the role of a patient, Laing concludes, he "tends to become defined as a nonagent, as a nonresponsible object, to be treated accordingly, and even comes to regard himself in this light," as Erving Goffman has shown at length from his look from within at asylums.[6]

The "committed" person labeled as patient, and specifically as "schizophrenic," is degraded from full existential and legal status as human agent and responsible person to someone no longer in possession of his own definition of himself, unable to retain his own possessions, precluded from the exercise of his discretion as to whom he meets, what he does. . . . More completely, more radically than anywhere else in our society, he is invalidated as a human being. . . . Once a "schizophrenic," there is a tendency to be regarded as always a "schizophrenic."[7]

Psychotic experience goes beyond the horizons of our common, communal sense and may therefore be judged as invalidly mad, Laing points out. But it may also be validly mystical. An exile from the scene of being as we know it, the psychotic "is an alien, a stranger signaling to us from the void in which he is foundering, a void which may be peopled by presences that we do not even dream of." Madness may be break-through as well as breakdown, liberation and renewal as well as enslave-ment and existential death. Laing also suggests that we do not meet true madness in our society any more than we ourselves are truly sane: "The madness of our patients is an artifact of the destruction wreaked on them by us and by them on themselves."[8]

Laing proposes that instead of the *degradation* ceremonial of psychi-atric examination, diagnosis, and prognostication, we need for those who are about to go into a schizophrenic breakdown an *initiation* ceremonial, through which the person will be guided with full social encouragement and sanction into inner space and time, by people who have been there and back again.[9] Laing has tried to make this a reality in Kingsley Hall and the other centers of the Philadelphia Association in London. The Jungian analyst John Weir Perry has taken a kindred approach in such books as *The Far Side of Madness*,[10] and in Diabasis House in San Francisco, where a small group of acute schizophrenics could go through their journey in dialogue with sympathetic attendants and without the deadening effect of drugs.

In *The Politics of Experience*, Laing sometimes falls into romanticiza-tion of the schizophrenic as the pioneer of the Twenty-First Century. Schizophrenics are often terribly literal, rather than imaginative or creative, as Leslie Farber has pointed out, and *most* of them, in part certainly because of the way our society treats them, do not break through to a higher level of integration. Nonetheless, what Laing says in his soberer moments is entirely consonant with the dialogue of touch-stones as an approach to human existence in general and to therapy in particular:

> Existence is a flame which constantly melts and recasts our theories. Existential thinking offers no security, no home for the homeless. It addresses no one except you and me. It finds its validation when, across the gulf of our idioms and styles, our mistakes, errings and perversities, we find in the other's communication an experience of relationship estab-lished, lost, destroyed, or regained.[11]

Freud and many of the analysts who have followed him have been concerned with "reality-testing," and Adler, Jung, Reich, Sullivan, Fromm, Glasser, and Mowrer have each, in his way, been concerned with what Glasser has called "reality therapy." Yet few if any of them have gone beyond a monological approach to reality to an understanding of the central place of the dialogue of touchstones of reality. Sullivan, to be sure, used to say to young psychiatrists when they came to work with him, "I want you to remember that in the present stage of our society, the patient is right, and you are wrong."[12] And Jung, as we have seen, had gone surprisingly far in the direction of taking fully seriously the dialogue between therapist and patient and the extent to which each learns and changes in this dialogue.

Ivan Boszormenyi-Nagy has perhaps come closest to an explicit rejection of the old formula of "reality-testing" in favor of a dialogue of touchstones. Boszormenyi-Nagy concludes an imaginary vignette in which one friend complains that he has been treated unfairly with the statement: "Even though you may not be aware of having violated any mutually shared ethical principle, our parallel subjective reactions have consensually validated the relative objectivity of my suffered injustice." Then Boszormenyi-Nagy comments:

> The importance of the argument illustrated by this vignette lies in its emphasis on the mutuality of an action dialogue which is more than the sum total of two persons' subjective experiences. Thus, while the concept of reality-testing in psychology is a comparatively monothetical notion (one is either reality-bound or subject to distortion), the concept of the just order of the human world is a dialectical [I would say dialogical] one. A man's betrayal of his friend involves more than the vicissitudes of his repressed childhood wishes, depressions, etc. To decide on the extent of distortion would depend on his friend's vantage point too.[13]

Hanna Colm has also explicitly portrayed a dialogue of touchstones in her report of her personal experience in the "therapeutic encounter." Instead of looking at the patient's disturbed behavior as "pathology," she asks herself what its meaning is for his whole living. She recognizes that neurotic behavior and neurotic symptoms often express the degree to which a patient can live *with integrity.* "I look not for his pathology but for his integrity." This approach helps her to find the thwarted, yet basically positive, angles in the patient's behavior, to overcome her own obstacles to entering into the struggle with the patient, and to observe what genuine reactions his behavior causes in her. She uses these observations "as a starting point towards experiencing him and me in interaction, in a back and forth process of questioning both of us."

> In this process we both must be open to correct our experience of each other where it belongs to our past and is not a genuine reaction to the other person. This is the process which gradually heals, most of all the patient, but also the therapist, from leftover childhood ideals of perfection and the resulting disappointment about oneself, others, and life in general.[14]

Sidney Jourard also offers what amounts to a summing up of confirmation and healing through meeting in terms of dialogue of touchstones. "In true encounter," he says, "there is a collapse of roles and self-concepts." The therapist's willingness to disclose himself to the client to drop his mask is a factor in the client's trusting him and daring to disclose himself. "As I disclose myself to you, I am your world, and this world discloses new possibilities to you—it evokes new challenges and invitations that may stir you and enliven your imagination." Jourard holds that if he remains in dialogue with his client, he "may actually lead him to the edge of going out of his mind, thus clearing the way for the emergence of a new self." (A rather Laingian note.)

> In dialogue at its best, the participants remain in contact and let their reciprocal disclosures affect one another. If the dialogue occurs in the context of letting be and confirmation, then the weaker of the two may indeed flip into raw experiencing, find it safe and emerge in a more awakened state.[15]

The most impressive confirmation of my insight concerning the dialogue of touchstones as an approach to therapy is the writings of Harold Searles. Like Kaplan and Laing, Searles recognizes that "reality" and, by extension, the ability to be of help, has mostly been considered the monopoly of the therapist:

> Psychoanalytic literature is written with the assumption that the analyst is healthy and therefore does not need psychological help from the patient, who is ill and is therefore in need of psychological help from, and unable to give such help to, the analyst . . . it is a source of lasting pain to me that my analyst [of his training analysis], like each of my parents long before,

maintained a high degree of unacknowledgment of my genuine desire to be helpful to him.[16]

From his earliest papers, Searles has consistently stressed that there is an element of reality in all the patient's distorted transference projections of the analyst and that the transference symbiosis can itself become so reality related that it can evolve into a therapeutic symbiosis that is mutually growth enhancing and can lead to a healthier individuation for both therapist and patient.[17]

It is in the last part of his discussion of the schizophrenic individual's experience of his world that Searles becomes startlingly explicit and richly concrete in his exposition of the dialogue of touchstones. No matter how unwittingly, the patient has an active part in the development and maintenance of his illness. It is only by making contact with this essentially assertive energy in him that the therapist can help him to become well.

Searles makes three suggestions concerning psychotherapeutic technique that offer us a range of specific approaches to the dialogue of touchstones in therapy that no one else, so far as I know, has articulated. First, the therapist must realize that the patient has arrived at his perceptual world over years of employing the best judgment of which he is capable and that it is a world deserving of our respect. The therapist cannot ask him to relinquish it in favor of the view of "reality" the therapist offers him. "Invariably, the better I come to know him, and his life, and myself in relation to him, the more I am impressed at how much accuracy, often powerfully incisive accuracy, there is in his perception of me."

Second, Searles found it wise early in therapy to endeavor to accept his patient's feelings about the world as he perceives it rather than challenge the accuracy of his perception of the world. By an active imagining of the real, Searles made present to himself how terrified he would be to find himself closeted with a therapist whom he perceived as a homicidal maniac bent on killing him. This enables the patient to share his feelings with his therapist, who never intimates that he is crazy for holding the worldview he holds. The therapist candidly acknowledges and confirms the increments of reality in the patient's distorted view of him—no matter how embarrassing or painful these may be. In this process, the patient comes to remember his own past, but he also is able to replace the repressed, fragmentary, and contradictory self-images derived from conflictual family roles with the therapist's growing perception of him as a single coherent, three-dimensional whole. Thus through identification with the feeling image the therapist is developing of him, the patient gradually becomes a whole and integrated human being.[18]

The clearest exposition of the dialogue of touchstones is the last step in the therapeutic process in which the therapist looks alternatively, and during varying lengths of time, at the patient's world, sharing it with him, and giving him glimpses of his own view of the world. Through this alternation, the therapist helps the patient realize that there is both an inner and an outer world—something that had been lost to him through the confusion of his perceptions because of the binds imposed upon him by his family. This not only gives the patient back his own sense of reality; it also confirms him as a human being:

> By helping him to see, and at times insisting upon the differences between *his* world and *ours*, we help him to realize that he is a human being among fellow human beings, each of whom has his own individual worldview, and that all these collective worldviews can coexist and be meaningfully interrelated.[19]

Gradually both the therapist and the patient become unafraid of each one's own and of the other's world, and this leads to a truly mutual individuation. Passing through the fear of suicide and incurable insanity, "both participants develop the trustful realization that their two worlds can be fully looked at and freely changed." Both come out of this "therapeutic symbiosis" and the mutual individuation that follows deeply changed. The patient, it is hoped, will never again be vulnerable to psychosis. But neither will the therapist ever again need to repress so fully his own more primitive processes, including the kind of nonintegration and nondifferentiation of experience that comprise the defenses of his formerly psychotic patient.

In the last paragraphs of his paper, Searles goes beyond the "normative limitation of mutuality" to focus on what we, the so-called sane, can learn from the schizophrenic. As the shadow of the emotional deficiencies of our culture, schizophrenia casts light on the hypocrisies and previously unquestioned, implicit assumptions in our "normal existence." Through our dialogue with the schizophrenic's touchstones of reality, "we are better equipped to achieve a healthier culture and to live more fully, freely, and knowingly." Just because the schizophrenic has been living on the sidelines of humanity, he is in a position to give us a perspective we could not otherwise attain. The schizophrenic individual has not been faced with the question of *how* but of *whether* to relate to his fellow man. Through the act of inclusion, or imagining his touchstones of reality, we can recognize "that in us, too, this has been, all along, a meaningful and alive and continuing conflict, heretofore hidden from ourselves." Not only shall we no longer take anything for granted about human beings and human behavior, but we shall come to realize "that silence between persons is not necessarily a gulf, a void, but may be a tangibly richer communion than any words could constitute."[20]

When I say that Searles goes beyond the "normative limitations of mutuality," I do not mean, for a moment, that he changes the structure of the therapy situation in which one person is basically there to help and the other to be helped. Rather he shows us in a most concrete and convincing way that the schizophrenic's touchstones of reality are not just "real for him." They represent a genuine dialogue with "reality" that can deeply enrich our own relation to reality. Put in the language of Buber's "What Is Common to All," the schizophrenic, even in his desire to have a world of his own apart from the common world, helps to build up the common world of speech-with-meaning. His voice cannot be excluded without impoverishing us all. Though his interpretation of his experiences falls outside the realm of the common, his experiences themselves are real and have a place in the common world.

It is in this spirit of respect for the unique reality that has emerged from even the most psychotic patient's dialogue with the world that I have tried to develop my own thinking concerning the dialogue of touchstones as an approach to therapy. To identify and isolate "reality" has been a problem not just for philosophers, but also for every living human being. I have always been deeply moved by the lines that the American poet Vachel Lindsay wrote in his otherwise joyous poem, "The Chinese Nightingale," not too long before his own suicide:

Years upon years I but half remember,
May and June and dead December,
Dead December, then again June.
Man is a torch, then ashes soon.
Life is a loom weaving illusion.
O who will end my dream's confusion?

"Each person is a more or less naive ontologist," writes Ronald Laing. "Each person has views of what is and what is not." But many have been caught in the tension of multiple "realities" and multiple "touchstones." Some have tried to escape this tension through taking refuge in one or another form of absolutism, others in one or another reductionist point of view, still others in that "common sense" that Whitehead called the bad philosophy of two centuries ago, some in occultism, and some in a crude relativism. Touchstones of reality and the dialogue of touchstones offer an alternative to the either/or's of objective versus subjective, absolute versus relative, mind versus body, and rejection of the "schizophrenic" and the romantic glorification of him.

From the standpoint of the dialogue of touchstones, much of what we call "mental illness" can be seen as something that has happened to distort, objectify, or make merely cultural our touchstones of reality. Touchstones and the dialogue of touchstones begin in and are renewed by immediacy. Sickness is what prevents the return to immediacy. From this standpoint, "health" is not "adjustment," becoming rational or emotional, but rather coming to a firmer grasp of one's own touchstones of reality in dialogue with the touchstones of others. In this sense, the dialogue of touchstones may be the goal of therapy as well as the means. This goal helps the therapist avoid three equally bad alternatives— adjusting the client to the culture, imposing his own values on the client, or accepting whatever the patient says and does as healthy and romantically celebrating it.

Heinz Kohut speaks of the self-injured patient's fear of disintegrating if he reveals his repressed archaic material to the analyst. But there is a more pervasive fear than that: Every client fears that in entering into therapy he will have to sacrifice his own touchstones of reality, that he will have to subordinate himself to an external authority and join in invalidating his own touchstones as "sick." What makes this fear all too real is not only the psychiatrist who sets up his own "reality" as the sole standard of health, but also the "responsible" and "helpful" person who tends to handle both sides of the dialogue and thus *disenables* the other person to bring his own touchstones into the dialogue.

The therapist in the dialogue of touchstones cannot be someone who merely analyzes or reflects what the client says. He must also be someone who brings his own touchstones into the dialogue. The therapist has no monopoly on reality. The normative limitation to mutuality in the therapeutic dialogue of touchstones lies not only in the structure—who comes to see whom for help—but also in the fact that the therapist brings something to the dialogue that the severely neurotic and psychotic patient cannot bring. It is not that his experience is more real, deeper, and certainly, not by a long shot, more intense. It is only that he has more experience in inclusion, in imagining the real, in experiencing the other side of the relationship as well as his own, in seeing through the other's eyes as well as through his own.

If we begin by honoring each person's unique relation to reality, then to say of a person that he or she is "sick" does not imply that this person is outside reality, but only that he or she needs help in being brought into the dialogue of touchstones. When and insofar as the patient is so brought in, he is brought in from where he is. Or rather, to use Jourard's language, the patient responds to an invitation and brings himself into the dialogue. Therefore, the uniqueness of the patient's touchstone remains of primal concern. A uniqueness that is not brought into the dialogue atrophies; for it reaches its reality only in being called into existence and in responding to what calls it.

The terrible dilemma of the "sick" person, we have seen, is having to choose between giving up his touchstones in order to communicate or giving up communication. But a touchstone that is not brought into the dialogue ceases to be a touchstone. Instead the person is divided into an outer "social" mask and an inner hidden reality, and both are less than real. It does not matter whether the outer mask is social conformity or the defenses and postures of the schizophrenic who regards others and/or him- or herself as unreal; it is still far less than a human reality.

It also does not matter whether the inner "reality" is one that is repressed from consciousness or is eagerly cherished as the most precious "inward" possession. It too is vestigial, atrophied, less than a fully human or even fully personal reality.

But such a person needs the help of someone who can glimpse and share the unique reality that has come from this person's life experience and can help this person find a way of bringing it into the common order of existence so that he or she too may raise what he or she has experienced as "I" into the communal reality of "We." Thinkers and artists like Blake, Kierkegaard, Nietzsche, Van Gogh, and Jung have had the courage to hold the tension between their faithfulness to their touchstones of reality and their need to enter into communication with others, *and* they have had the genius to create bridges—of poetry, art, theology, philosophy, or psychology—by which a dialogue of touchstones could take place between them and the world. For ordinary persons who experience the gap between their unique experience and the common world, this is usually not possible. Such persons need the help of a therapist who can "imagine the real" and practice inclusion in order to help them enter into a dialogue of touchstones. Harold Searles offers us an example of such therapy from his own training analysis:

> Early in our third session, my first training analyst had suddenly stood up and permanently dismissed me. The despair which I brought into the first session with Dr. Hadley [his subsequent training analyst] was despair lest I would prove hopelessly unable to communicate my innermost feelings to any human being. At the end of that first session . . . I asked, "Do you see any reason why we can't work together?" He assured me, briefly but emphatically, "Hell no!"[21]

The help of the therapist is not, in the first instance, a matter of finding the right words, still less techniques of communication. It is a matter of the dialogue of touchstones coming into being between one who cannot reach out and one who can. "When one person is singing and cannot lift his voice," said a Hasidic rabbi, "and another comes and sings with him, another who can lift his voice, then the first will be able to lift his voice." "That," said the rabbi, "is the secret of the bond between spirit and spirit." The title that Martin Buber gave this Hasidic story of healing was not "The Helper" but "When Two Sing." It might also be called "Healing through Meeting" or even "A Dialogue of Touchstones." For this *is* the secret of the bond between spirit and spirit.

The helpfulness of the therapist does not lie in the fact that he or she is a better Socratic dialectician or that he or she articulates better, but rather that he or she can help the patient out of the unfruitful either/or of choosing between faithfulness to one's own emergent touchstones and relation with the community. Yet this is only possible in a situation of mutual trust. If the patient fears to expose himself for fear that the therapist or his family or his friends will invalidate what he has to contribute as worthless, then he will not be able to enter into the venture of the dialogue of touchstones. The goal of healing through meeting, of confirmation, and of the dialogue of touchstones is, therefore, the same—to establish a dialogue on the basis of trust. There is something the patient brings that no one else in the world can—his uniqueness.

The "confirmation of otherness" that the dialogue of touchstones assumes and brings into existence means that no voice is without value, no witness without reality. Every voice needs to be heard precisely because it represents a unique relationship to reality. Even though that voice may be distorted, "sick," and miserable, it still contains the nucleus of a unique touchstone that its very negativity both bears and conceals. People in our culture, especially the educated and the cultured, fear being put down because the emphasis in our culture is on the quick and facile response. The "community of affinity" protects itself through the either/or. Either you are one of us or you are not. If you are one of us, we do not need to hear you because we already know and represent your point of view. If you are different and if you disagree, we do not want to hear you because you "make waves"—you disturb the harmony of our likemindedness. Our society itself is sick—polarized into communities of affinity. Because this is so, the individual cannot help being sick, since he or she does not have the ground on which to stand and from which to enter into a genuine dialogue of touchstones.

Confirming the other, in the end, cannot mean just healing in the negative sense of making a single person whole. It must also mean a movement in the direction of a climate of trust, a caring community, a community that confirms otherness. Thus we can say of healing through meeting what we said of the dialogue of touchstones: It is not only the means to the goal; it is itself the goal. The third alternative to the sickness of conformity and the sickness of rebellion is the community that confirms otherness. Such a community gives each person a ground of his own, a ground from which he can touch the other's touching, a ground in which mutual confirming and healing through meeting can take place in spiraling circles that bring more and more of each person's touchstones—whether born of trauma or of ecstasy—into the reality of life together. This is the secret of the bond between person and person.

NOTES

CHAPTER 1

1. For a fuller interpretation of Job and biblical faith, see Maurice Friedman, *Problematic Rebel; Melville, Dostoievsky, Kafka, Camus*, 2nd rev. and expanded ed. (Chicago: University of Chicago Press, Phoenix Books, 1970).
2. Herman Melville, *The Confidence-Man: His Masquerade* (New York: Grove Press, 1949), 187.
3. Martin Buber, *Pointing the Way: Collected Essays*, ed. & trans. with an Introduction by Maurice Friedman (Atlantic Highlands, NJ: Humanities Press International, 1990), 223 f., 229.
4. Martin Buber, *Between Man and Man*, trans. by Ronald Gregor Smith with an Introduction by Maurice Friedman (New York: Macmillan Books, 1985), "What Is Man?" 196 f.
5. Martin Buber, *The Knowledge of Man: A Philosophy of the Interhuman*, ed. with an Introductory Essay by Maurice Friedman, trans. by Maurice Friedman and Ronald Gregor Smith (Atlantic Highlands, NJ: Humanities Press International, 1988), "Elements of the Interhuman," Sec. 3, "Personal Making Present."
6. *Ibid.*, "What is Common to All," trans. by Maurice Friedman, Sec. 8.
7. Buber, *Between Man and Man*, "The Question to the Single One," 60–62.

CHAPTER 2

1. With the exception of the section on Buber's "The Way of Man," this

chapter is based upon Maurice Friedman, *A Dialogue with Hasidic Tales: Hallowing the Everyday* (New York: Human Sciences Press, 1988).

2. Martin Buber, *Hasidism and Modern Man*, trans. & ed. with an Introduction by Maurice Friedman (Atlantic Highlands, NJ: Humanities Press International, 1988), Book IV—"The Way of Man. According to the Teachings of Hasidism," 173 f.

3. Buber, *Hasidism and Modern Man*, Book IV—"The Way of Man," 142.

4. Martin Buber, *Ten Rungs: Hasidic Sayings*, trans. by Olga Marx (New York: Schocken Books, 1947), 37 f.—"In the Dust"; Martin Buber, *The Tales of the Hasidim: The Early Masters*, trans. by Olga Marx (New York: Schocken Books, 1961), 66—"The Limits of Advice"; Martin Buber, *The Origin and Meaning of Hasidism*, ed. & trans. with an Introduction by Maurice Friedman (Atlantic Highlands, NJ: Humanities Press International, 1988), 166 f.; Martin Buber, *Tales of the Hasidim: The Later Masters*, trans. by Olga Marx (New York: Schocken Books, 1961), 17—"Everywhere."

5. Buber, *Hasidism and Modern Man*, 176.

6. *Ibid.*, 42 f.

7. *Ibid.*, 175.

8. *Ibid.*, 38–40.

9. Martin Buber, *The Tales of the Hasidim: The Early Masters*, trans. by Olga Marx (New York: Schocken Books, 1961), 277—"Climbing Down."

10. Martin Buber, *The Origin and Meaning of Hasidism*, ed. & trans. with an Introduction by Maurice Friedman (Atlantic Highlands, NJ: Humanities Press International, 1988), 142 f.

11. *Early Masters*, 109 f.—"The List of Sins."

12. Cf. Tamar Kron and Rafi Yungman, "Martin Buber's 'Inclusion'—An Answer to a Dilemma of the Psychotherapist," *Israel Journal of Psychiatry and Allied Professions*, Spring 1988.

13. *Early Masters*, 196—"The Letter."

14. *Ibid.*, 255 f.—"The Penitent."

15. Maurice Friedman, *The Healing Dialogue in Psychotherapy* (New York: Jason Aronson, 1985)—"Empathy, Identification, Inclusion, Intuition," 203.

16. *Early Masters*, 53.

17. Martin Buber, *Tales of the Hasidim: The Later Masters*, trans. by Olga Marx (New York: Schocken Books, 1961), 111—"Turning Point."

18. *Later Masters*, 288 f.—"The Sacred Goat."

19. *Early Masters*, 126—"When Two Sing."

CHAPTER 3

1. Martin Buber, *Between Man and Man*, trans. by Ronald Gregor Smith with an Introduction by Maurice Friedman (New York: Macmillan Paperbacks, 1985), 114.
2. *Ibid.*, 52.
3. Martin Buber, *The Knowledge of Man: A Philosophy of the Interhuman*, ed. with an Introductory Essay by Maurice Friedman (Atlantic Highlands, NJ: Humanities Press International, 1988), "Elements of the Interhuman," trans. by Ronald Gregor Smith, 74 f.
4. Martin Buber, *Eclipse of God. Studies in the Relation of Religion and Philosophy* with an Introduction by Robert M. Seltzer (Atlantic Highlands, NJ: Humanities Press International, 1988), "Religion and Philosophy," trans. by Maurice Friedman, 35.
5. Martin Buber, *Good and Evil: Two Interpretations* (New York: Scribner's Paperbacks [Macmillan], 1980), 129.
6. *The Worlds of Existentialism: A Critical Reader*, ed. with Introductions and a Conclusion by Maurice Friedman (Atlantic Highlands, NJ: Humanities Press International, 1991), 497.
7. Leslie H. Farber, *The Ways of the Will: Toward a Psychology and Psychopathology of the Will* (New York: Basic Books, 1966), "Will and Willfulness in Hysteria," "Despair and the Life of Suicide," "The Therapeutic Despair," and "Schizophrenia and the Mad Psychiatrist." See also Leslie H. Farber, *lying, despair, jealousy, envy, sex, suicide, drugs, and the good life* (New York: Basic Books, 1976).
8. Maurice Friedman, *The Healing Dialogue in Psychotherapy* (New York: Jason Aronson, 1985, reprinted 1989).
9. Richard Hycner, *Between Person and Person: Toward a Dialogical Psychotherapy* (Highland, NY: The Center for Gestalt Development, 1991).
10. See Buber, *The Knowledge of Man*, Chap. 1—Maurice Friedman's "Introductory Essay" and Chap. 2—"Distance and Relation," trans. by Ronald Gregor Smith.

CHAPTER 4

1. Sigmund Freud, *New Introductory Lectures on Psycho-Analysis*, trans. by J.H. Sprott (New York: W.W. Norton, 1933), "A Philosophy of Life," Chap. 7, 217–219, 229 f.

2. Sigmund Freud, *The Future of an Illusion*, translated by W.D. Robson-Scott (New York: The International Psychoanalytical Library, 1953); 33, 56.
3. Sigmund Freud, *New Introductory Lectures on Psycho-Analysis*, 217–219.
4. *Ibid.*
5. Cf. Sigmund Freud, *Totem and Taboo & Other Works. The Complete Psychological Works of Sigmund Freud*, Vol. XIII, trans. under the editorship of James Strachey, Anna Freud, *et. al.* (London: The Hogarth Press & the Institute of Psycho-Analysis, 1955), 157 f.
6. Maurice Friedman, *Touchstones of Reality: Existential Trust and the Community of Peace* (New York: E.P. Dutton, 1972); Maurice Friedman, *The Human Way: A Dialogical Approach to Religion and Human Experience* (Chambersburg, PA: Anima Publications, 1982).
7. Maurice Friedman, *The Human Way*, 4.
8. *Ibid.*, 29 f.
9. *Ibid.*, 7 f.
10. Maurice Friedman, *To Deny Our Nothingness: Contemporary Images of Man*, 3rd rev. ed. with a new Preface and Appendix (Chicago: University of Chicago Press, Phoenix Books and Midway Books, 1978), 18. I have amended the text slightly to remove what today would be considered "sexist" language.
11. Friedman, *Touchstones of Reality*, 311 f.

CHAPTER 5

1. "Looked at theologically, my concept of the anima . . . is pure Gnosticism; hence I am often classed among the Gnostics. On top of that, the individuation process develops a symbolism whose nearest affinities are to be found in folklore, in Gnostic, alchemical, and suchlike 'mystical' conceptions, not to mention shamanism. When material of this kind is adduced for comparison, the exposition fairly swarms with 'exotic' and 'farfetched' proofs, and anyone who merely skims through a book instead of reading it can easily succumb to the illusion that he is confronted with a Gnostic system. In reality, however, individuation is an expression of that biological process . . . by which every living thing becomes what it was destined to become from the beginning. This process naturally expresses itself in man as much psychically as somatically. On the psychic side it produces those well-known quaternity symbols, for instance, whose parallels are found in mental asylums as well as in Gnosticism. . . . Hence it is by no means a case of mystical speculations, but of clinical observations

and their interpretation, through comparison with analogous phenomena in other fields." C. G. Jung, *Psychology and Religion: East and West. Collected Works*, Vol. XI, translated by R. F. C. Hull (New York: Pantheon Books, Bollingen Series XX, 1958), 306 f. The material in the long paragraph above where this note appears in my text is also based on *Psychology and Religion: East and West.*

2. C. G. Jung, *Modern Man in Search of a Soul*, trans. by W. S. Dell & Carl F. Baynes (New York: Harcourt Brace & Co., 1934), 239.

3. *Ibid.* (Harvest: HBJ book, undated); 212.

4. C. G. Jung, *Memories, Dreams, Reflections*, recorded & ed. by Aniela Jaffe, trans. by Richard & Clara Winston (New York: Pantheon Books, 1961), 206; italics added.

5. C. G. Jung, *Psychology and Alchemy Collected Works*, Vol. XII, translated by R. F. C. Hull (New York: Pantheon Books, Bollingen Series XX, 1953), 31, 35.

6. *Ibid.*, 36.

7. C. G. Jung, *Aion: Researches into the Phenomenology of the Self Collected Works*, Vol. IX, Part II, translated by R. F. C. Hull (New York: Pantheon Books, Bollingen Series XX, 1959), 35.

8. *Ibid.*, 70.

9. *Ibid.*, 198, 204, 190, 196, 195.

10. *Ibid.*, 223.

11. *Ibid.*, 269, 221.

12. *Ibid.*, 255 f.

13. C. G. Jung, *The Development of Personality Collected Works*, Vol. XVII, translated by R. F. C. Hull (New York: Pantheon Books, Bollingen Series, 1954), 174 f.

14. *Ibid.*, 175 to 177.

15. *Ibid.*, 183; italics added.

16. *Ibid.*, p. 179.

17. *Ibid.*, 184, 180.

18. C. G. Jung, *Psychology and Religion: West and East Collected Works*, Vol. XI, translated by R. F. C. Hull (New York: Pantheon Books, Bollingen Series, 1958), 82, 96, 157; italics added.

19. C. G. Jung, *Two Essays on Analytical Psychology Collected Works*, Vol. VII, translated by R. F. C. Hull (New York: Pantheon Books, Bollingen Series, 1953), 237.

20. C. G. Jung, *Answer to Job*, translated by R. F. C. Hull (Cleveland and New York: The World Publishing Co., a Meridian Book, 1960), 53; italics added. *Answer to Job* is included in Jung, *Psychology and Religion, op. cit.*

21. For my interpretation of the Book of Job, see Maurice Friedman, *Problematic Rebel: Melville, Dostoievsky, Kafka, Camus*, 2nd rev. & radically reorganized ed. (Chicago: University of Chicago Press, Phoenix Books, 1970), 12–22.
22. Jung, *Answer to Job*, 95 f.
23. *Ibid.*, 96, 178.
24. *Ibid.*, 183; italics added.
25. *Ibid.*, 133, 108, 155.
26. *Ibid.*, 118, 136, 176.
27. *Ibid.*, 179, 186.
28. *Ibid.*, 186.
29. *Ibid.*, 203.
30. That Jung may not have entirely escaped from this danger is suggested by his celebration in *Answer to Job* of the new Roman Catholic dogma of the Assumption of Mary. He considers this dogma "to be the most important religious event since the Reformation"—not because of any of the reasons that the Catholic Church would hold to be important, but because it gives the feminine principle the place in the deity that Jung's psychology calls for!
31. Martin Buber, *Eclipse of God: Studies in the Relation between Religion and Philosophy* (Atlantic Highlands, NJ: Humanities Press International, 1988), "Religion and Modern Thinking," trans. by Maurice Friedman, 79, 83 f.
32. *Ibid.*, 88 f.
33. Viktor E. Frankl, *The Unconscious God: Psychotherapy and Theology* (New York: Simon & Schuster, 1975), 63–65.

CHAPTER 6

1. Erich Fromm, *Man for Himself: An Inquiry into the Psychology of Ethics* (New York: Rinehart & Co., 1947), 7.
2. Erich Fromm, *The Art of Loving, World Perspectives*, Vol. IX (New York: Harper & Brothers, 1956), 28.
3. *Ibid.*, 55 f.
4. *Ibid.*, 45.
5. Erich Fromm, *The Heart of Man, Its Genius for Good and Evil*, Vol. XII of *Religious Perspectives*, ed. by Ruth Nanda Anshen (New York: Harper & Row, 1964).

CHAPTER 7

1. Edward Hoffman, *The Right to Be Human: A Biography of Abraham Maslow* (Los Angeles: Jeremy P. Tarcher, 1988), 109 f., 256 f.
2. Abraham H. Maslow, *Toward a Psychology of Being*, 2nd ed. (New York: D. Van Nostrand Co., 1968), 5.
3. Abraham H. Maslow, *Religions, Values, and Peak-Experiences* (New York: Penguin Books, 1976), 95, 99.
4. *Ibid.*, 7.
5. Maslow, *Toward a Psychology of Being*, 7.
6. Hoffman, *Right to Be Human*, 266 f.
7. Maslow, *Toward a Psychology of Being*, 76–96.
8. *Ibid.*, 104–106, 108–111.
9. *Ibid.*, 114.
10. *Ibid.*, 115–123.
11. Maslow, *Religions, Values, and Peak-Experiences*, 16, 19–21, 27 f., 85 f.
12. *Ibid.*, 54.
13. *Ibid.*, 54–56, 60, 65.
14. *Ibid.*, viii f.
15. *Ibid.*, ix–xiii.
16. *Ibid.*, xiv.
17. *Ibid.*, xvi.
18. Maurice Friedman, *The Hidden Human Image* (New York: Delacorte Press, 1974), 289.

CHAPTER 8

1. Viktor E. Frankl, *Man's Search for Meaning*, rev. & updated (New York: Washington Square Press, 1985), 125 f.; Viktor E. Frankl, *The Unconscious God: Psychotherapy and Theology* (New York: Simon & Schuster, 1975), 21.
2. Viktor E. Frankl, *Psychotherapy and Existentialism: Selected Papers on Logotherapy* (New York: Washington Square Press, 1967), 15.
3. Frankl, *Man's Search for Meaning*, 88.
4. Viktor E. Frankl, *The Doctor and the Soul: From Psychotherapy to Logotherapy*, 2nd rev. & expanded ed. with added chapter in English by author, trans. by Richard & Clara Winston (New York: Alfred A. Knopf, 1972), xx.
5. I have written elsewhere of the bewildering intermixture of personal

freedom and psychological compulsion that characterizes modern man. See Maurice Friedman, *Contemporary Psychology: Revealing and Obscuring the Human* (Pittsburgh, PA: Duquesne University Press, 1984), Chap. 13.

6. Frankl, *Man's Search for Meaning*, 98.
7. Frankl, *The Doctor and the Soul*, x, 55.
8. Viktor E. Frankl, *The Will to Meaning: Foundations and Applications of Logotherapy* (New York & Cleveland: The World Publishing Co., 55 f., 63; Frankl, *The Unconscious God*, 56.
9. Frankl, *Psychotherapy and Existentialism*, 11, 67, 136.
10. Frankl, *Man's Search for Meaning*, 143, 162.
11. Frankl, *The Will to Meaning*, 18 f.; Frankl, *The Doctor and the Soul*, 136 f.
12. *Will to Meaning*, 8 f.
13. *Psychotherapy and Existentialism*, 81 f.
14. Viktor E. Frankl, *The Unheard Cry for Meaning: Psychotherapy and Humanism* (New York: Simon & Schuster, 1978), 66 f.; italics added.
15. *Ibid.*, 66 f., 72.
16. *Psychotherapy and Existentialism*, 51.
17. Martin Buber, *The Knowledge of Man: The Philosophy of the Interhuman*, ed. with an Introductory Essay (Chap. 1) by Maurice Friedman (Atlantic Highlands, NJ: Humanities Press, 1988), "What Is Common to All," trans. by Maurice Friedman, Secs. 1, 4, 7, pp. 81, 88, 94.
18. *The Doctor and the Soul*, p. x; *Psychotherapy and Existentialism*, 57, 72; *The Will to Meaning*, 145.
19. *The Doctor and the Soul*, 62 n., 270 n.
20. *The Will to Meaning*, 154.
21. *The Unconscious God*, 25, 31, 38, 57.
22. *Ibid.*, 61 f., 66 f.
23. *The Unconscious God*, 72, 74; *The Doctor and the Soul*, xv, 270, 272 f., 276 f.
24. In the postscript to his classic work *I and Thou*, Buber writes that we must take care not to understand our dialogue with God as taking place solely alongside or above the everyday.

God's speech to men penetrates what happens in the life of each one of us, and all that happens in the world around us, biographical and historical, and makes it for you and me into instruction, message, demand. Happening upon happening, situation upon situation, are enabled and empowered by the personal speech of God to demand of the human person that he take his stand and make his decision.

Martin Buber, *I and Thou*, 2nd rev. ed. with Postscript by the Author added, trans. by Ronald Gregor Smith (New York: Charles Scribner's Sons, 1958), 136 f.

CHAPTER 9

1. Maurice Friedman, *To Deny Our Nothingness: Contemporary Images of Man*, 3rd rev. ed with new Preface & Appendix (Chicago: The University of Chicago Press, 1978), 211.
2. Maurice Friedman, *The Human Way: A Dialogical Approach to Religion and Human Experience* (Chambersburg, PA: Anima Publications, 1982), 117.
3. An excellent early example of the latter is Joseph E. Havens, ed., *Religion and Psychology* (New York: Van Nostrand Insight Books, 1968). Since then a good deal more has been written on psychology and religion, one of the best of which is Don S. Browning, *Religious Thought and the Modern Psychologies: A Critical Conversation in the Theology of Culture* (Philadelphia: Fortress Press, 1987).
4. Maurice Friedman, *Touchstones of Reality: Existential Trust and the Community of Peace* (New York: E.P. Dutton, 1972), 23.

CHAPTER 10

1. Friedrich Nietzsche, *Thus Spake Zarathustra*, trans. Thomas Common (New York: Modern Library, 1927), 56 f.
2. Nietzsche, *Thus Spake Zarathustra*, 63 f.
3. Martin Buber, *A Believing Humanism: Gleanings*, trans. with an Introduction and Explanatory Comments by Maurice Friedman (New York: Simon & Schuster, 1969), "On the Psychologizing of the World," 148. This book has been reprinted under the title *A Believing Humanism: My Testament* (Atlantic Highlands, NJ: Humanities Press International, 1990).
4. Martin Buber, *Between Man and Man*, trans. by Ronald Gregor Smith with an Introduction by Maurice Friedman (New York: Macmillan, 1985), "Dialogue," 21–14.
5. Buber, *Believing Humanism*, "On the Psychologizing of the World," 150. (See note 3 above.)

CHAPTER 11

1. Ernst Cassirer, *Language and Myth*, trans. by Suzanne Langer (New York: Harper and Brothers, 1946), 11, 18, 27.

2. H. and H.A. Frankfort, *et. al., The Intellectual Adventure of Ancient Man: An Essay on Speculative Thought in the Ancient Near East* (Chicago: University of Chicago Press, 1946), 4 ff. and concluding chapter, "The Emancipation of Thought from Myth," which is also found in H. and H.A. Frankfort, *et. al., Before Philosophy*, Chapter 8 (New York: Penguin Books), 241–48.

3. Martin Buber, *Prophetic Faith*, trans. from the Hebrew by Carlyle Witton-Davies (New York: Macmillan, 1986), 46.

4. Martin Buber, *Moses: The Revelation and the Covenant* (Atlantic Highlands, New Jersey: Humanities Press International, 1988), 16 f.

5. Martin Buber, *Hasidism and Modern Man*, ed. and trans. with an Introduction by Maurice Friedman (Atlantic Highlands, NJ: Humanities Press International, 1988), 26.

6. Harry M. Buck, Jr., "From History to Myth: A Comparative Study," *The Journal of Bible and Religion*, Vol. XXIX, July 1961, 219 f.

7. Mircea Eliade, *Cosmos and History: The Myth of the Eternal Return*, trans. by Willard Trask (New York: Harper Torchbooks, 1959), 85.

8. *Ibid.*, 106 f.

9. *Ibid.*, 156.

10. *Ibid.*, 162.

11. *Ibid.*, 154 f.

12. *Ibid.*, 132.

13. Martin Buber, *Pointing the Way*, trans. and ed. by Maurice Friedman (Atlantic Highlands, NJ: Humanities Press International, 1990), "Prophecy, Apocalyptic, and the Historical Hour," 200. See 192–207: Martin Buber, *Israel and the World: Essays in a Time of Crisis* (New York: Schocken Books, 1963), "The Two Foci of the Jewish Soul," 36.

14. Eliade, *Cosmos and History*, 158 f.

15. Joseph Campbell, 2nd ed., *The Hero with a Thousand Faces* (Princeton, NJ: Princeton University Press, 1968), 9.

16. *Ibid.*, 121.

17. *Ibid.*, 19.

18. *Ibid.*, 257, 259.

19. *Ibid.*, 260, 386, 388.

20. *Ibid.*, 386, 388.

21. *Ibid.*, 164 f.

22. *Ibid.*, 236–238, 243.

23. *Ibid.*, 12 f.

24. Joseph Campbell, *Myths to Live By* (New York: Bantam Books, 1973), 10, 25, 29.

25. Joseph Campbell, *The Power of Myth* with Bill Moyers, ed. by Betty Sue Flowers (New York: Doubleday, 1988), 154.
26. Martin Buber, *Tales of the Hasidim: The Early Masters*, trans. by Olga Marx (New York: Schocken Books, 1961), 156.
27. Campbell, *The Power of Myth*, 159.
28. Campbell, *Myths to Live By*, 92 f.
29. Campbell, *The Power of Myth*, 91, 118, 120, 229.
30. *Ibid.*, 120.

CHAPTER 12

1. Letter from Ivan Boszormenyi-Nagy to Maurice Friedman, June 21, 1974.
2. C. G. Jung, *The Undiscovered Self*, trans. by R. F. C. Hull (Boston: Little, Brown), 1958, 12.
3. Viktor E. Frankl, "The Image of Man in Psychotherapy," trans. by William Hallo, in *The Worlds of Existentialism: A Critical Reader*, ed. with Introductions and a Conclusion by Maurice Friedman (Atlantic Highlands, NJ: Humanities Press International, 1991), 468.
4. Rollo May, *Power and Innocence: A Search for the Sources of Violence* (New York: Norton, 1972).
5. Ferdinand Ebner, "The Word and Spiritual Realities" in Maurice Friedman, *The Worlds of Existentialism*, 294–296.
6. Martin Buber, *I and Thou*, 2nd ed., trans. by R. G. Smith (New York: Scribner's, 1958), 69 f. Ebner's and Buber's intuition of the origin of insanity have been confirmed by Viktor von Weizsäcker, a German psychiatrist who made an important contribution to psychosomatic medicine. See Maurice Friedman, *The Worlds of Existentialism*, 405–410.
7. Martin Buber, *Between Man and Man*, trans. by Ronald Gregor Smith with an Introduction by Maurice Friedman (New York: Macmillan Books, 1985).
8. Marvin J. Spiegelman, "Some Implications of the Transference" in *Speculum Psychologiae, Festschrift für C. A. Meier* (Zurich: Raschon Verlag, 1965).
9. Martin Buber, *A Believing Humanism: My Testament*, trans. with Explanatory Comments by Maurice Friedman (Atlantic Highlands, NJ: Humanities Press International, 1990), "The Unconscious," notes taken by Maurice Friedman at the seminars on the unconscious and dreams given by Buber for the Washington (D.C.) School of Psychiatry in the Spring of 1957, 153–173.
10. Buber, *Between Man and Man*, 196 f., italics added.

11. Hans Trüb, "Healing through Meeting" in Friedman, *The Worlds of Existentialism*, 504.

12. Buber, *A Believing Humanism*, "The Unconscious," 167 f.

13. Maurice Friedman, *The Confirmation of Otherness: In Family, Community, and Society* (New York: Pilgrim Press, 1983), Chaps. 5–8.

14. Ivan Boszormenyi-Nagy, "Intensive Family Therapy as Process," in Ivan Boszormenyi-Nagy and J. L. Framo, eds., *Intensive Family Therapy: Theoretical and Practical Aspects* (New York: Harper & Row, Hoeber Medical Division, 1965), 120.

15. See Maurice Friedman, *The Healing Dialogue in Psychotherapy* (New York: Jason Aronson, 1985), Chap. 11—"Disconfirmation and 'Mental Illness.' "

16. Maurice Friedman, "Introductory Essay" to Buber, *The Knowledge of Man: A Philosophy of the Interhuman*, trans. by Maurice Friedman and Ronald Gregor Smith (Atlantic Highlands, NJ: Humanities Press International, 1988) 28 f.; Buber, *A Believing Humanism*, "The Unconscious," 169–173.

17. Carl R. Rogers, *On Becoming a Person: A Therapist's View of Psychotherapy* (Boston: Houghton Mifflin, 1961), 55 f.

18. Buber, *Believing Humanism*, "The Unconscious," 169–173; Maurice Friedman, "Introductory Essay" to Buber, *The Knowledge of Man*, 28 f.

19. Buber, *Knowledge of Man*, Appendix: "Dialogue between Martin Buber and Carl R. Rogers," Moderated by Maurice Friedman, 169 f. This dialogue has now been reprinted as the first of a number of dialogues in *Carl Rogers: Dialogues*, ed. by Howard Kirschenbaum and Valerie Henderson (Boston: Houghton Mifflin, 1989).

20. *Ibid.*, 180 f.

21. *Ibid.*, 181 f.

22. *Ibid.*, 182 f.

23. *Ibid.*

24. Maurice Friedman, *The Confirmation of Otherness*, Chaps. 6–7.

25. Leslie H. Farber, *lying, despair, jealousy, envy, sex, suicide, drugs, and the good life* (New York: Basic Books, 1976), 165.

26. Buber, *Pointing the Way*, "Bergson's Concept of Intuition," 86.

27. Buber, *I and Thou*, 132 f.

28. Harry Stack Sullivan, *Conceptions of Modern Psychiatry* (New York: W. W. Norton, 1940), 90.

29. Leslie H. Farber, "Martin Buber and Psychotherapy" in Paul Arthur Schilpp and Maurice Friedman, eds., *The Philosophy of Martin Buber*

volume of *The Library of Living Philosophers*, ed. Paul A. Schilpp (LaSalle, Illinois: Open Court Publishing Co., 1967), 581.

CHAPTER 13

1. Ivan Boszormenyi-Nagy and Geraldine Spark, *Invisible Loyalties: Reciprocity in Intergenerational Family Therapy* (New York: Harper & Row, 1973; Brunner/Mazel, 1984), 24.
2. Ivan Boszormenyi-Nagy and Barbara R. Krasner, *Between Give and Take: A Clinical Guide to Contextual Therapy* (New York: Brunner/Mazel, 1986), 27.
3. *Ibid.*, 37.
4. Ivan Boszormenyi-Nagy, *Foundations of Contextual Therapy: Collected Papers of Ivan Boszormenyi-Nagy, M.D.* (New York: Brunner/Mazel, 1987), 255.
5. Boszormenyi-Nagy and Spark, *Invisible Loyalties*, 248; Boszormenyi-Nagy and Krasner, *Between Give and Take*, 61.
6. Boszormenyi-Nagy and Krasner, *Between Give and Take*, 102.
7. *Ibid.*, 218.
8. *Ibid.*, 326.
9. *Ibid.*, 27, 60, 383.
10. Boszormenyi-Nagy and Spark, *Invisible Loyalties*, p. 77; Boszormenyi-Nagy and Krasner *Between Give and Take*, 27, 61, 102, 189, 208, 368.
11. *Ibid.*, 28, 38, 58, 74 f., 88.
12. Boszormenyi-Nagy and Spark, *Invisible Loyalties*, 61, 69.
13. Boszormenyi-Nagy and Krasner, *Between Give and Take*, 176, 306 f.
14. *Ibid.*, 29, 396.
15. Biszormenyi-Nagy and Sparks, *Invisible Loyalties*, 370 f.
16. Boszormenyi-Nagy and Krasner, *Between Give and Take*, 400.
17. Ivan Boszormenyi-Nagy, *Foundations of Contextual Therapy*, 230, 162.
18. *Ibid.*, 231.
19. *Ibid.*, 74.
20. Boszormenyi-Nagy and Sparks, *Invisible Loyalties*, 13.
21. Boszormenyi-Nagy and Krasner, *Between Give and Take*, 407.

CHAPTER 14

1. Martin Buber, *A Believing Humanism: My Testament*, trans. with Explanatory Comments by Maurice Friedman (Atlantic Highlands, NJ: Humanities Press International, 1990), 140–142.

2. Martin Buber, *The Knowledge of Man: A Philosophy of the Interhuman*, ed. with an Introductory Essay by Maurice Friedman, trans. by Maurice Friedman and Ronald Gregor Smith (Atlantic Highlands, NJ: Humanities Press International, 1988). "Guilt and Guilt-Feelings," trans. by Maurice Friedman.

3. *Ibid.*, "What Is Common to All," trans. by Maurice Friedman.

4. *Ibid.*, 90.

5. *Ibid.*, "Guilt and Guilt-Feelings."

6. Quoted in Rollo May, "Contributions of Existential Psychotherapy," in Rollo May, Ernest Angel, Henri F. Ellenberger, eds., *Existence: A New Dimension in Psychiatry and Psychology* (New York: Basic Books, 1958), 53.

7. Buber, *Knowledge of Man*, "Guilt and Guilt-Feelings."

8. Ivan Boszormenyi-Nagy and Geraldine Spark, *Invisible Loyalties: Reciprocity in Intergenerational Family Therapy* (New York: Harper & Row, Hoeber Medical Division, 1973; New York: Brunner/Mazel, 1984), 184. I refer to Boszormenyi-Nagy alone in the text because he is the author of the main theoretical chapters of *Invisible Loyalties*.

9. *Ibid.*, 8, 55–58, 60 f., 67.

10. *Ibid.*, 69, 78–81.

11. *Ibid.*, 61.

12. *Ibid.*, 148.

13. *Ibid.*, 95.

14. *Ibid.*, 91.

15. *Ibid.*, 66, 74.

16. Ivan Boszormenyi-Nagy, *Foundations of Contextual Therapy: Collected Papers of Ivan Boszormenyi-Nagy, M.D.* (New York: Brunner/Mazel, 1987), 306 f.

17. *Ibid.*, 311.

18. *Ibid.*, 160.

19. *Ibid.*, 261.

20. Ivan Boszormenyi-Nagy and Barbara R. Krasner, *Give and Take: A Clinical Guide to Contextual Therapy* (New York: Brunner/Mazel, 1986), 329.

21. Ivan Boszormenyi-Nagy, "Contextual Therapy: Therapeutic Leverages in Mobilizing Trust" in R. F. Green and J. L. Framo, eds., *Family Therapy: Major Contributions* (New York: International Universities Press, 1981).

22. A. David Feinstein, "Self-Responsibility in Illness and the Issue of Guilt" (unpublished).

CHAPTER 15

1. Dan Wilson, *An Opening Way, Pendle Hill Pamphlet* (Wallingford, PA: Pendle Hill Publications, 1961).

2. Carl R. Rogers, *A Way of Being* (Boston: Houghton Mifflin, 1980), 166.

3. Lyman C. Wynne, "The Injection and Concealment of Meaning in the Family Relationships and Psychotherapy of Schizophrenics in S. Euvinarwin & Y. O. Alenen, eds., *Psychotherapy of Schizophrenia*, Proceedings of the IVth International Symposium, Turku, Finland, August 4–7, 1971 (Amsterdam, The Netherlands: Excerpta Medica, 1971), 180–193.

4. R. D. Laing, *The Politics of Experience* (New York: Ballantine Books, 1967), 108.

5. Bert Kaplan, ed., *The Inner World of Mental Illness* (New York: Harper & Row, 1964), "Editor's Introduction," vii.

6. Erving Goffman, *Asylum: Essays on the Social Situation of Mental Patients and Other Inmates* (New York: Doubleday [Anchor Books], 1961).

7. Laing, *The Politics of Experience*, 122.

8. *Ibid.*, 132 f., 144 f.

9. *Ibid.*, 128 f.

10. John Weir Perry, *The Far Side of Madness* (Englewood Cliffs, NJ: Prentice Hall, 1974).

11. Laing, *The Politics of Experience*, 56.

12. *Ibid.*, 109.

13. Ivan Boszormenyi-Nagy and Geraldine Spark, *Invisible Loyalties, Reciprocity in Intergenerational Family Therapy* (New York: Harper & Row, Hoeber Medical Division, 1973; New York: Brunner Mazel, 1984).

14. Hanna Colm, "The Therapeutic Encounter," *Review of Existential Psychology and Psychiatry*, Vol. V (1965), 139.

15. Sidney Jourard, *Disclosing Man to Himself* (New York: D. Van Nostrand, 1968), 124 f.

16. Harold F. Searles, "The Patient as Therapist to His Analyst" in P. L. Giovacchini, ed., *Tactics and Techniques in Psychoanalytic Psychotherapy*, Vol. II (New York: Jason Aronson, 1975), 96.

17. *Ibid.*, 97 f.

18. Harold F. Searles, "The Schizophrenic's Experience of His World," *Psychiatry*, Vol. XXX (1967), 128–130.

19. *Ibid.*, 130.

20. *Ibid.*, 131.

21. Robert J. Langs and Harold F. Searles, *Intrapsychic and Interpersonal Dimensions of Treatment: A Clinical Dialogue* (New York: Jason Aronson, 1980), 62.

INDEX

AUG 10 '95	6-6-04		
NOV 03 '95			
JAN 30 '96		DISCARDED	
MAY 03 '96			
DEC 02 '96			
NOV 08 '97			
APR 2 6 '99			
DEC 1 9 '99			
NOV 2 2000			